AUDREY HEPBURN

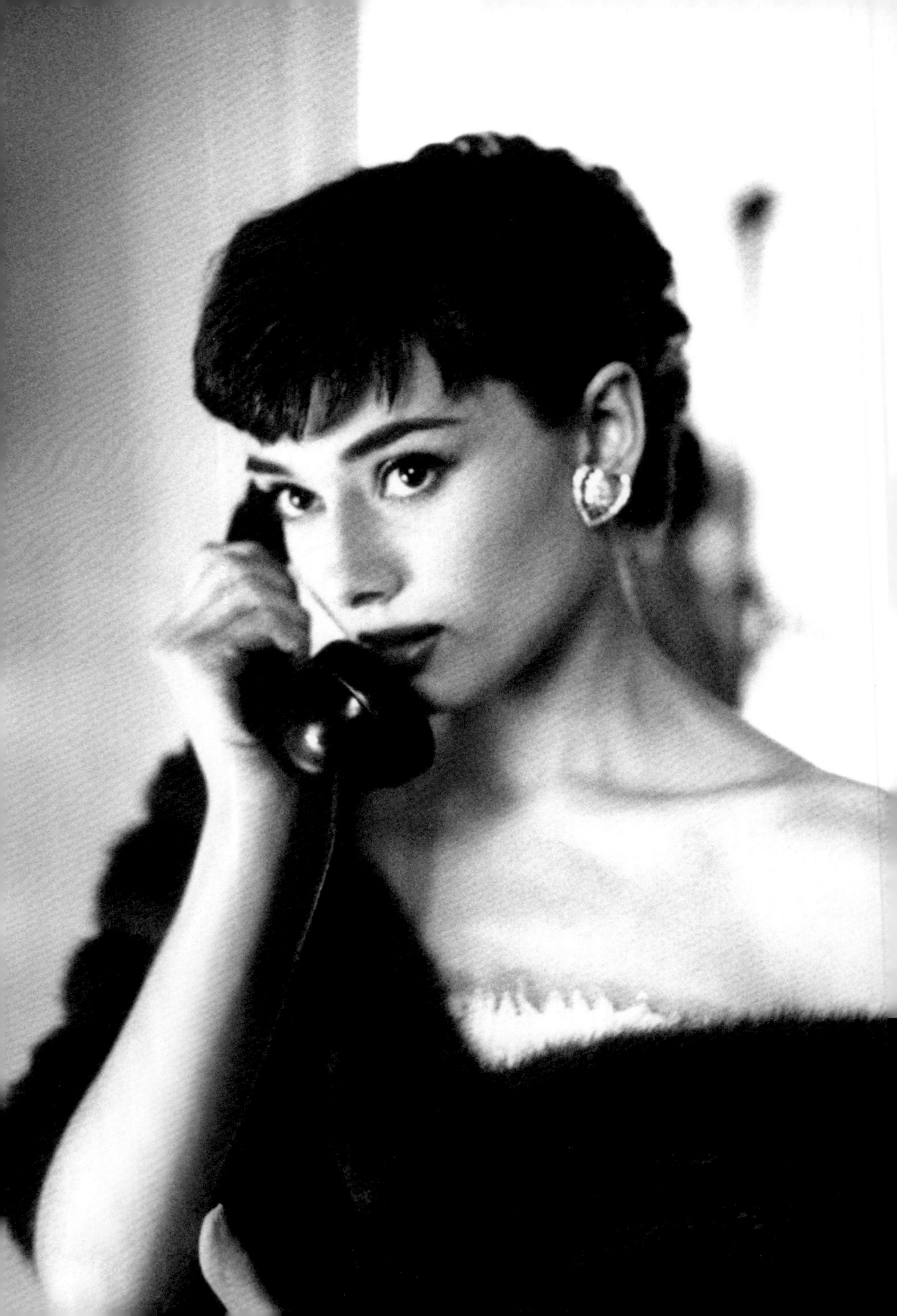

Bob Willoughby

AUDREY HEPBURN

Photographs 1953–1966

TASCHEN

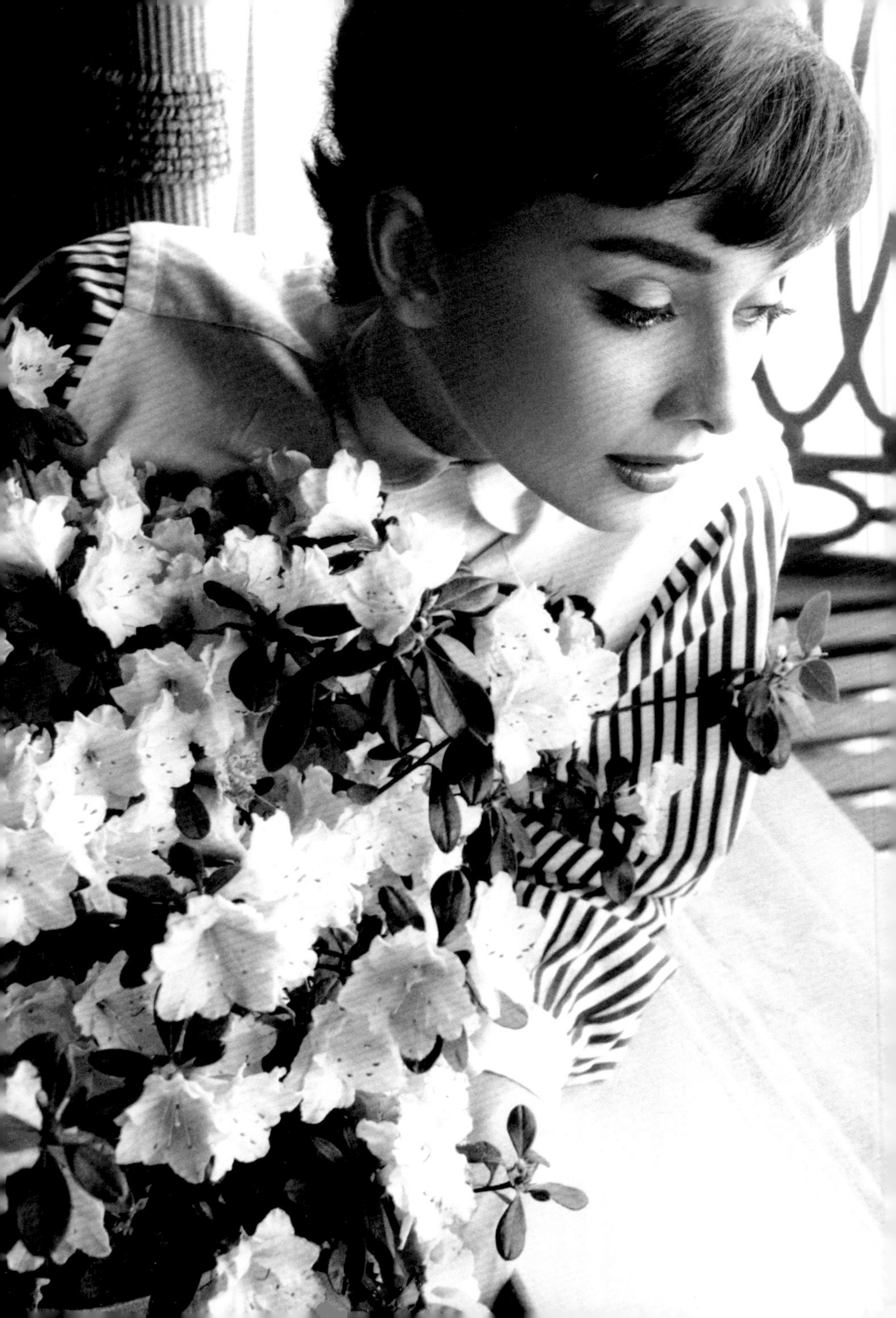

TO HAVE KNOWN AUDREY HEPBURN WAS A GRACE

I could never have guessed this when I first photographed her at Paramount Studios in 1953. The new girl in town. She had just completed the filming of *Roman Holiday*, and was at Paramount in Hollywood for publicity photographs.

I really didn't know quite what to make of Audrey when I first saw her. She certainly was not the typical image of a young starlet, for that was what I had been sent to photograph. I watched her across the room as she was being photographed by Bud Fraker, and she did have something…but I couldn't quite put my finger on it until I was finally introduced to her.

Then that radiant smile hit me right between the eyes, warming me inside like a shot of whisky. That amazing instant contact she made, a remarkable gift that everyone who met her felt. She exuded some magic warmth that was hers alone.

Happily our lives would intersect many times over the years we knew each other. Our first born would celebrate their first birthdays together, and I would photograph her in so many different places as you can see from this collection.

While many of these photographs of Audrey are well known, they have never before been seen together as a complete collection. I would like this book to be my salute to that magic sprite. A forest creature who, before one's eyes, could transform herself into a princess. A rare human being, whom I respected and loved.

Bob Willoughby, Vence, France

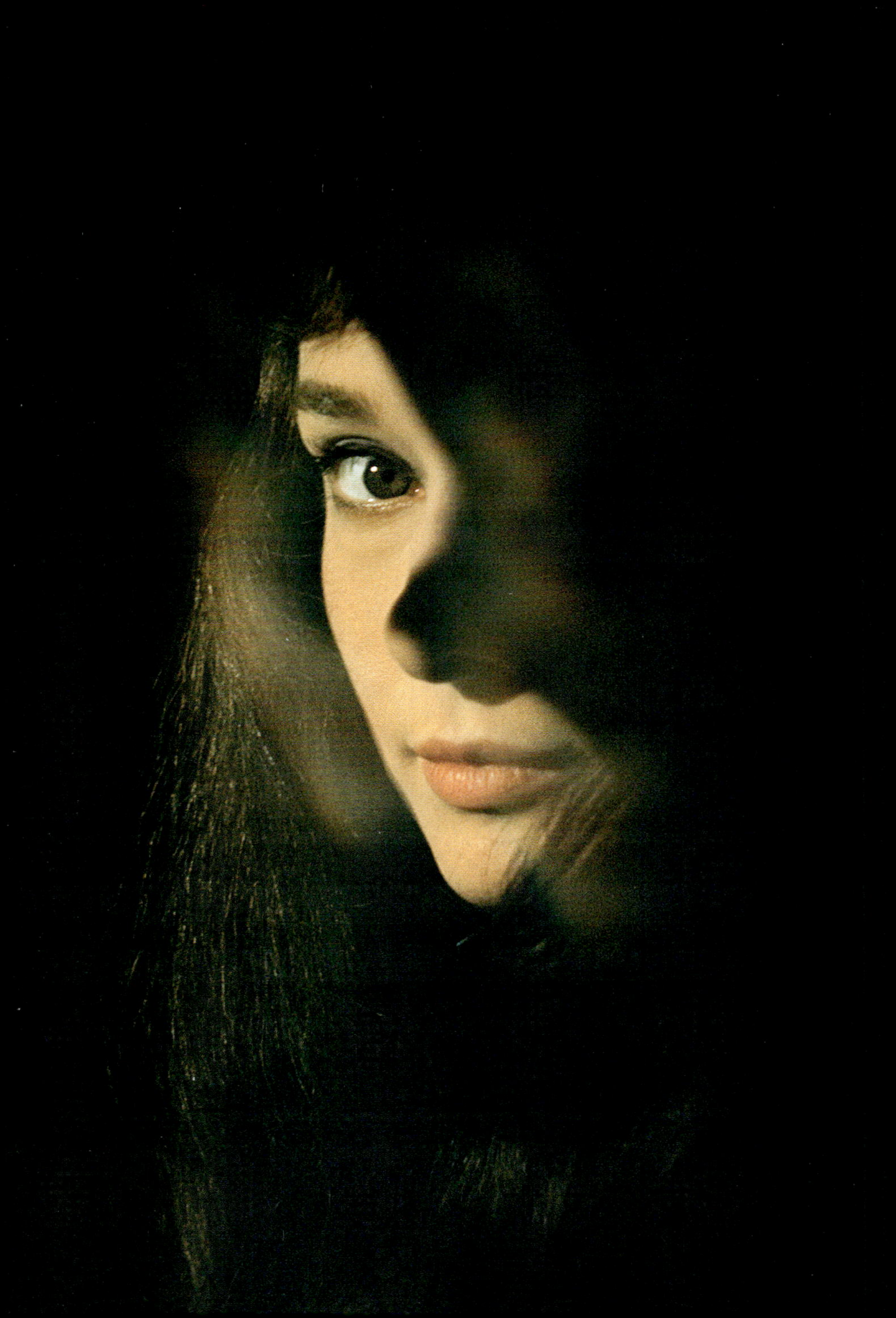

CONTENTS

PARAMOUNT STUDIOS

1953

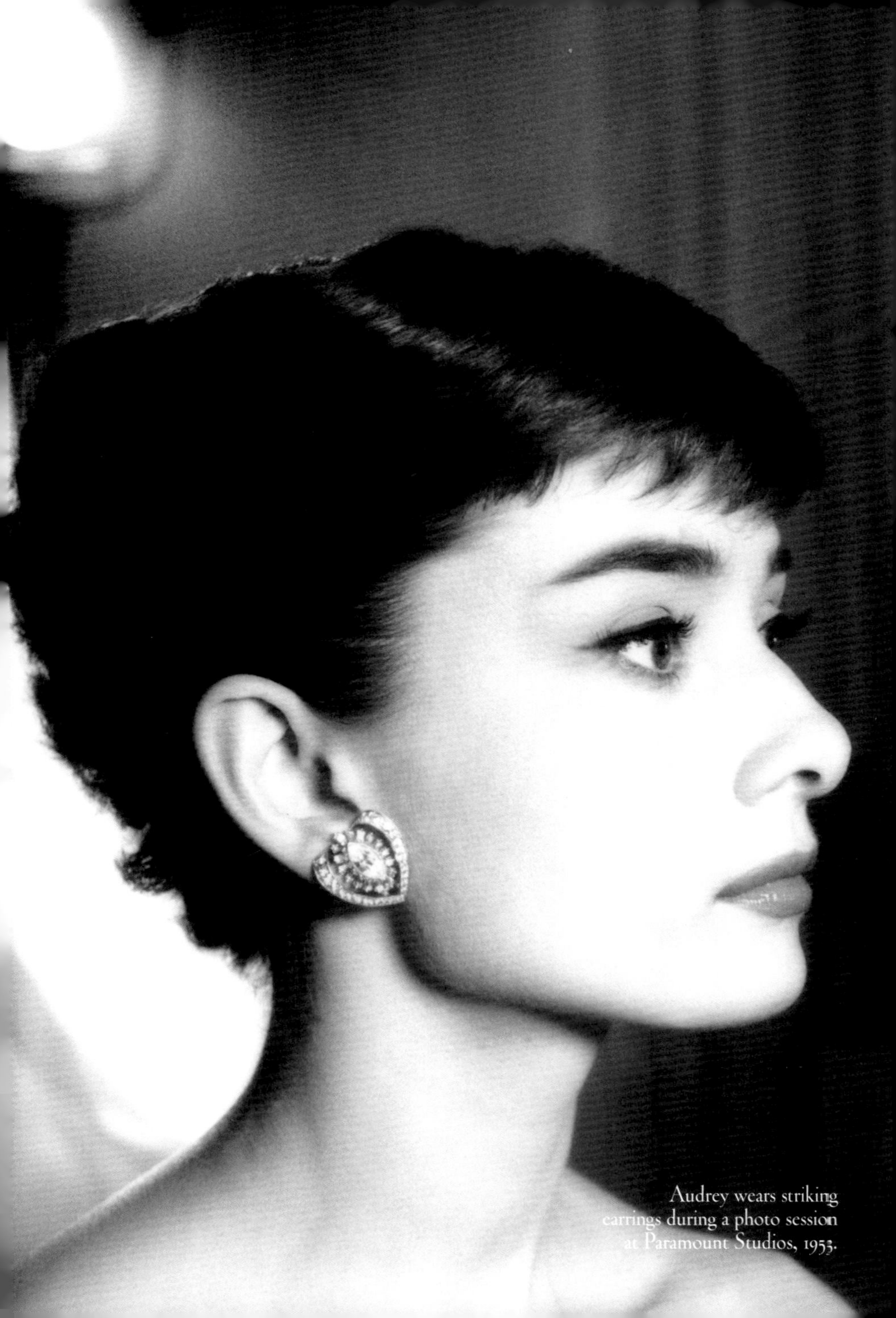

Audrey wears striking earrings during a photo session at Paramount Studios, 1953.

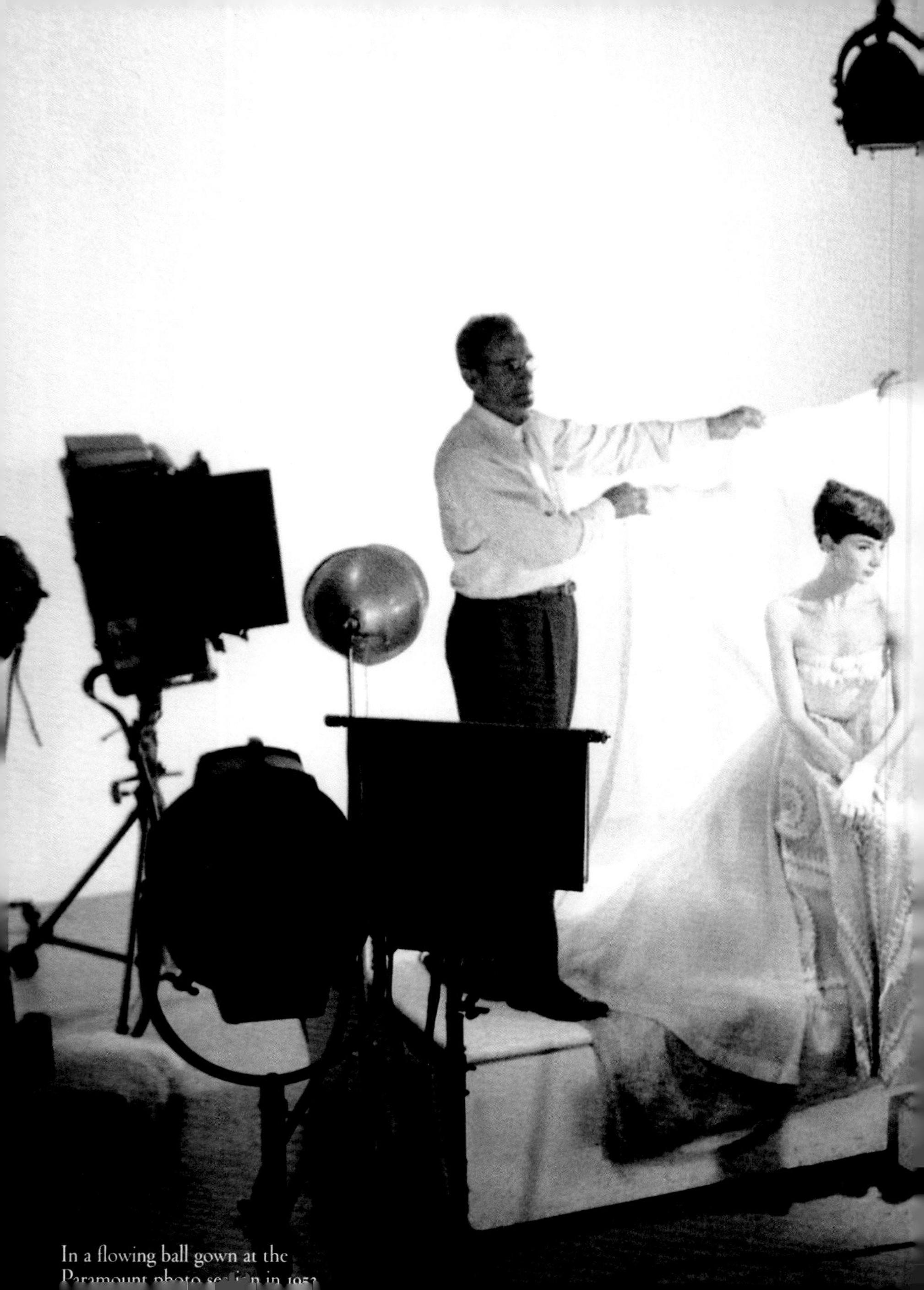

In a flowing ball gown at the
Paramount photo session in 1953

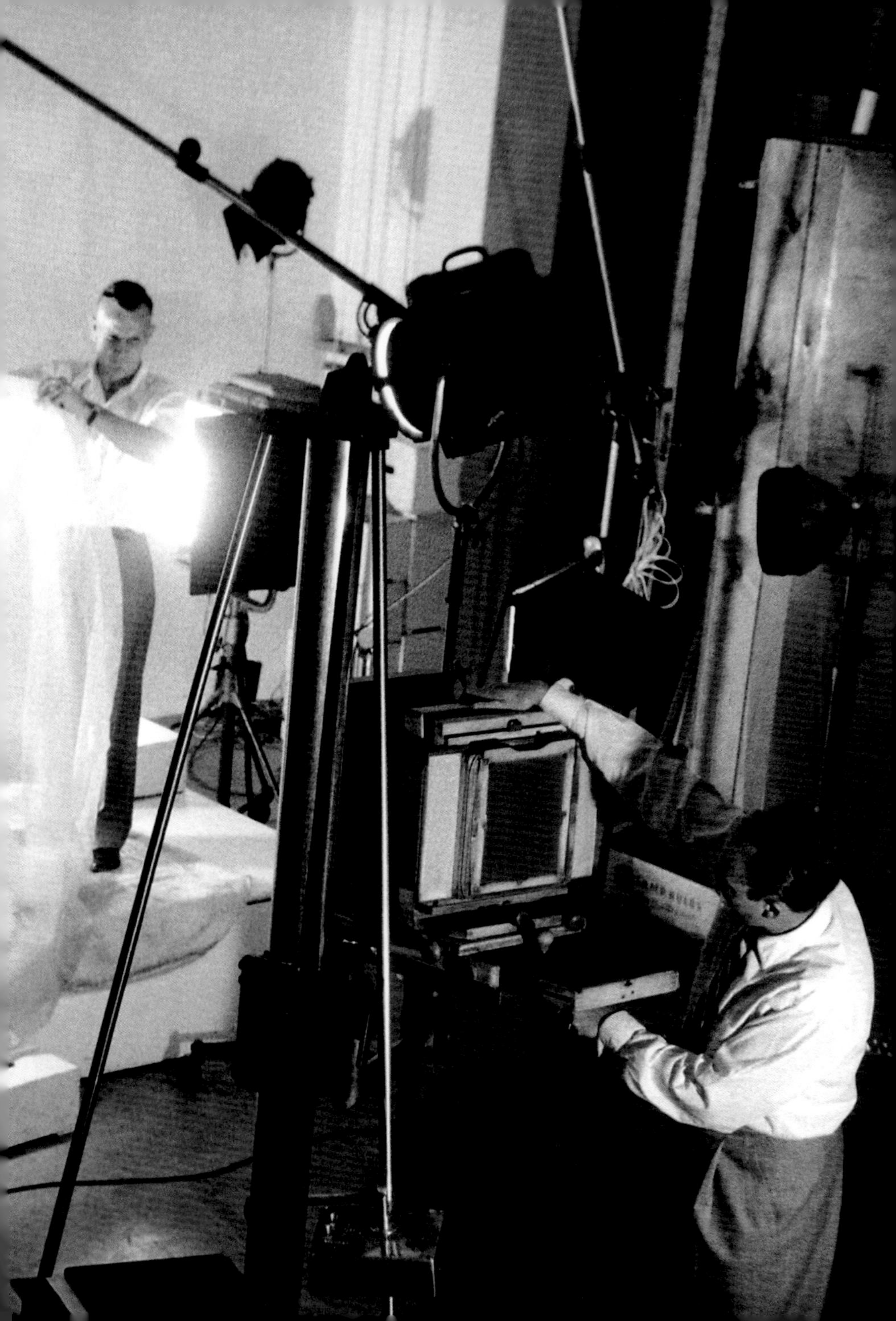

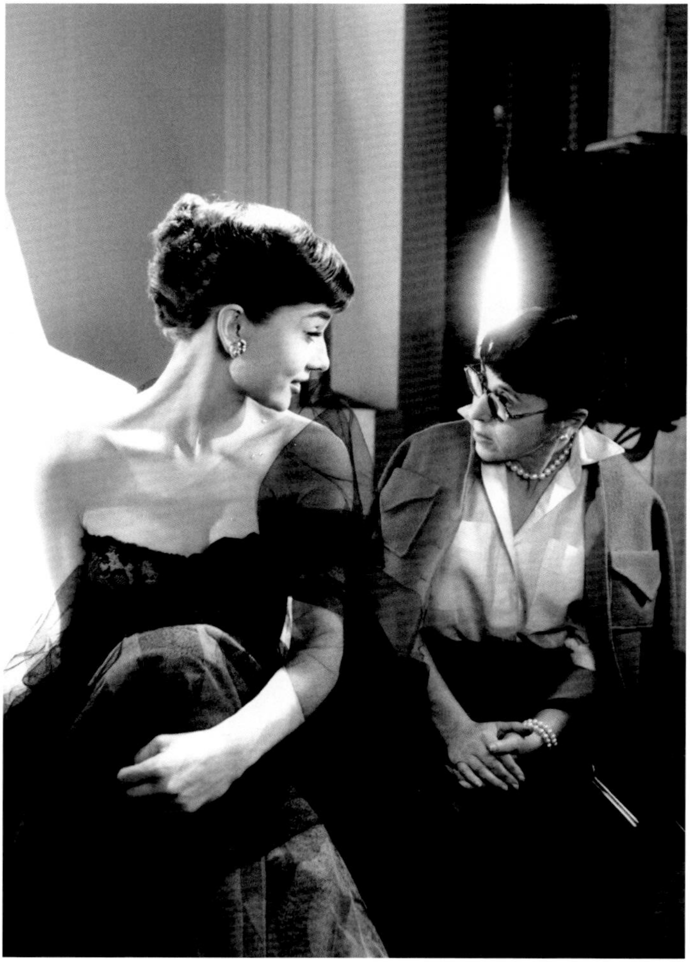

Audrey chats with Edith Head, who designed the costumes for *Roman Holiday*, at Paramount Studios, 1953.

In earrings and gown at the Paramount photo session in 1953.

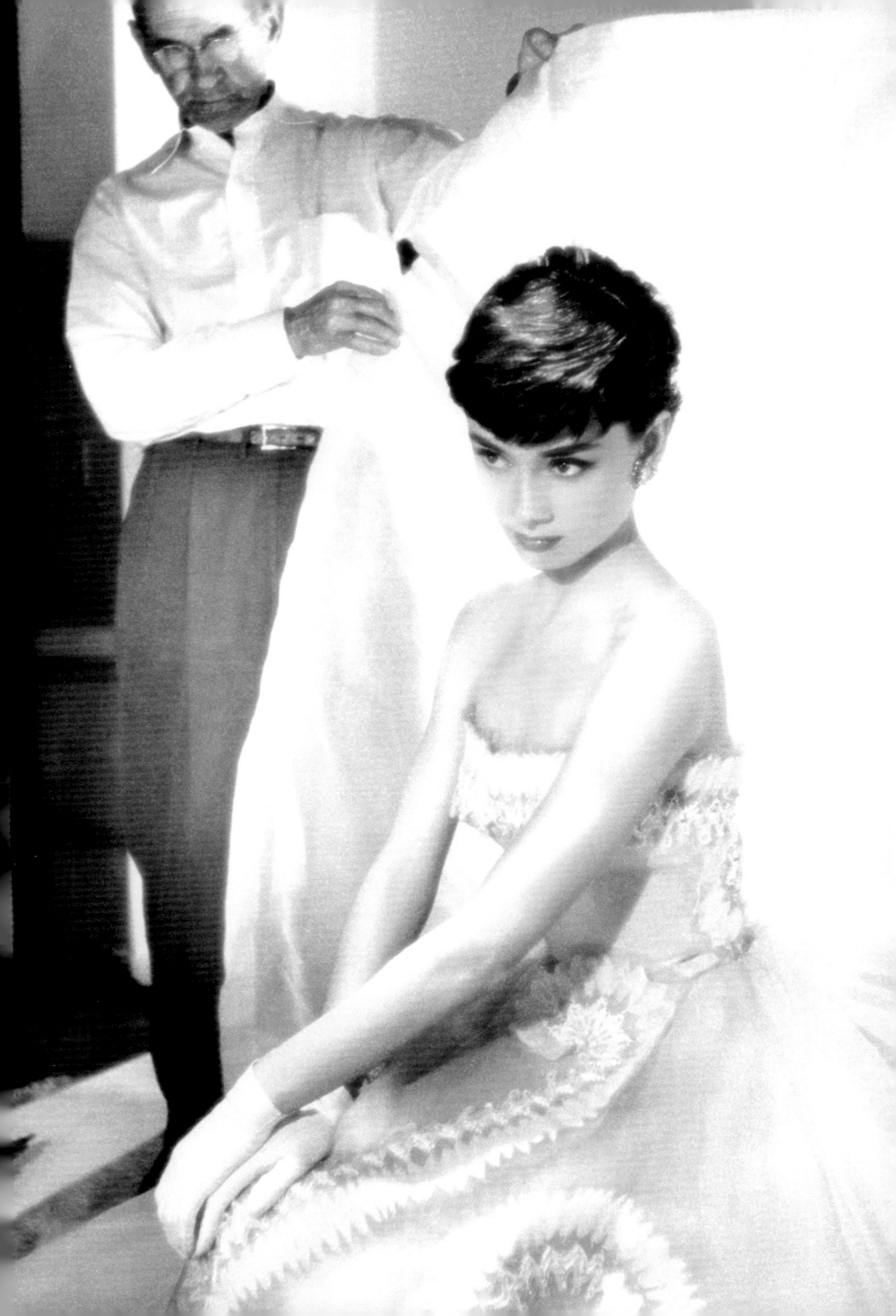

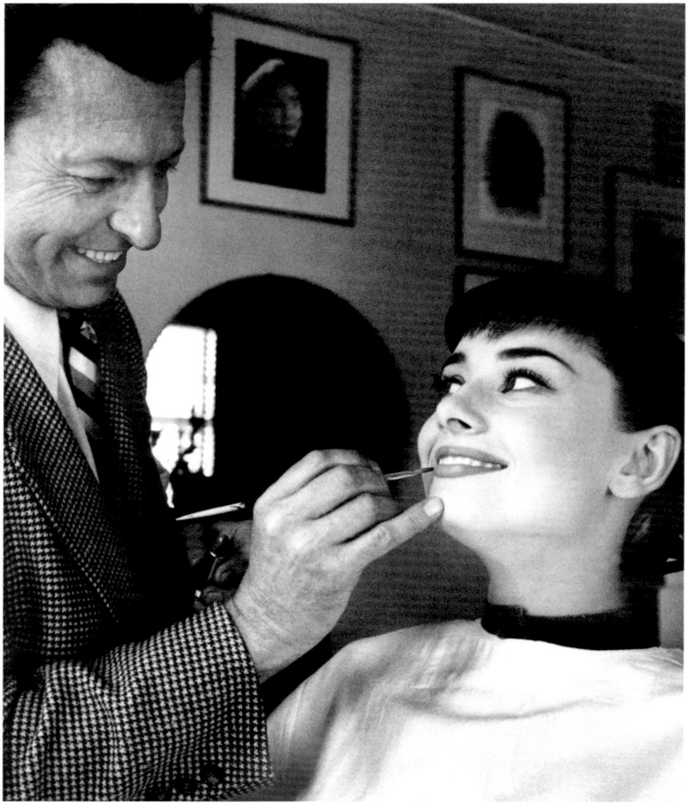

Makeup artist Wally Westmore prepares Audrey for her first publicity shoot at Paramount.

Bud Fraker positions Audrey for a shot.

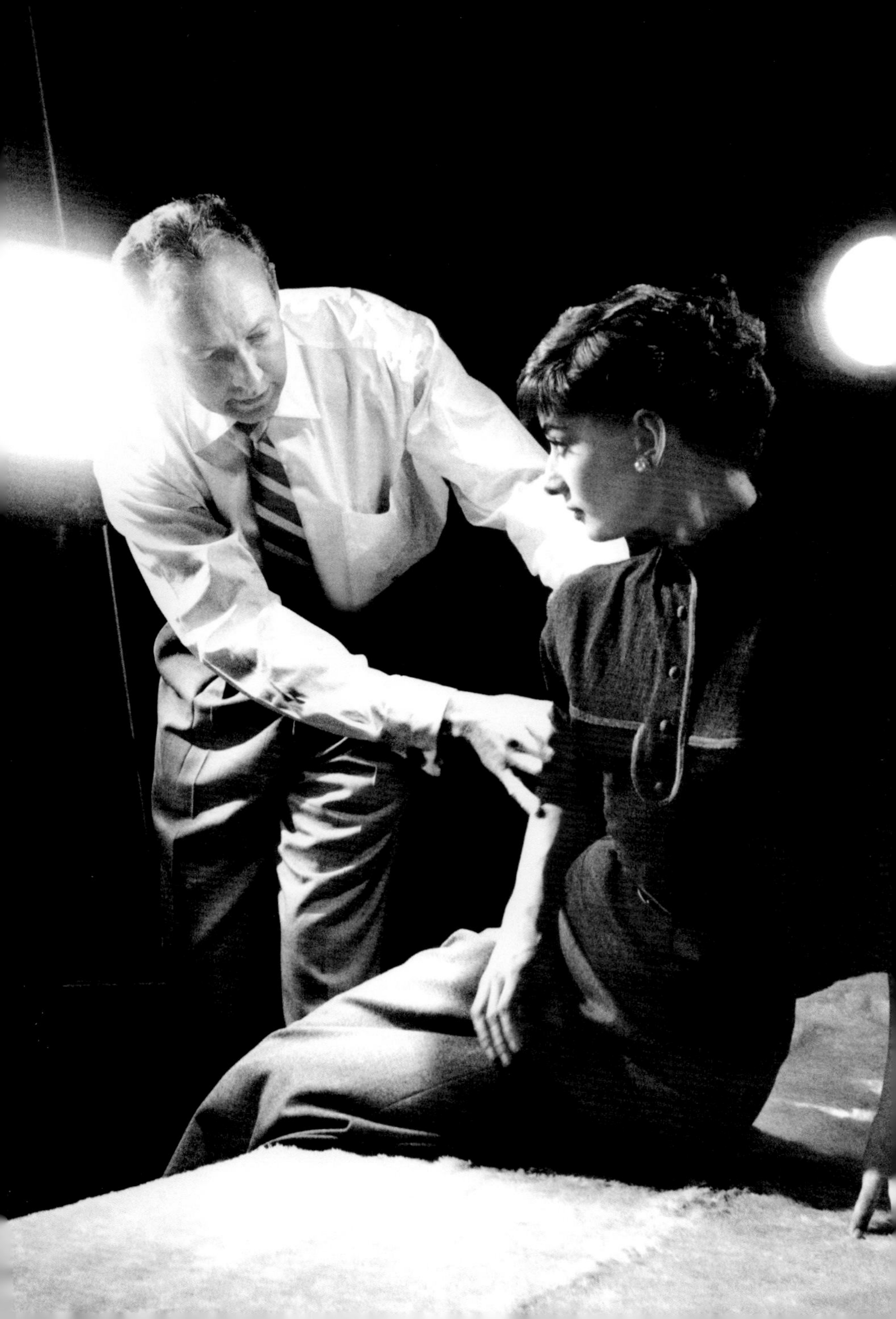

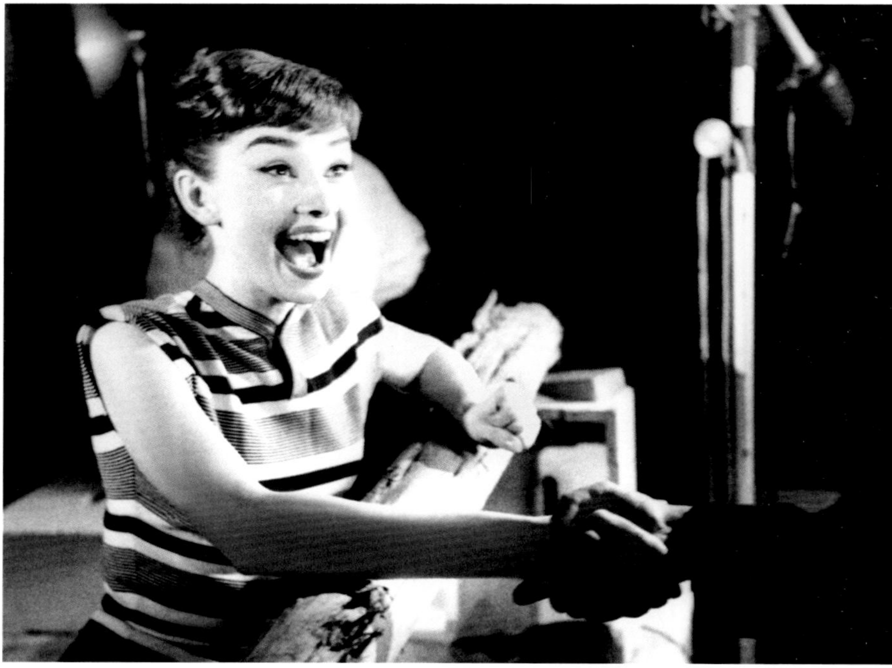

Above:
Photo session at Paramount, 1953.

Opposite:
Audrey reads a letter from home in her hotel room in Los Angeles, where she is playing the lead role in *Gigi*.

Following spread:
Audrey wears her own nightgown for a photo session at Paramount in 1953.

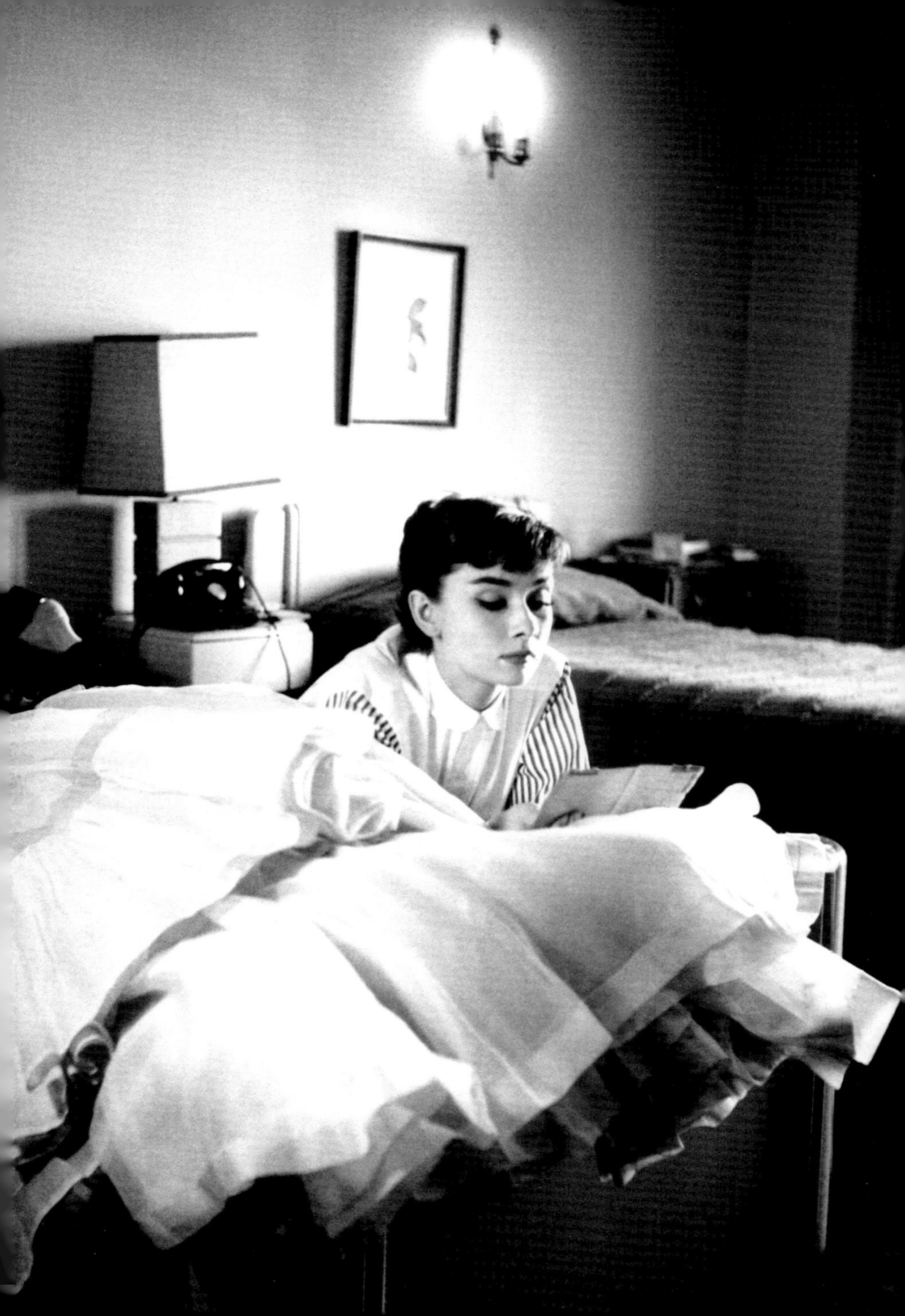

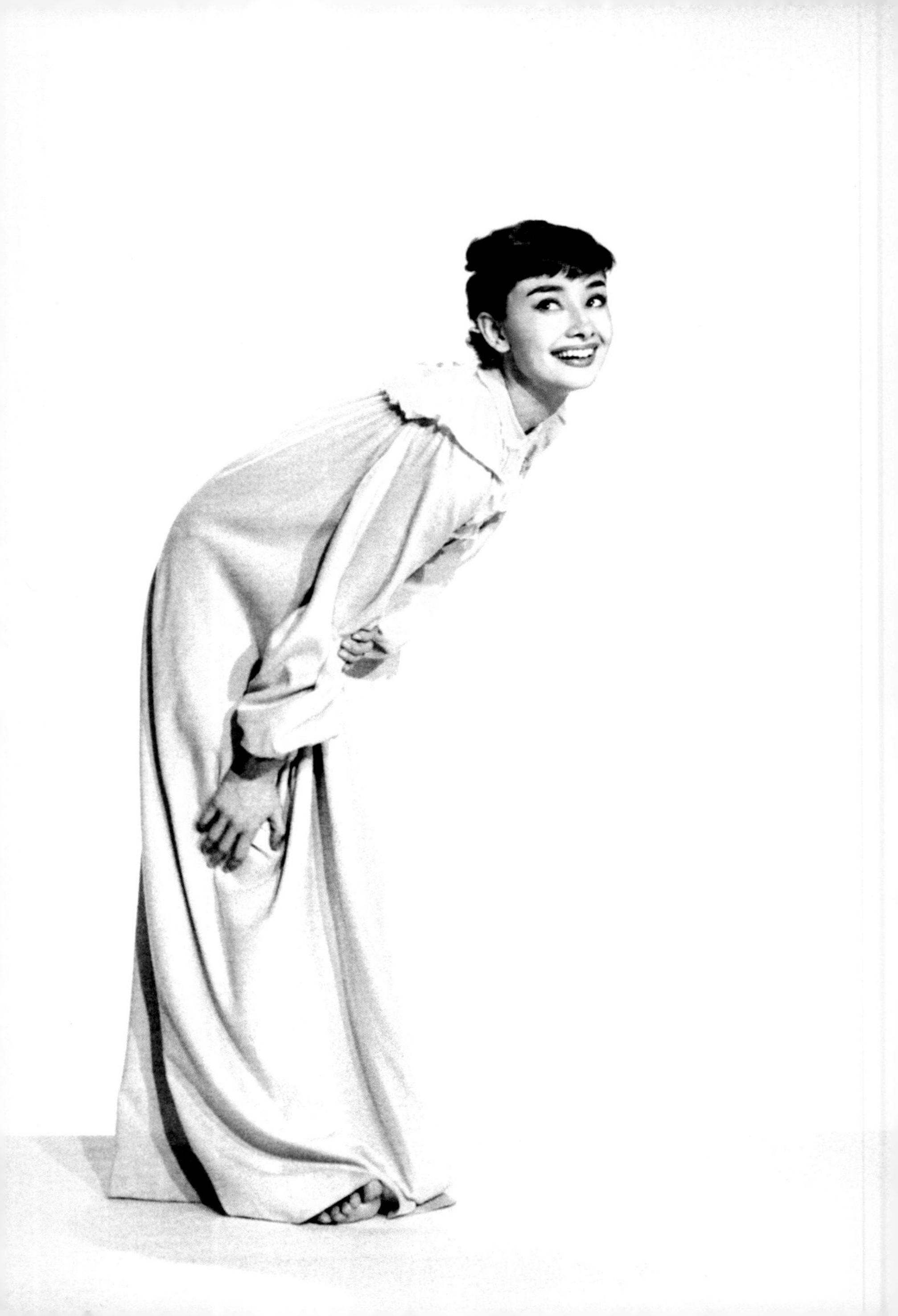

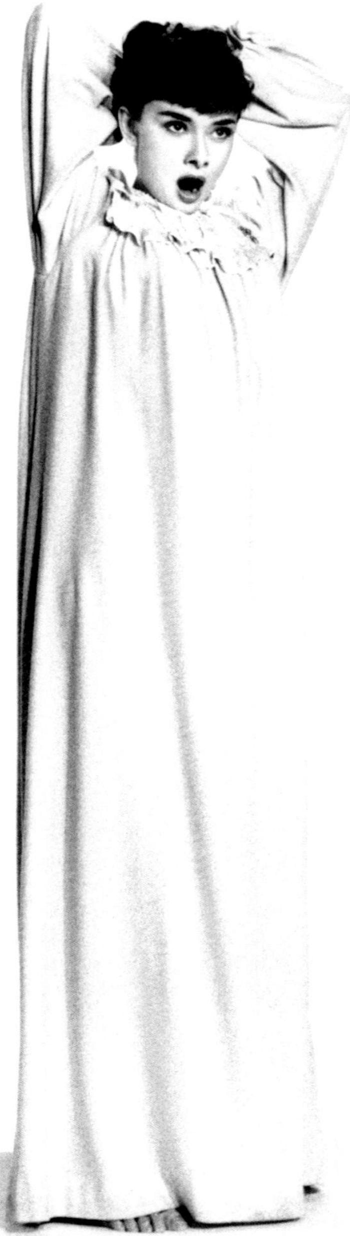

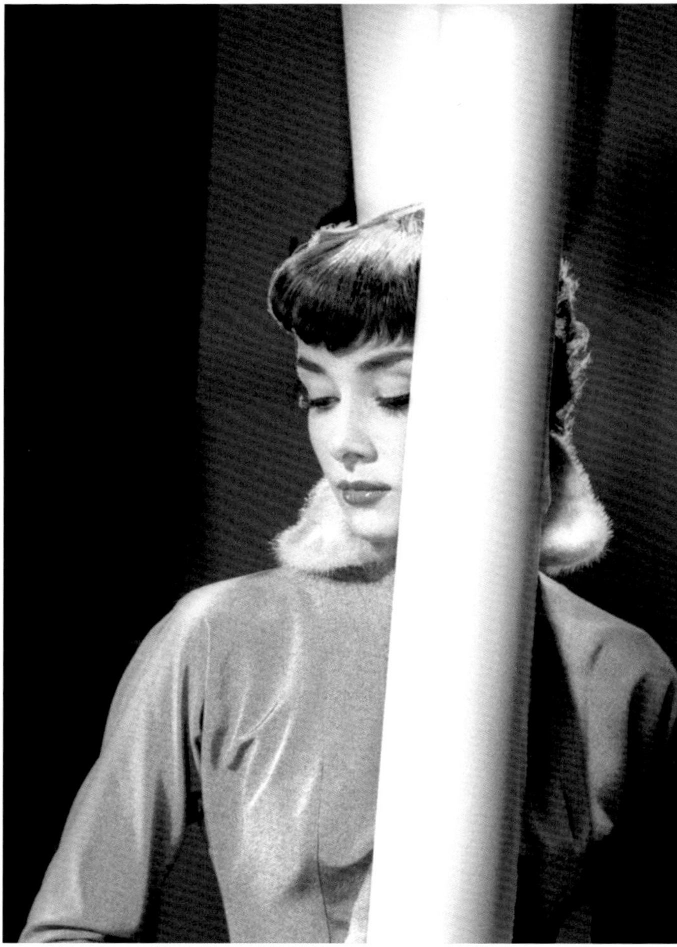

Audrey looks downcast.

Leading portrait photographer Bud Fraker says goodbye to Audrey at the end of the 1953 session at Paramount.

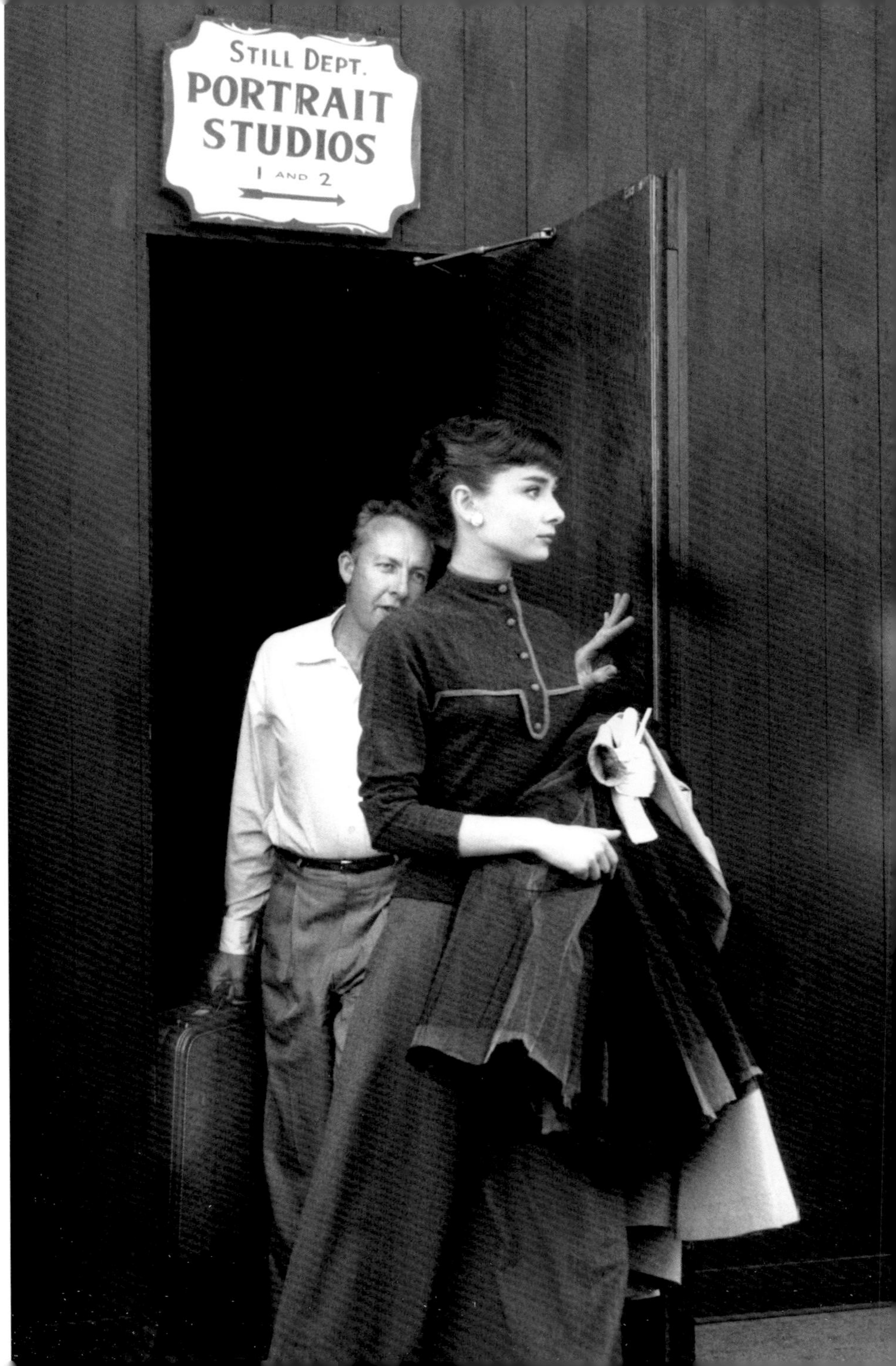
STILL DEPT.
PORTRAIT
STUDIOS
1 AND 2

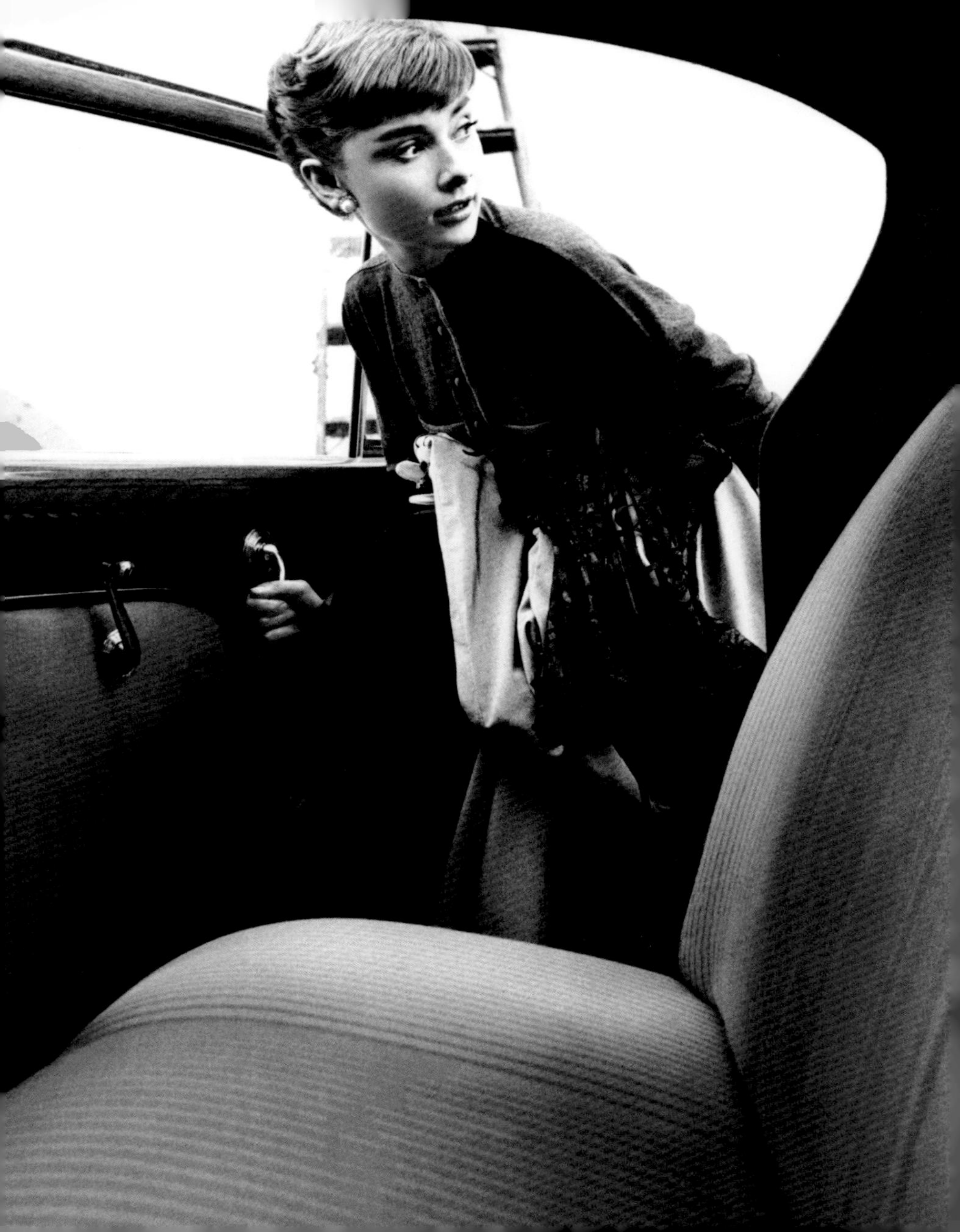

"I remember the 50s as a time of renewal and of regained security. There was a rebirth of opportunity, vitality, and enthusiasm ... a return to laughter and gaiety—the world was functioning again. Above all there was a wonderful quality of hope, born from relief and gratitude for those greatest of all luxuries—freedom and peace."

Audrey Hepburn

Audrey climbs into the Paramount Studios car waiting to return her to the hotel after the photo session with Bud Fraker.

AUDREY & IP

1958

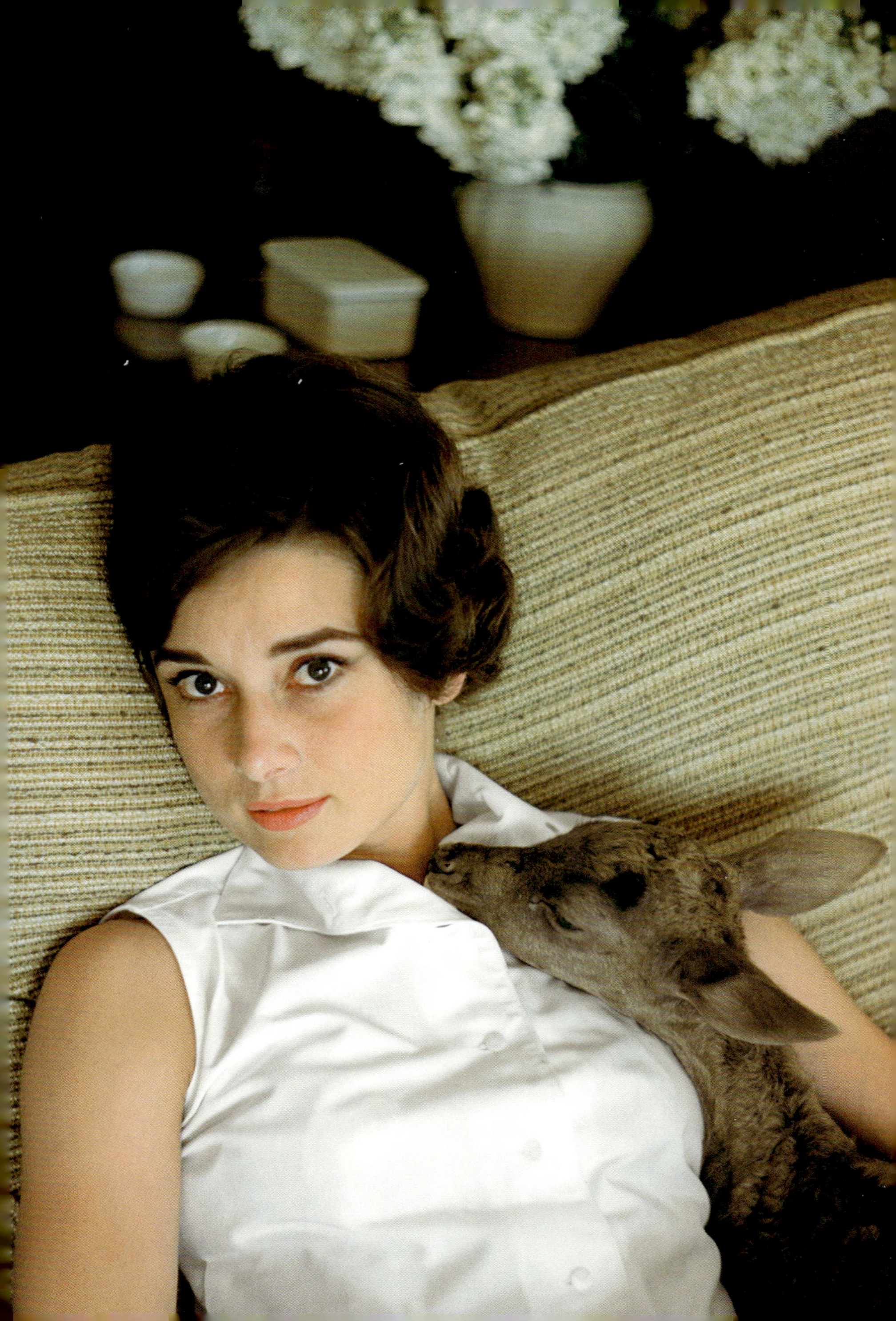

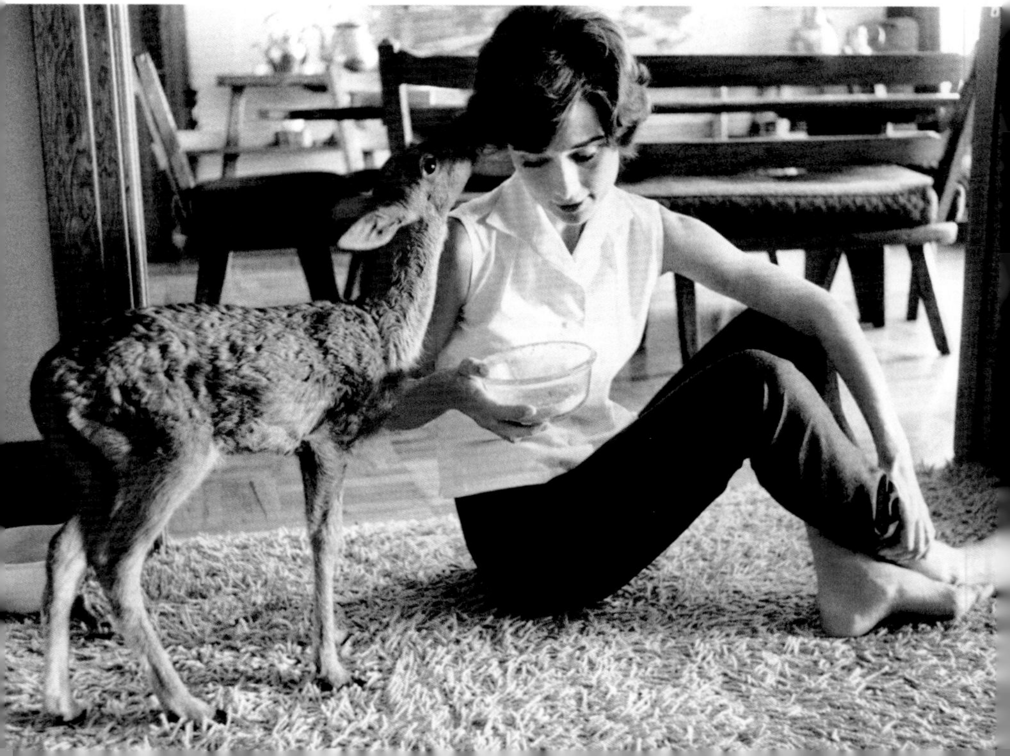

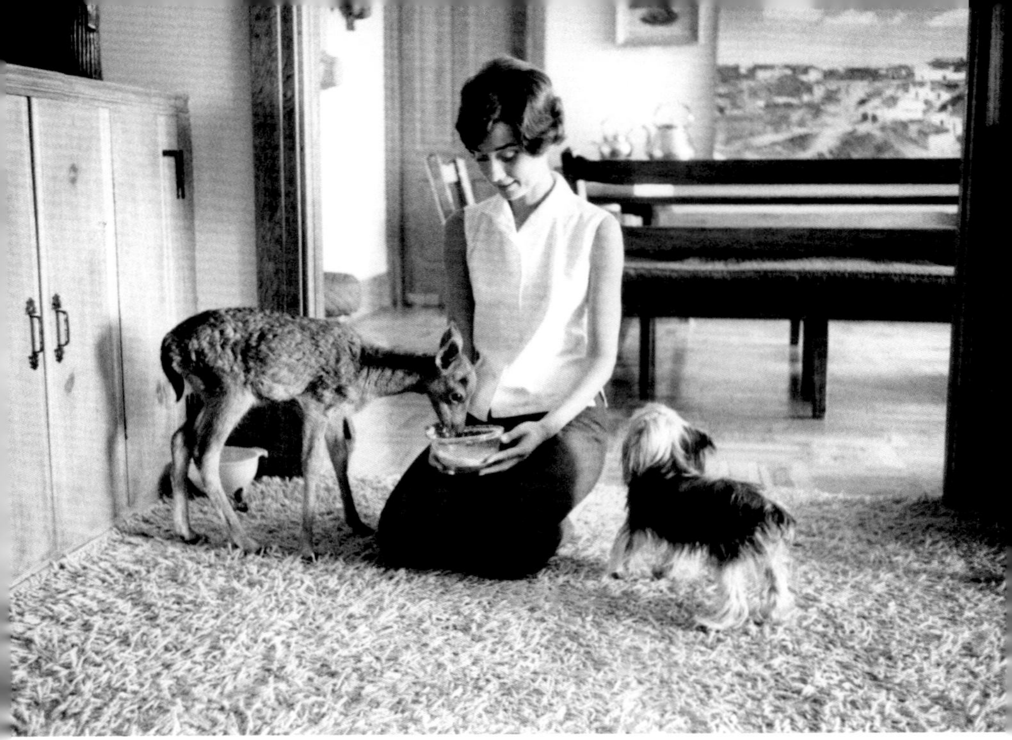

Previous spread:
Audrey and Ip—the fawn, whose full name was Pippin, lived with Audrey as a pet in order to become tame before shooting for *Green Mansions* began.

Opposite:
Audrey feeds Pippin the fawn.

Above:
Audrey's Yorkshire terrier, Famous, is jealous of the attention given to the new addition to the family.

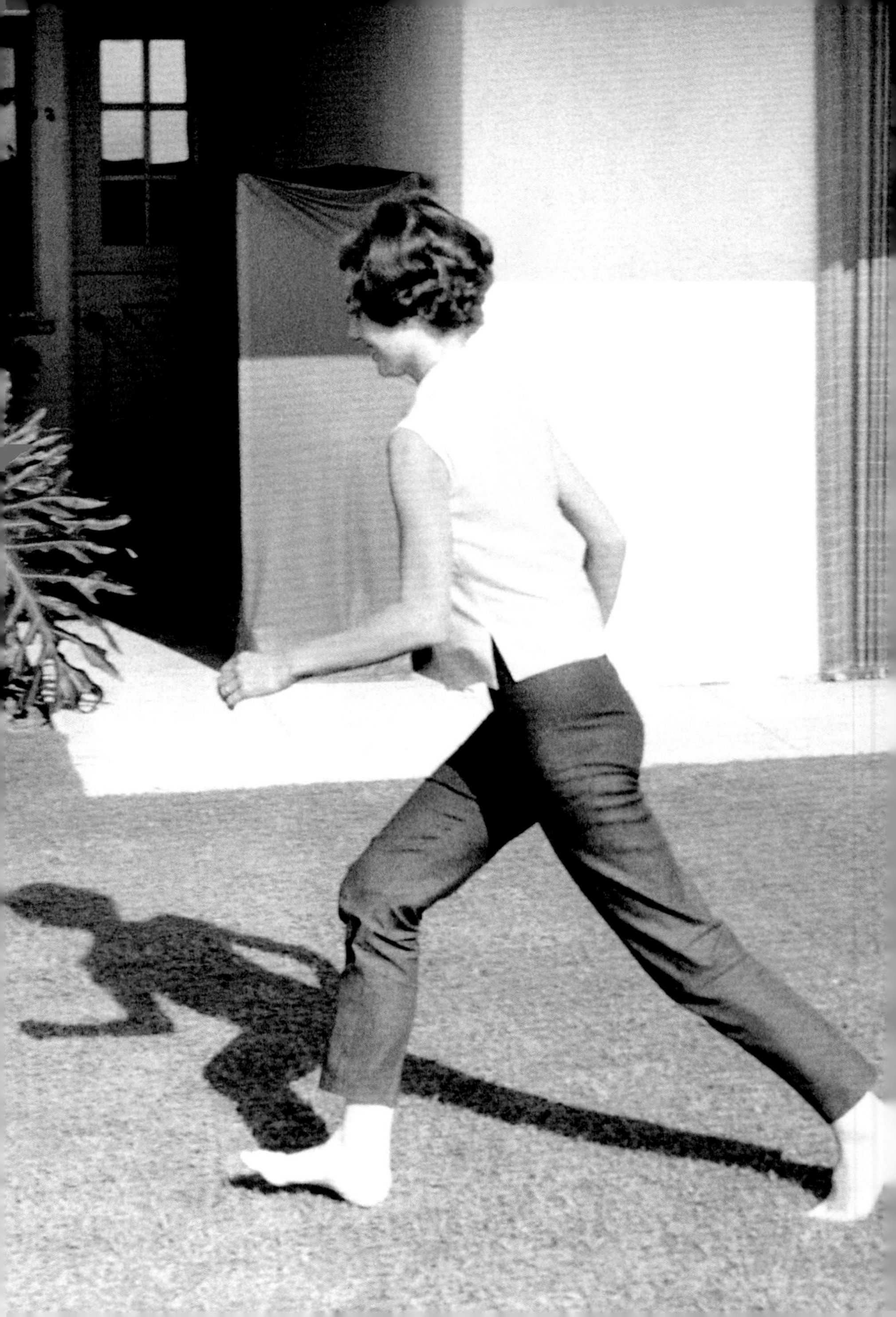

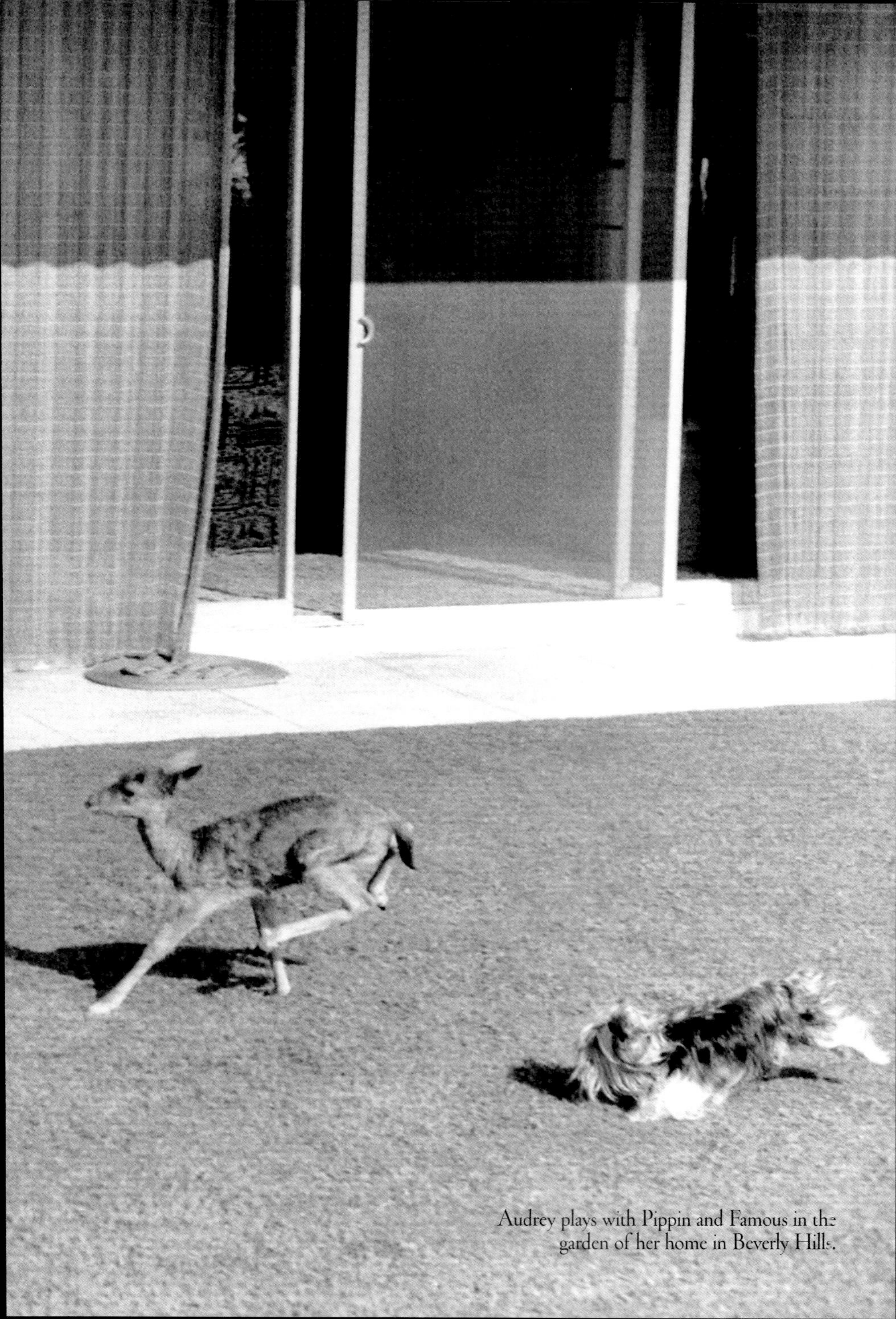

Audrey plays with Pippin and Famous in the garden of her home in Beverly Hills.

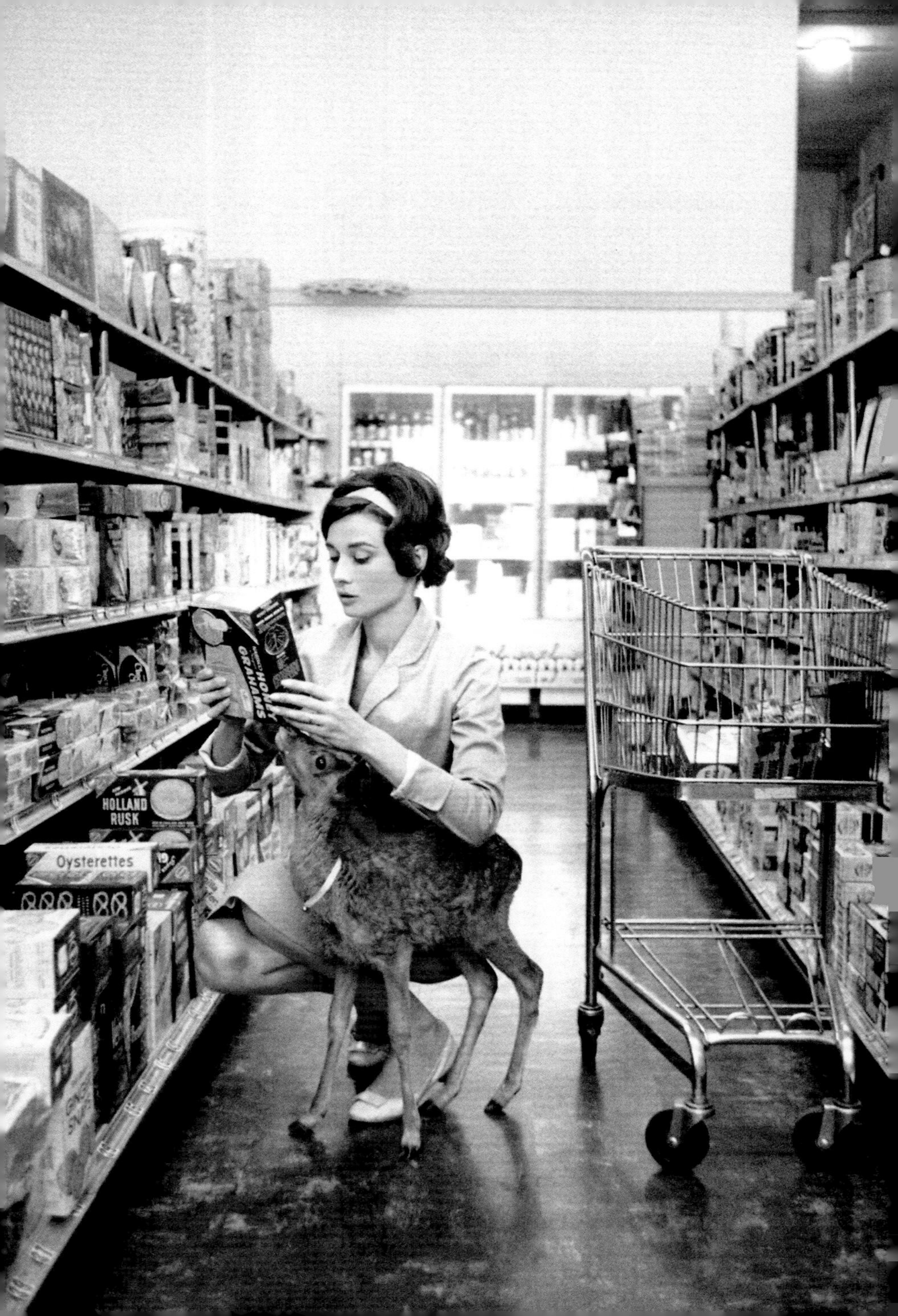
GRAHAMS
HOLLAND
RUSK
Oysterettes

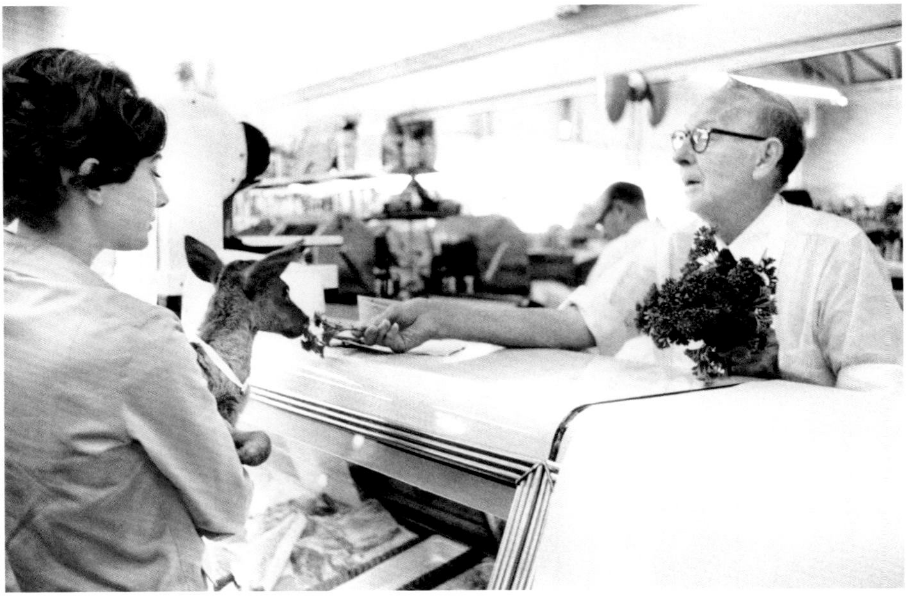

Opposite:
Audrey takes Ip shopping in Gelson's supermarket, Beverly Hills.

Above:
The butcher at Gelson's supermarket offers Ip a sprig of parsley.

Following spread:
Ip loves to sleep close to Audrey.
Famous has his own corner of the sofa.

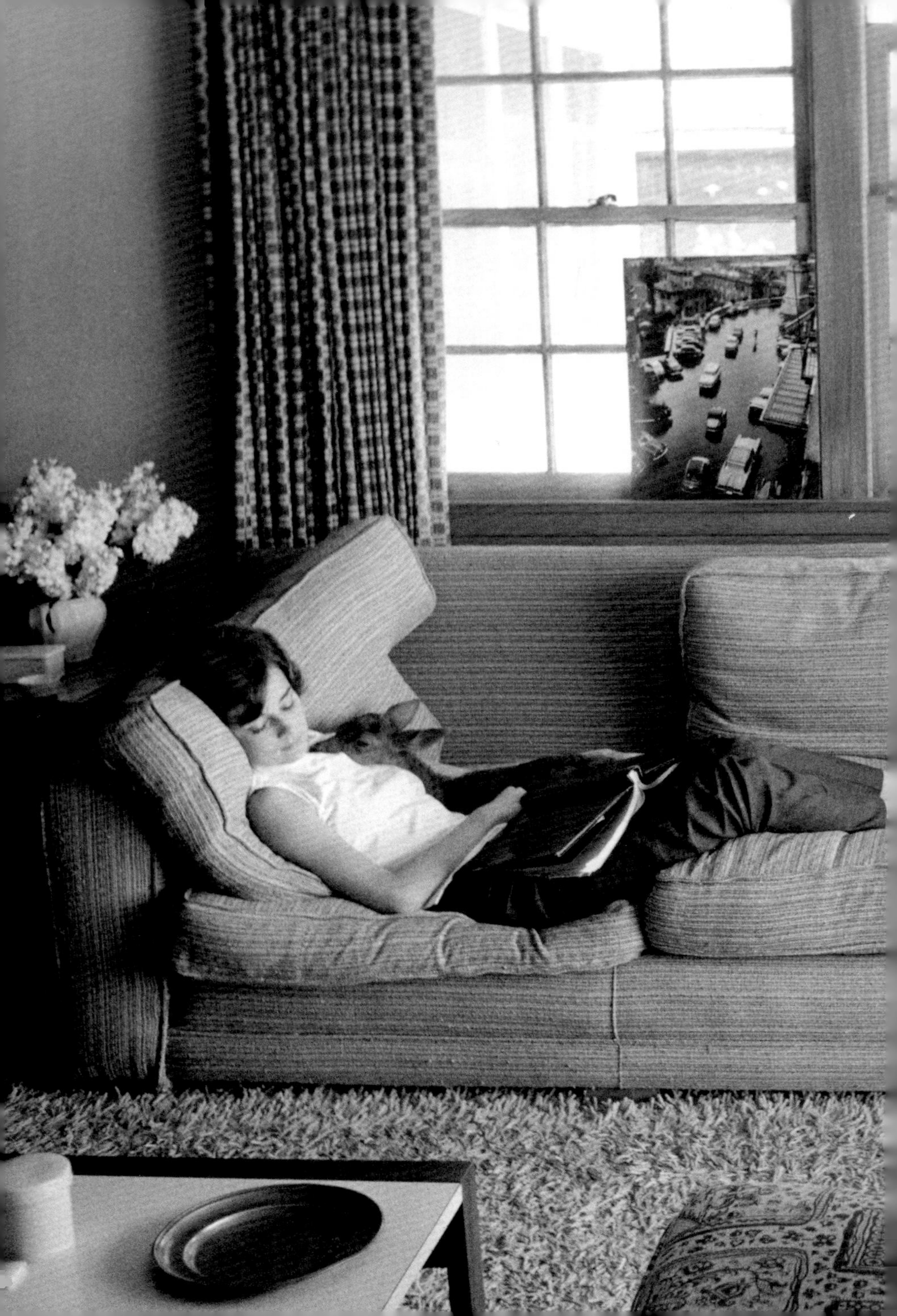

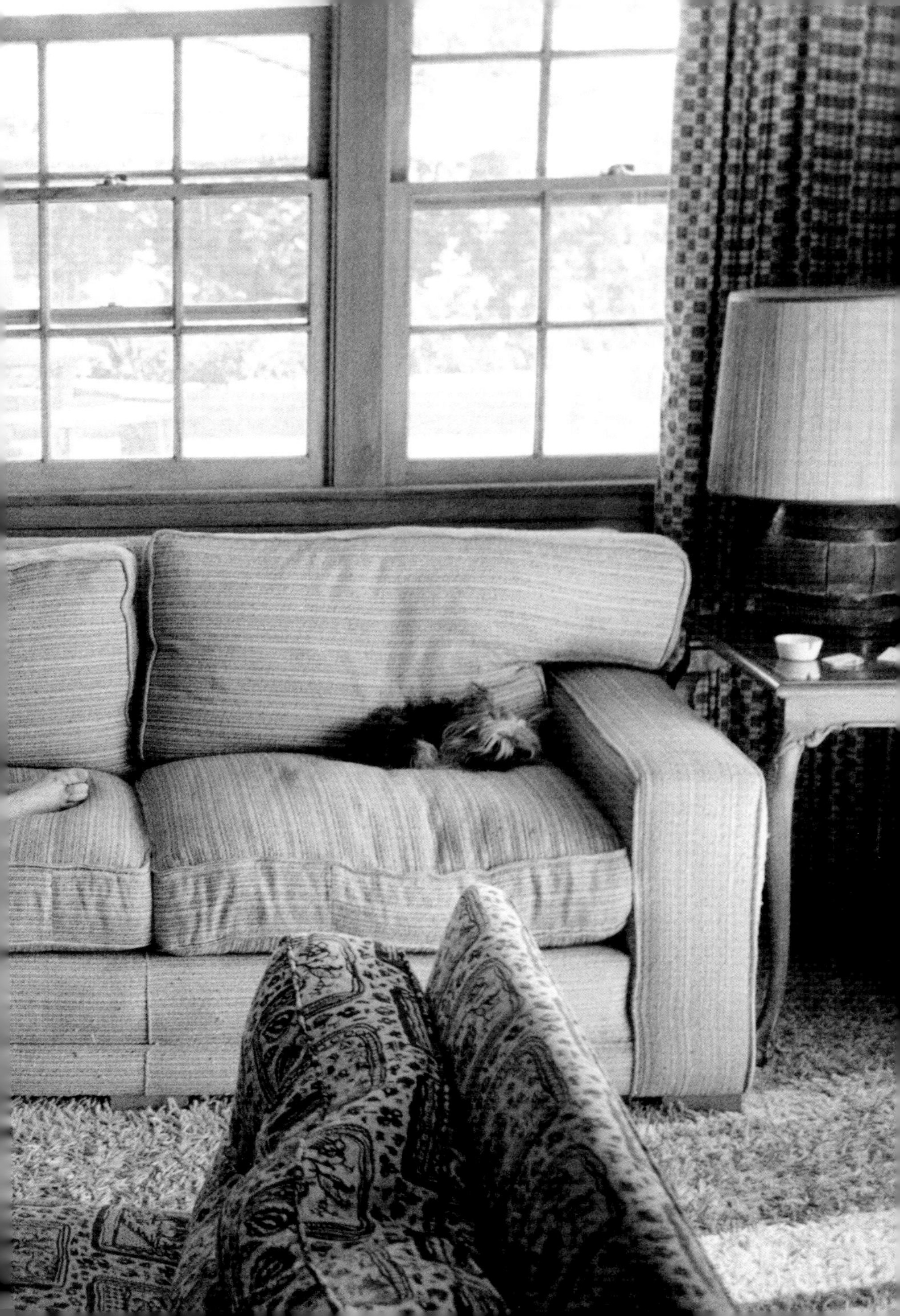

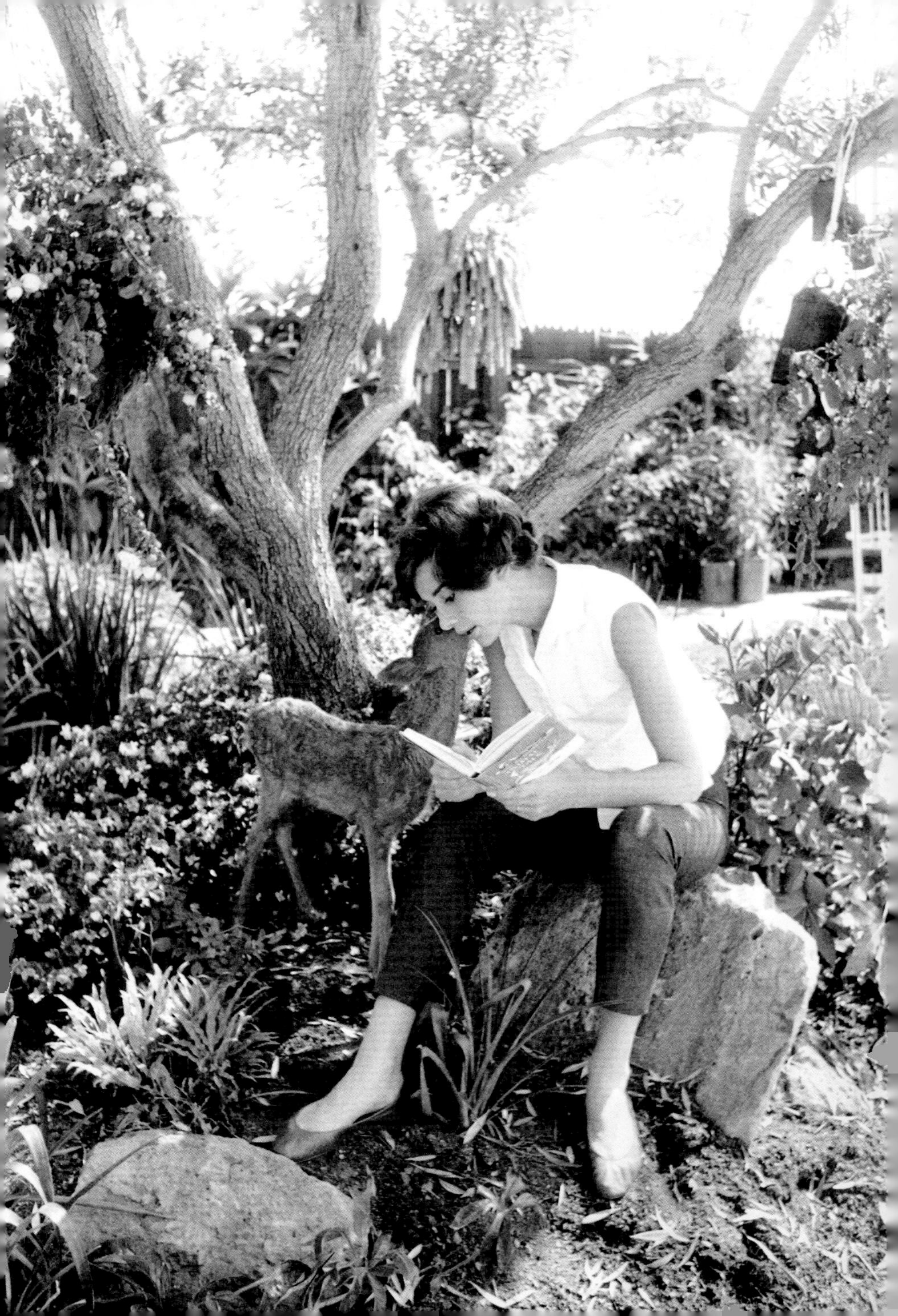

"For two and a half months it lived in our house.
It ate its bowl of pabulum with us in the dining room,
and at night it slept in our bathroom.
It got so it actually thought Audrey was its mother;
professional animal trainers were amazed
at the way it followed her around."

Mel Ferrer

Pippin and Audrey relaxing in
the garden of her Beverly Hills home.

Following spread:
Audrey plays the jungle girl Rima opposite Anthony Perkins
in *Green Mansions*, 1958.

GREEN MANSIONS

1958

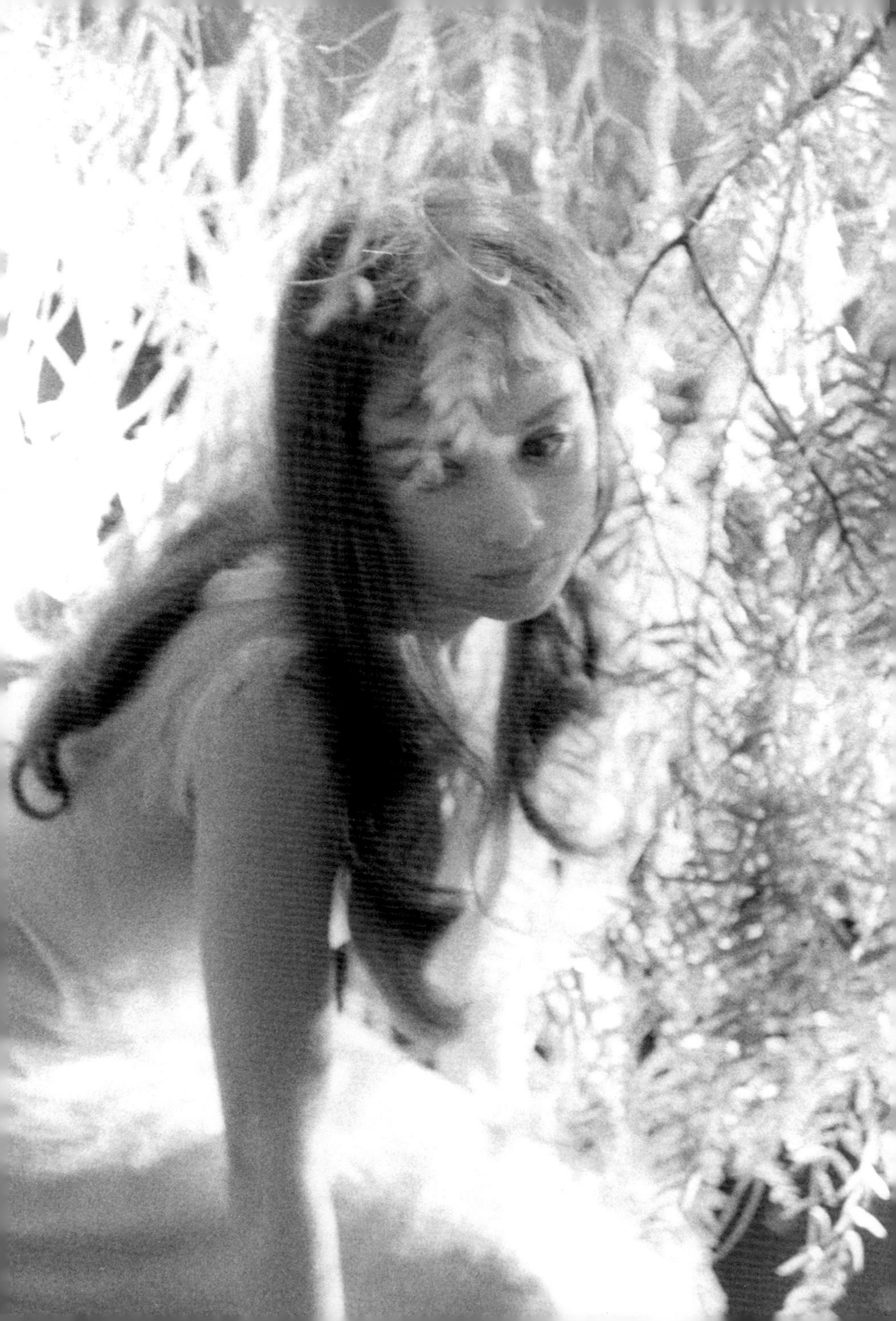

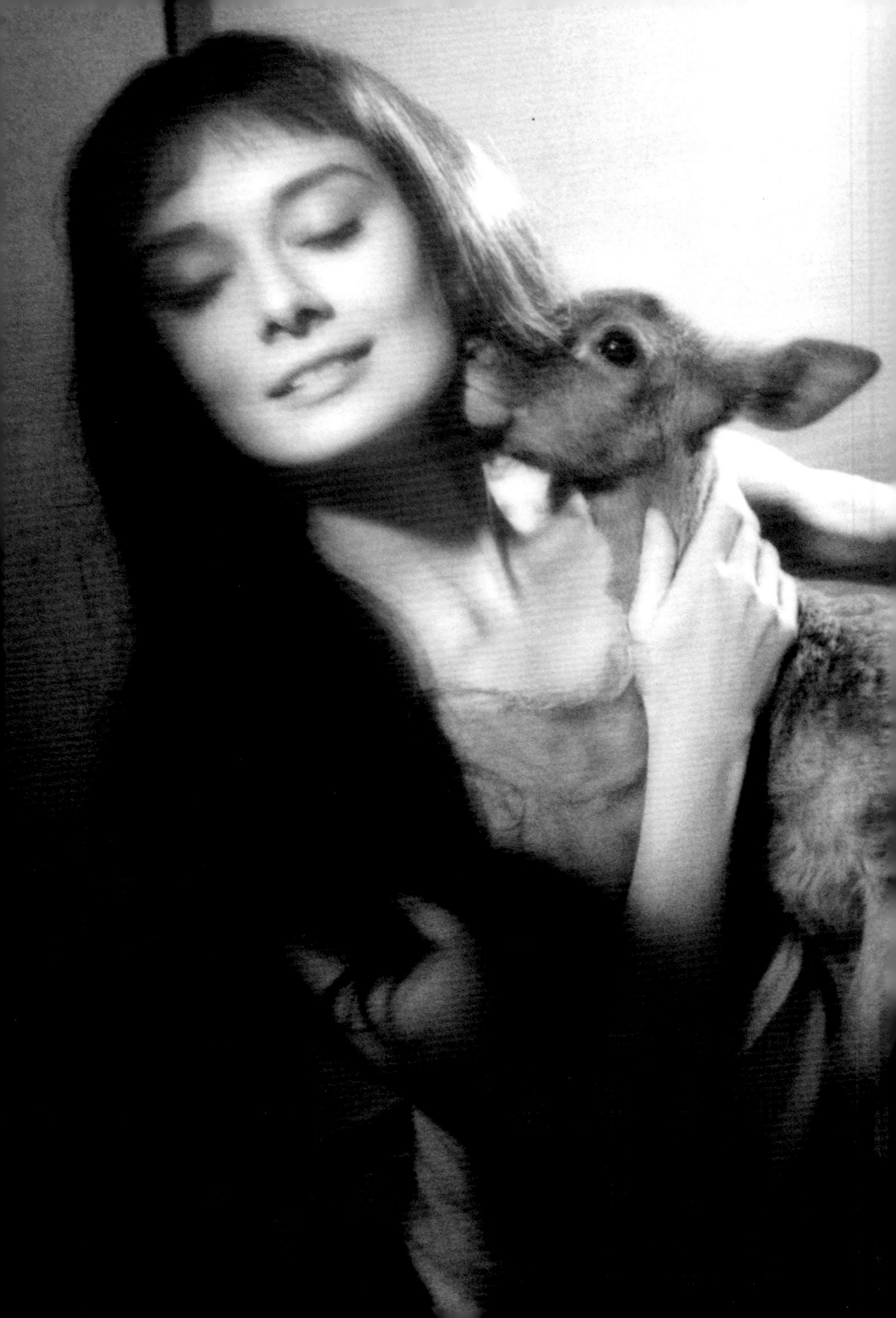

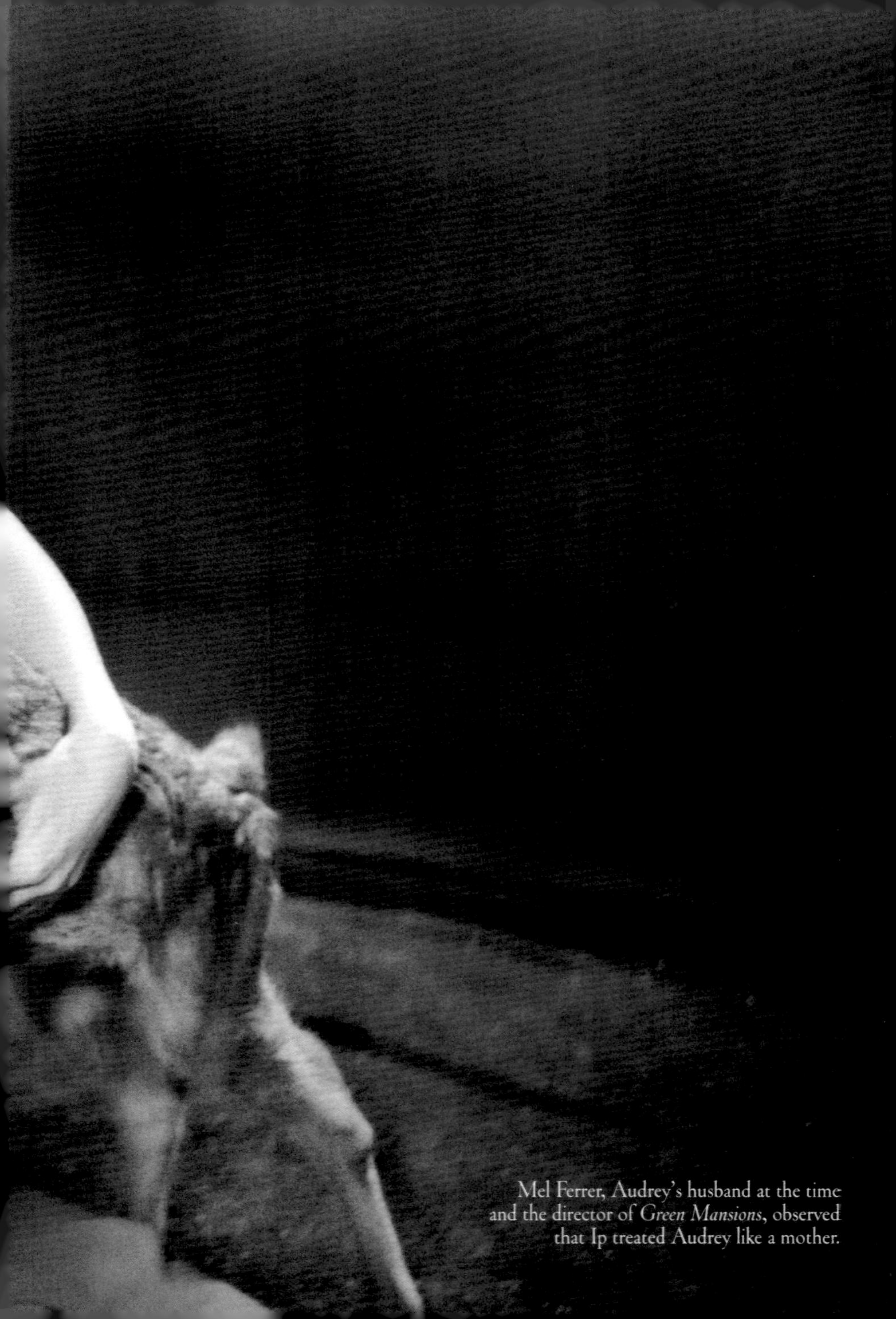

Mel Ferrer, Audrey's husband at the time and the director of *Green Mansions*, observed that Ip treated Audrey like a mother.

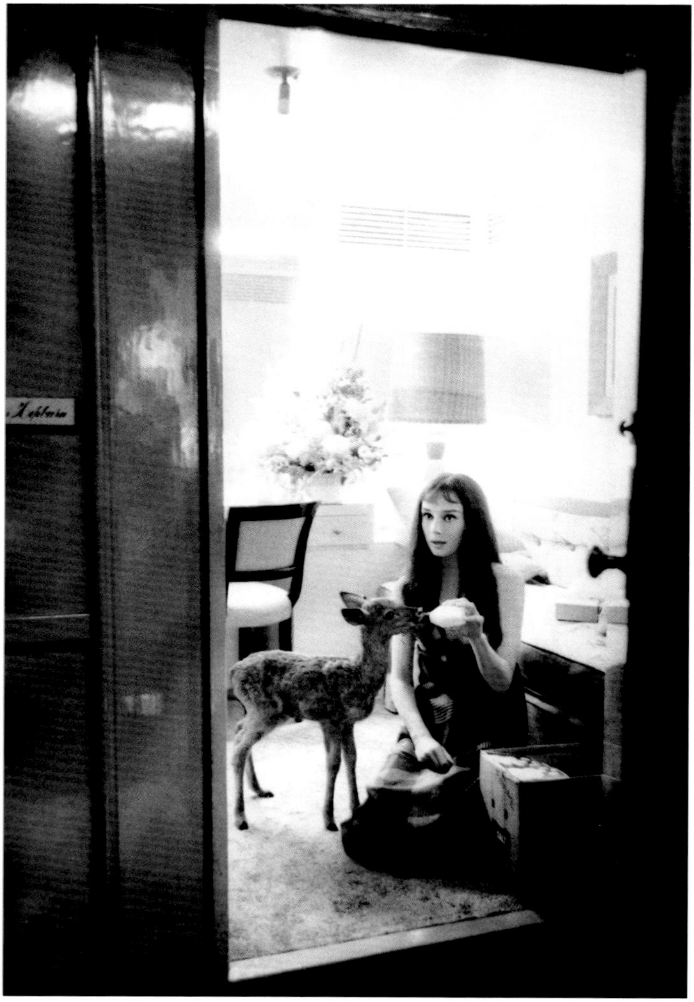

Feeding time for Ip in Audrey's dressing room.

Audrey knots her shirt during the filming of *Green Mansions.*

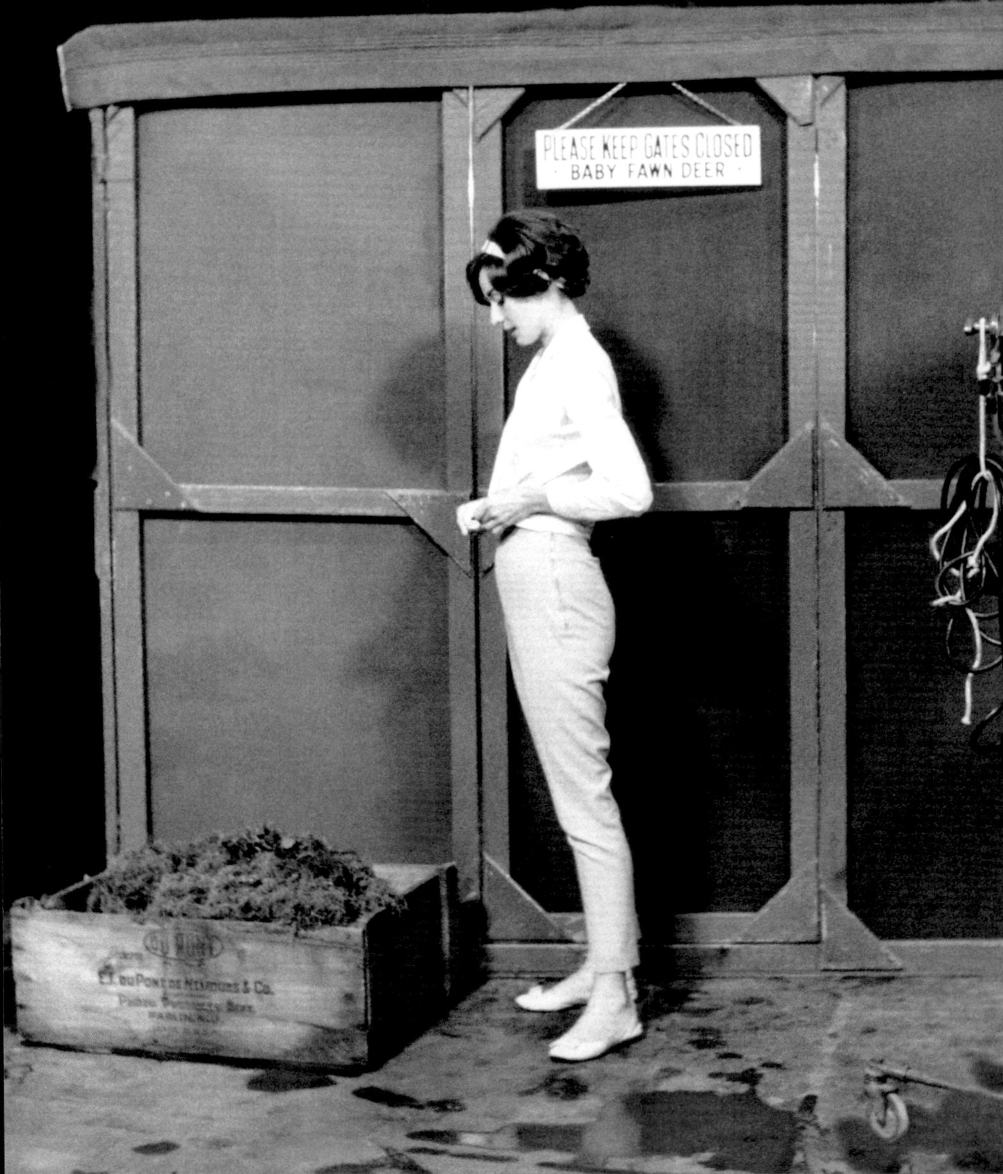
PLEASE KEEP GATES CLOSED
· BABY FAWN DEER ·

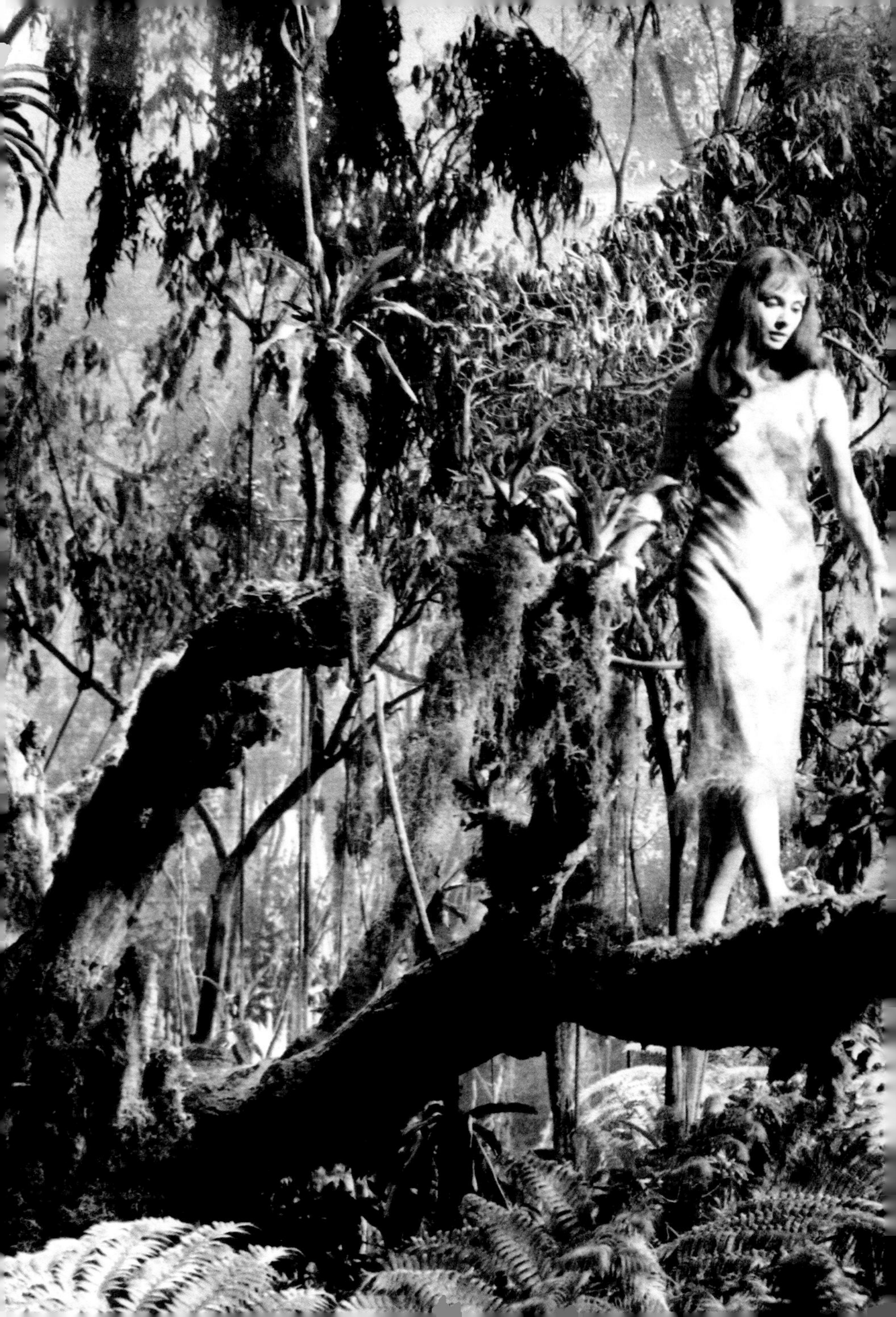

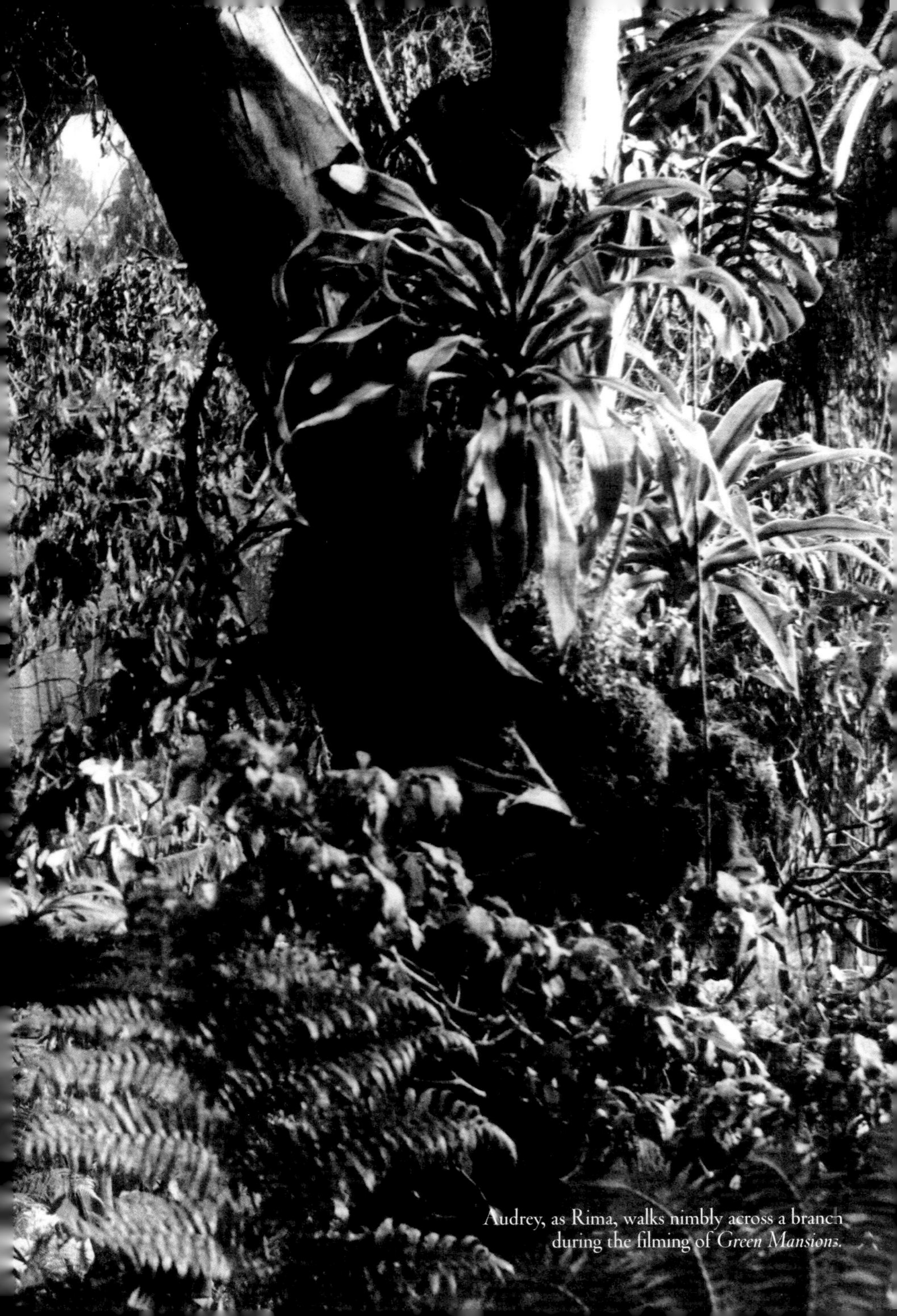

Audrey, as Rima, walks nimbly across a branch during the filming of *Green Mansions.*

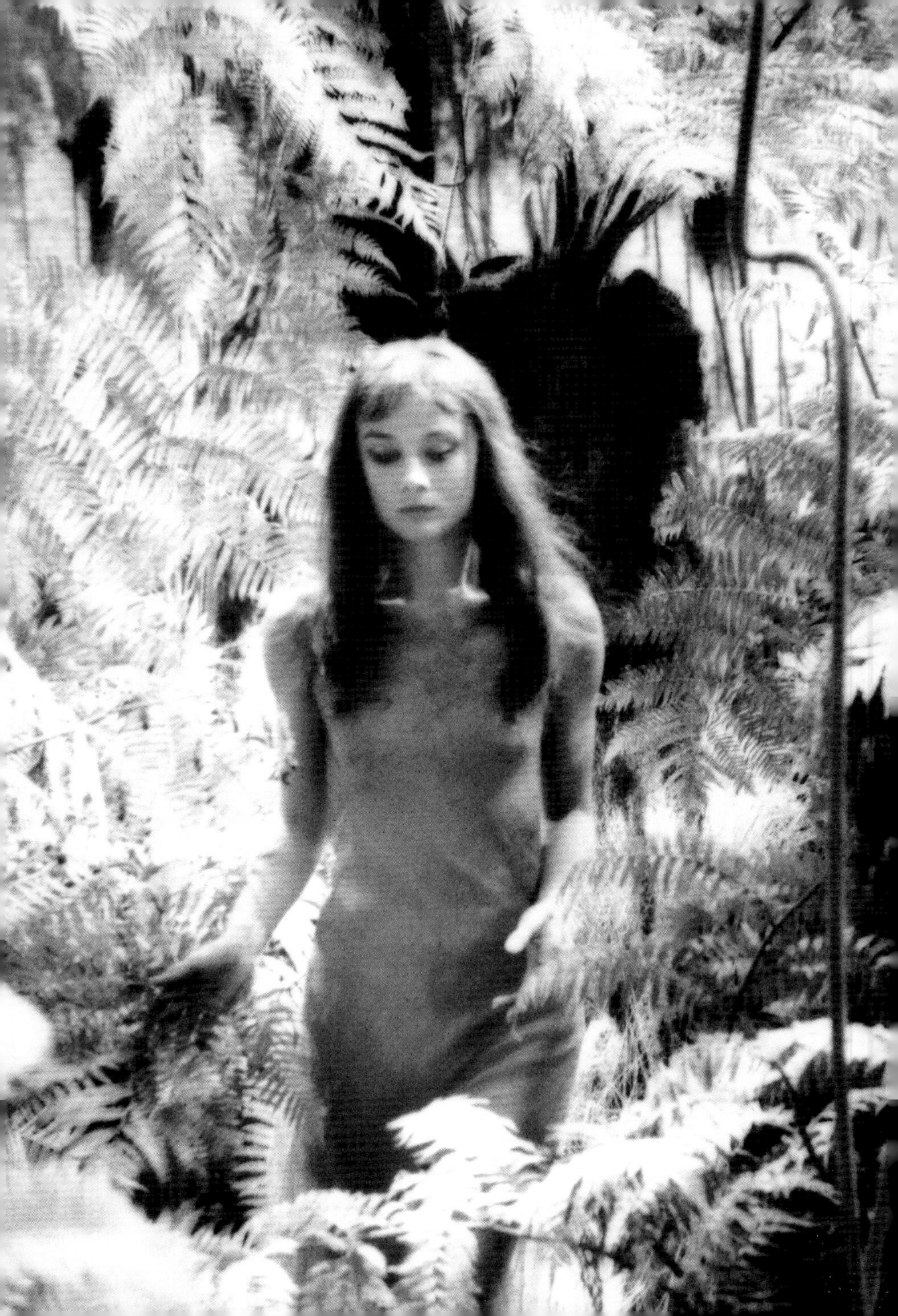

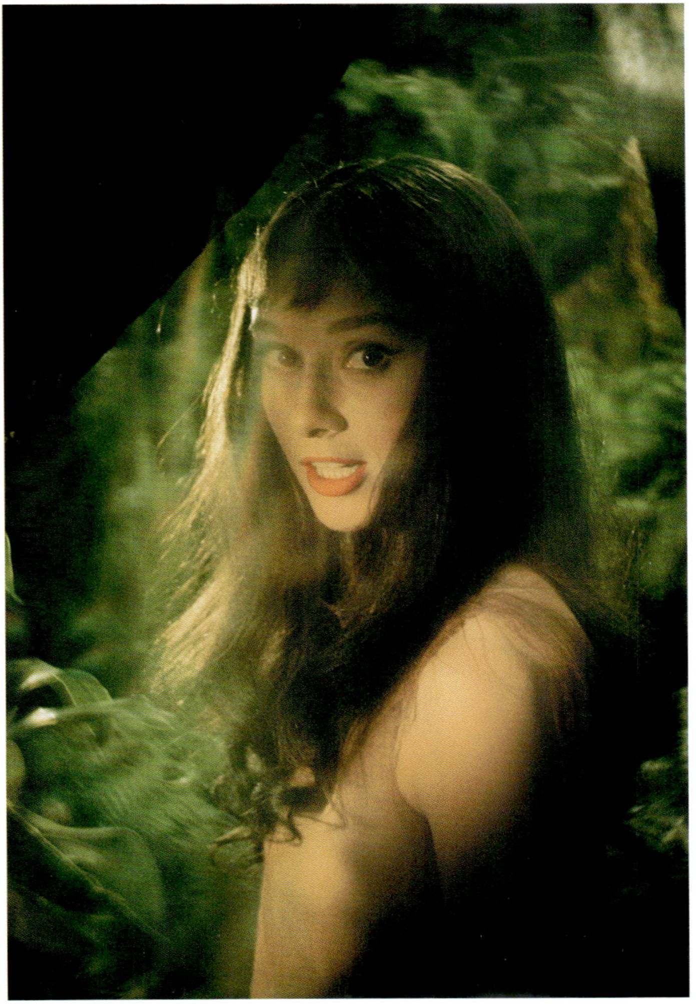

Rima makes her way through the ferns.

Photo taken on the set of *Green Mansions.*

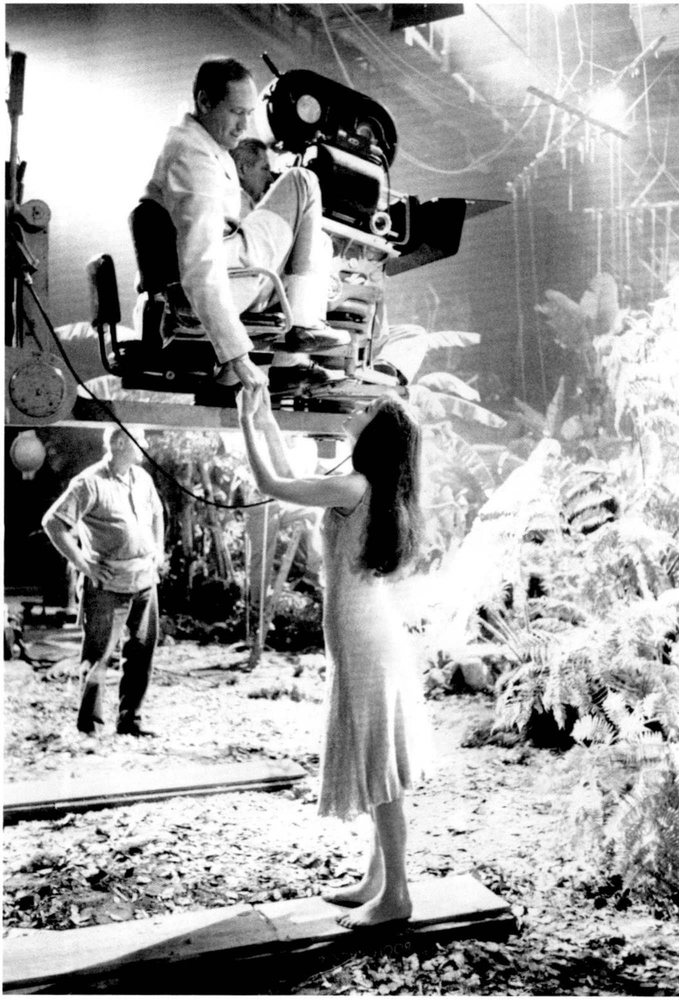

Mel and Audrey are very loving toward each other on set.

Audrey poses in the branches of a tree.

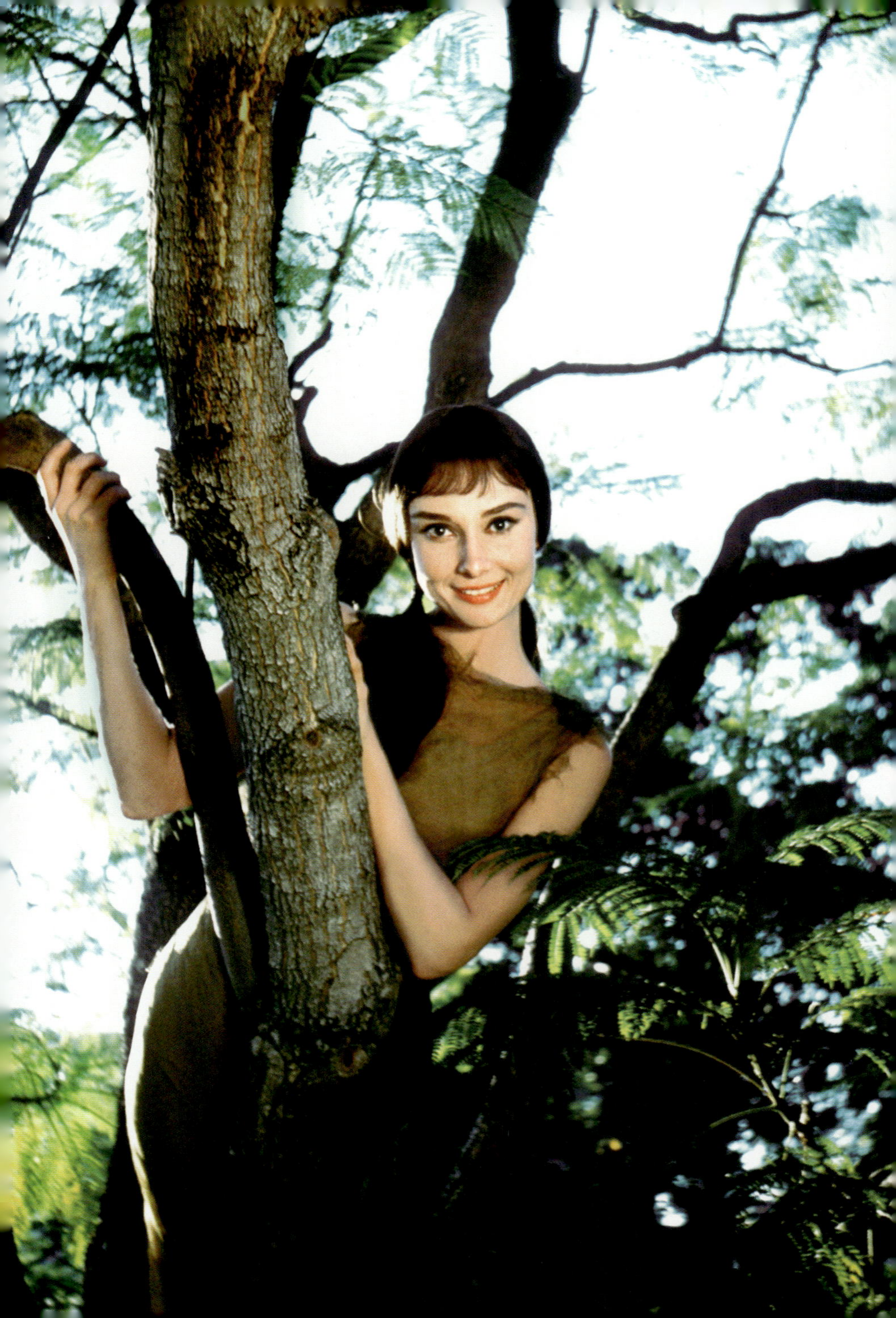

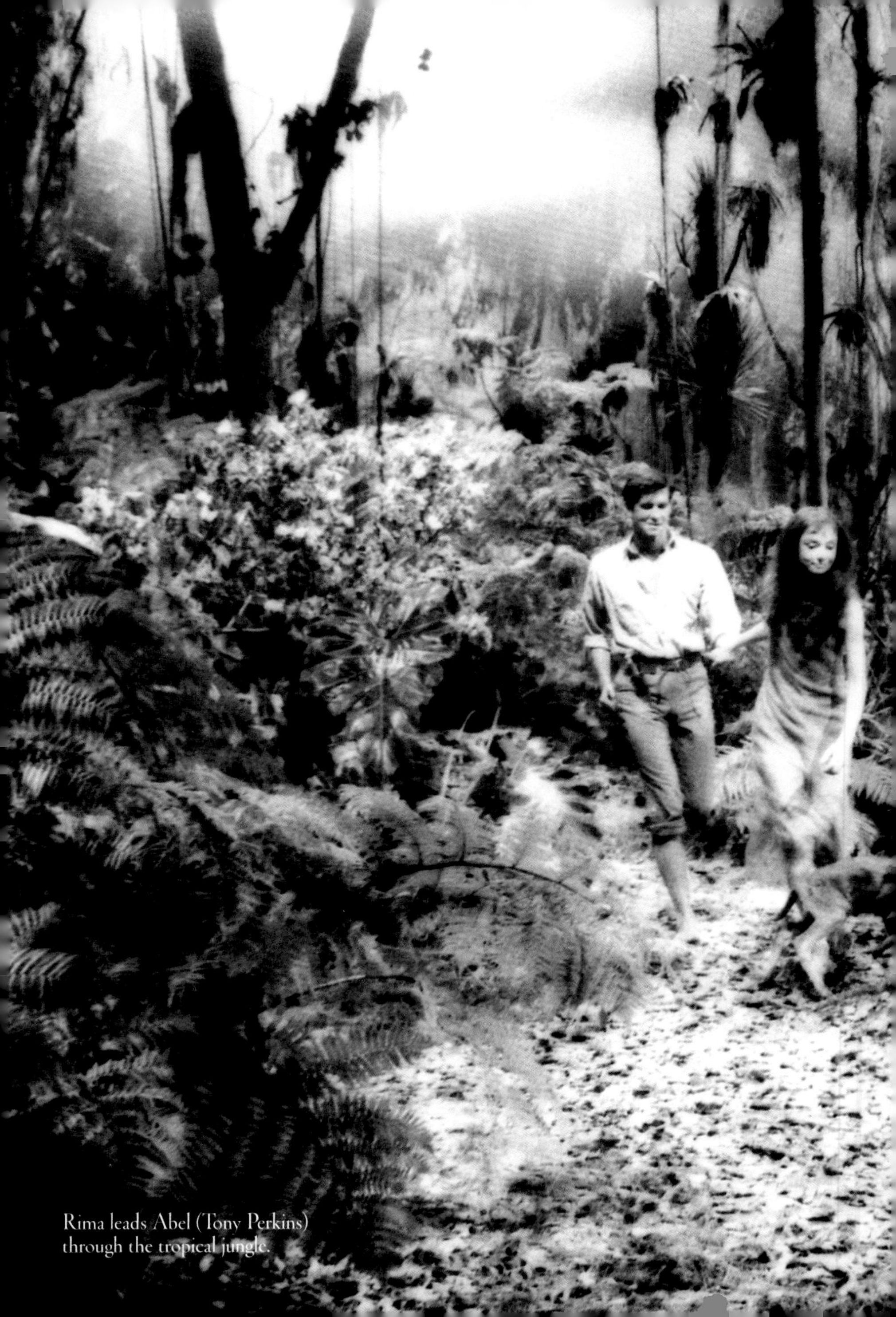

Rima leads Abel (Tony Perkins) through the tropical jungle.

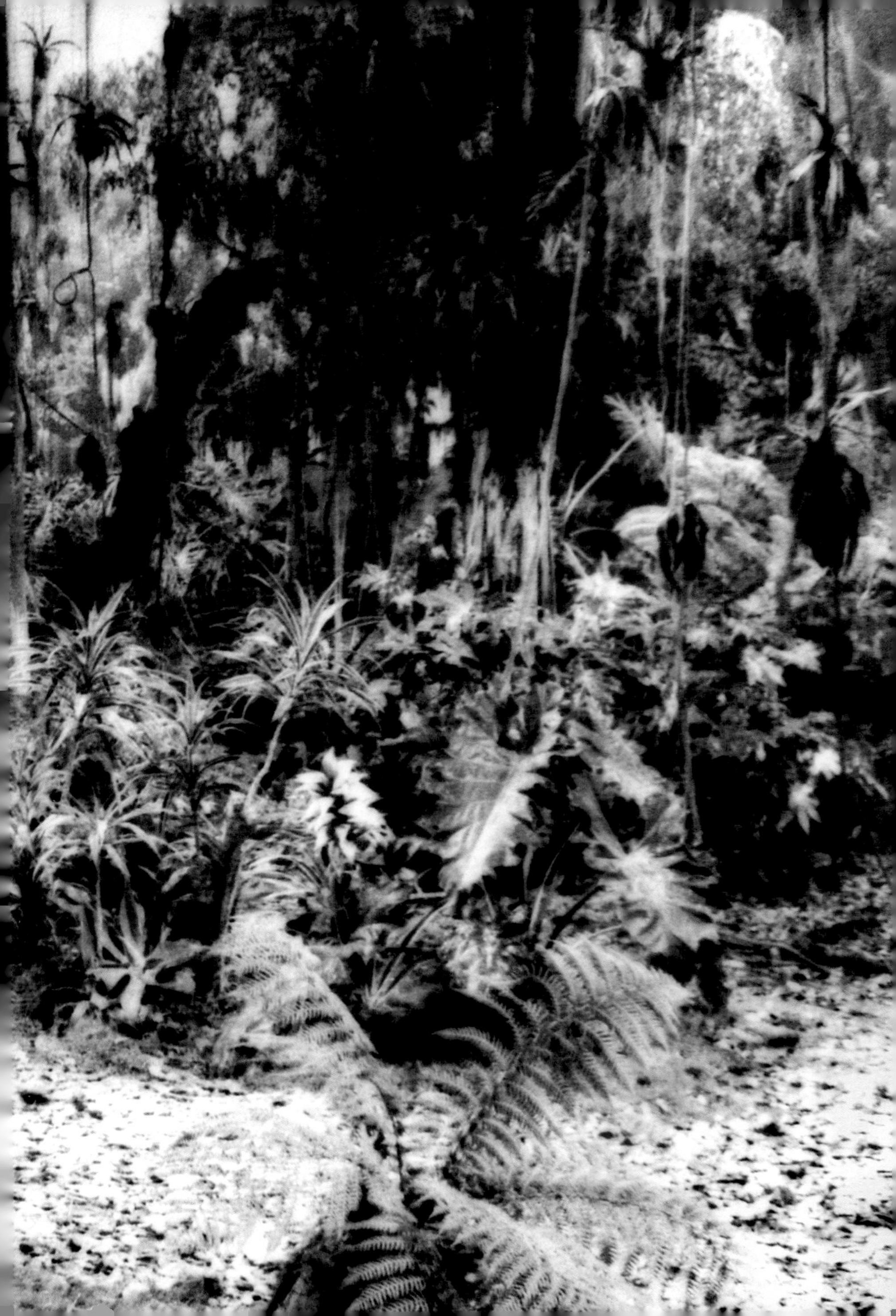

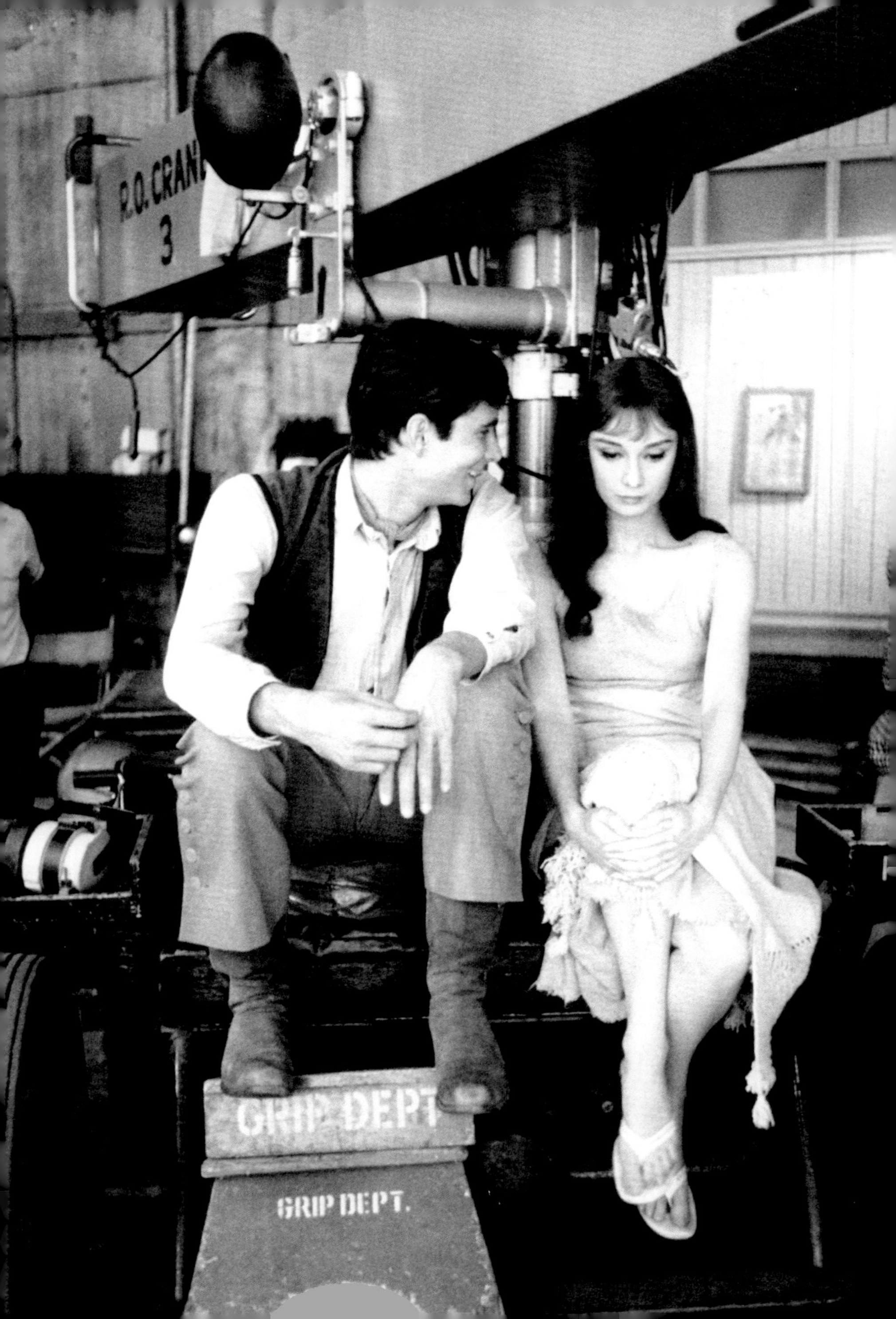
R.O. CRAN
3
GRIP DEPT
GRIP DEPT.

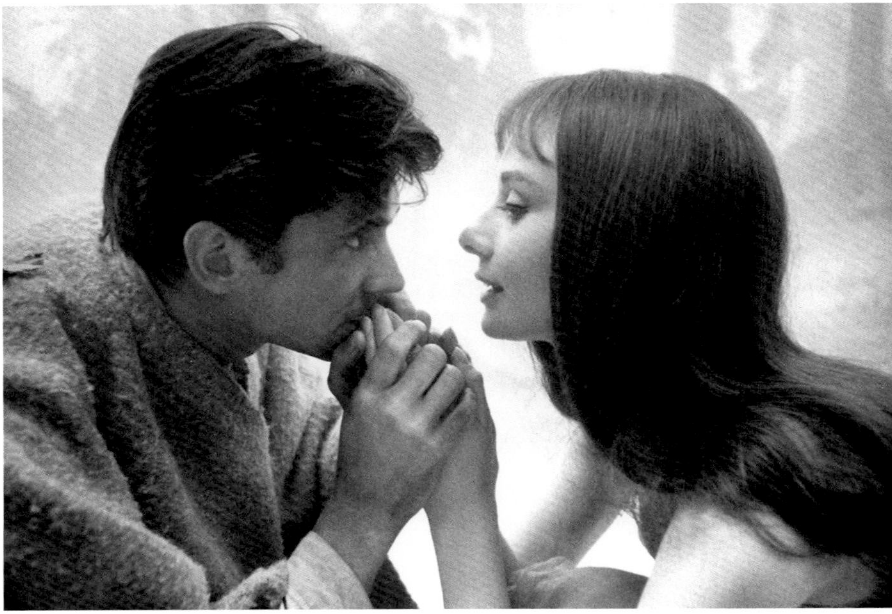

Tony Perkins tries to cheer up a sad-looking Audrey as the pair sit together on a camera boom.

Audrey and Tony had a very close relationship. He took good care of her, made her laugh and was like a brother to her.

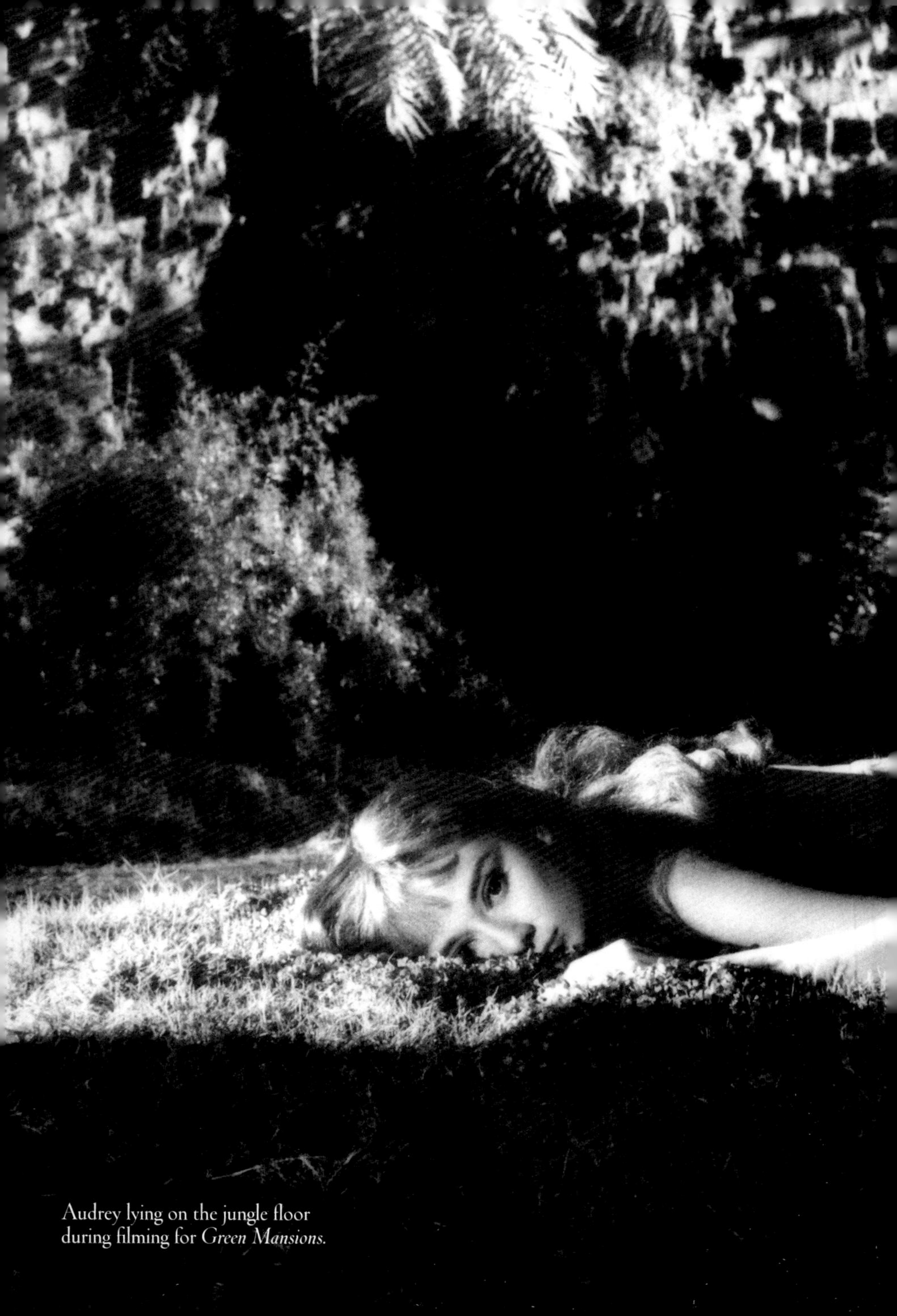

Audrey lying on the jungle floor during filming for *Green Mansions.*

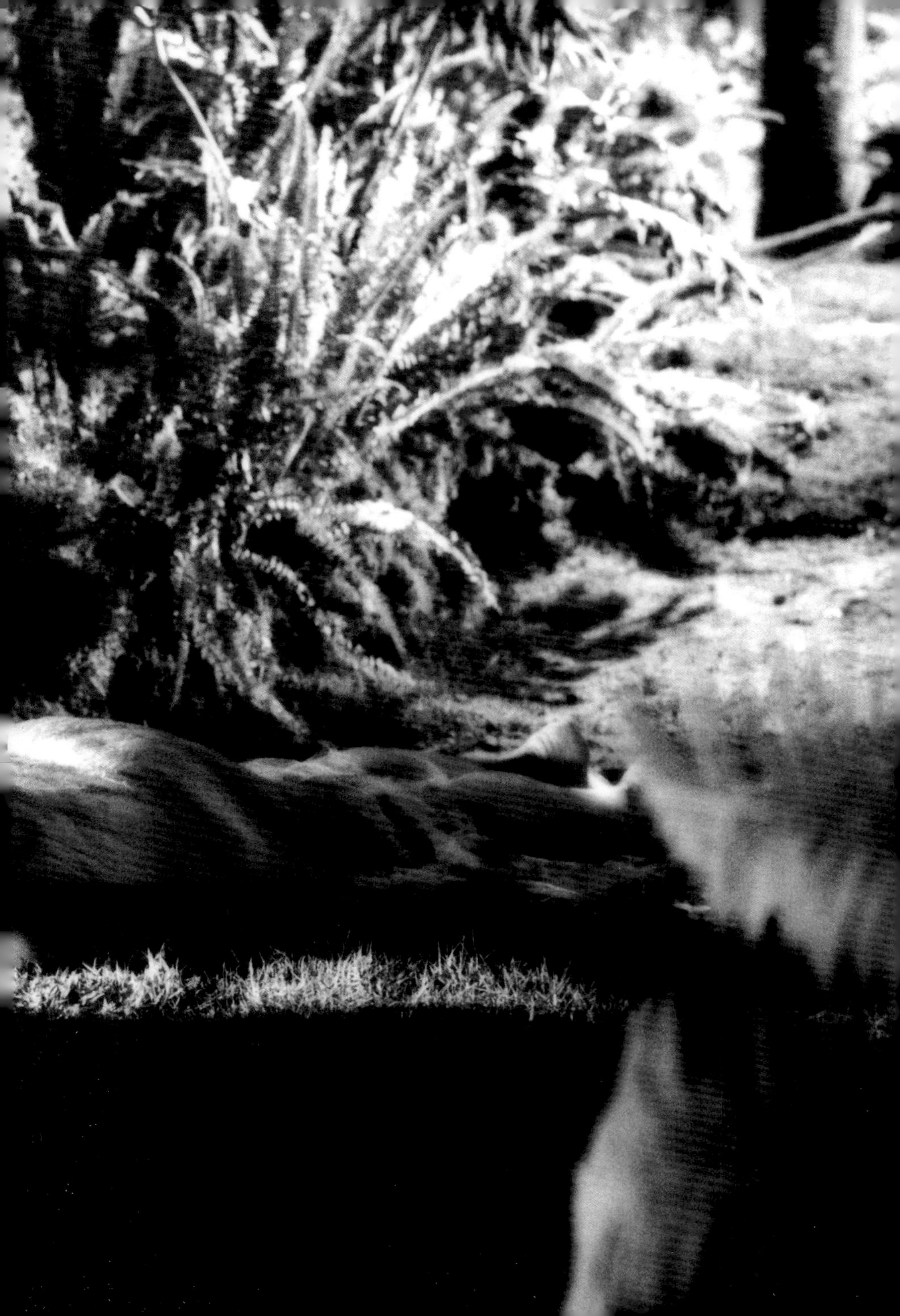

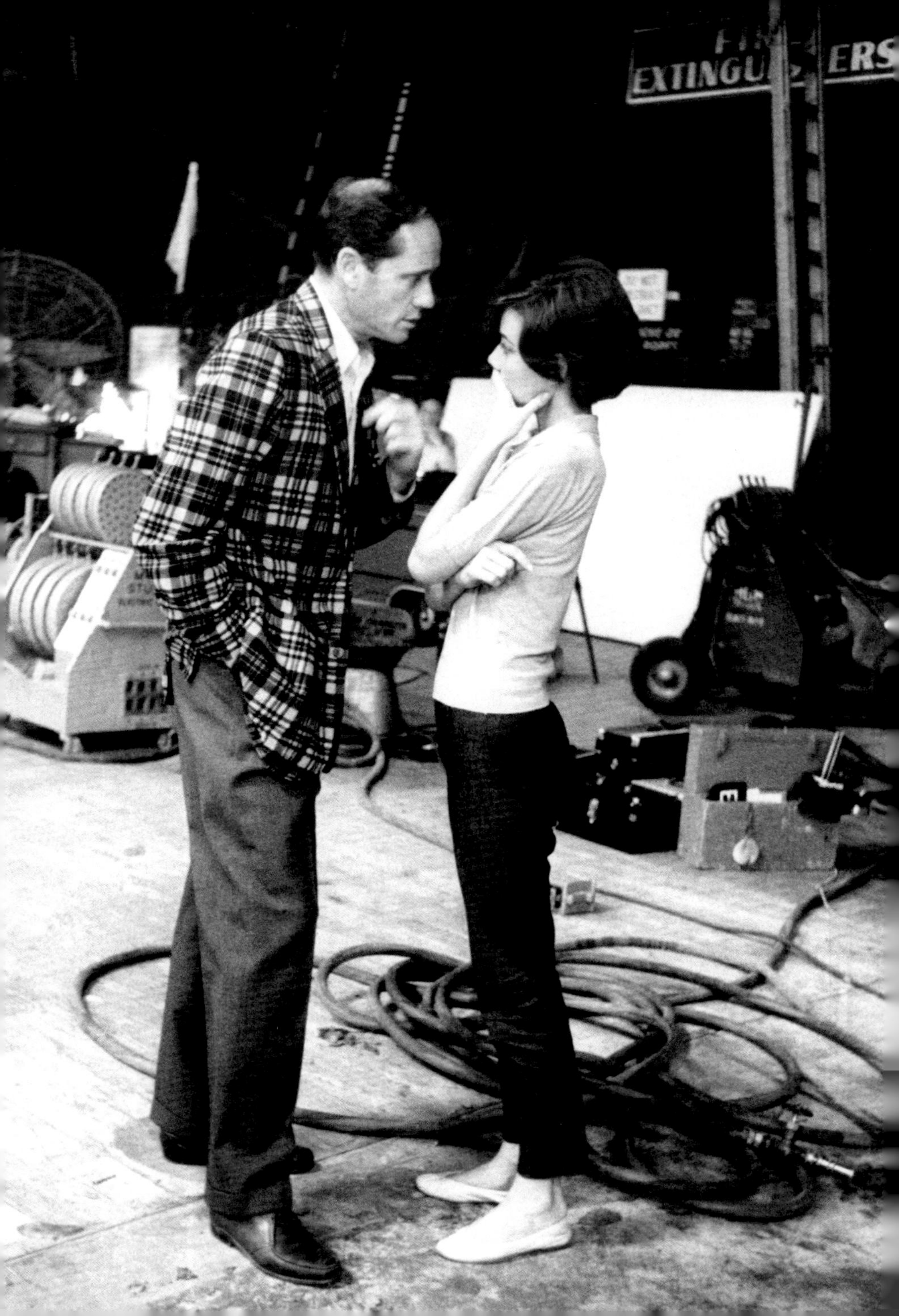

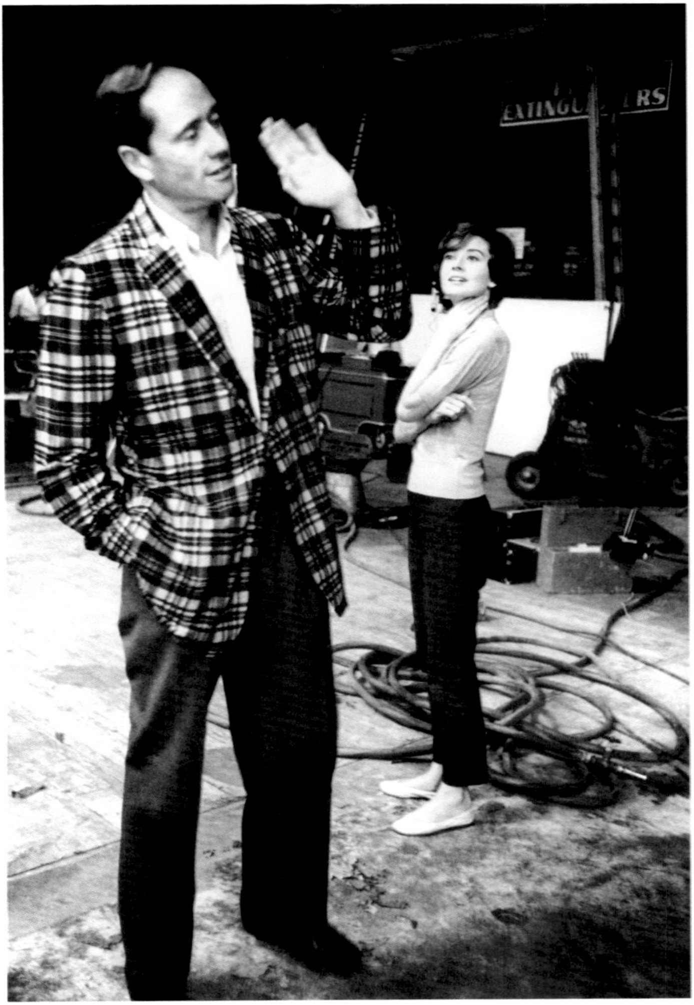

Green Mansions is Mel Ferrer's first film as director.
Audrey never criticizes her husband, nor does she complain or offer suggestions.

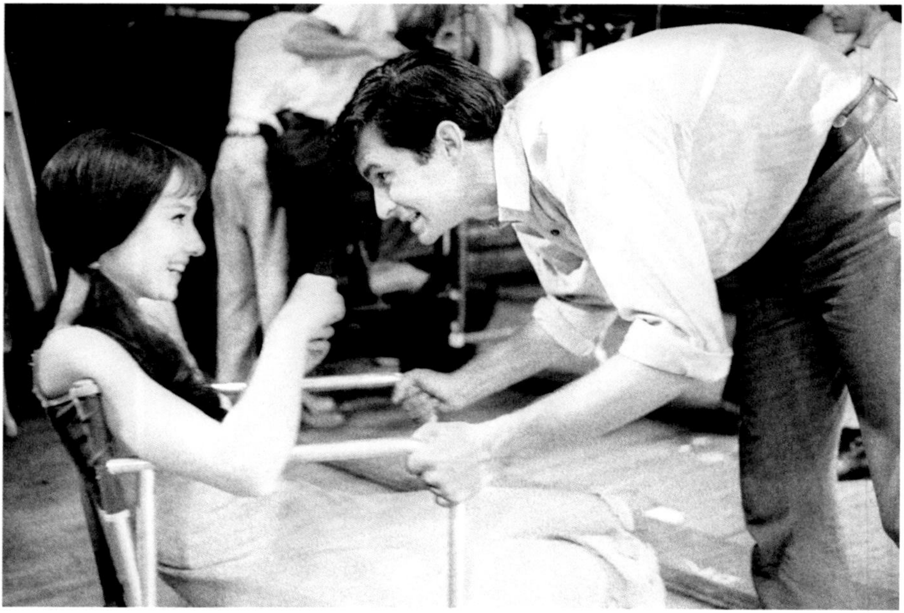

Above:
Tony Perkins could always put a smile on Audrey's face.

Opposite:
Audrey consoles her Yorkshire terrier, Famous. He is jealous of the attention she gives to Ip, the fawn.

Following spread:
Audrey and Famous relax together on the couch at home.

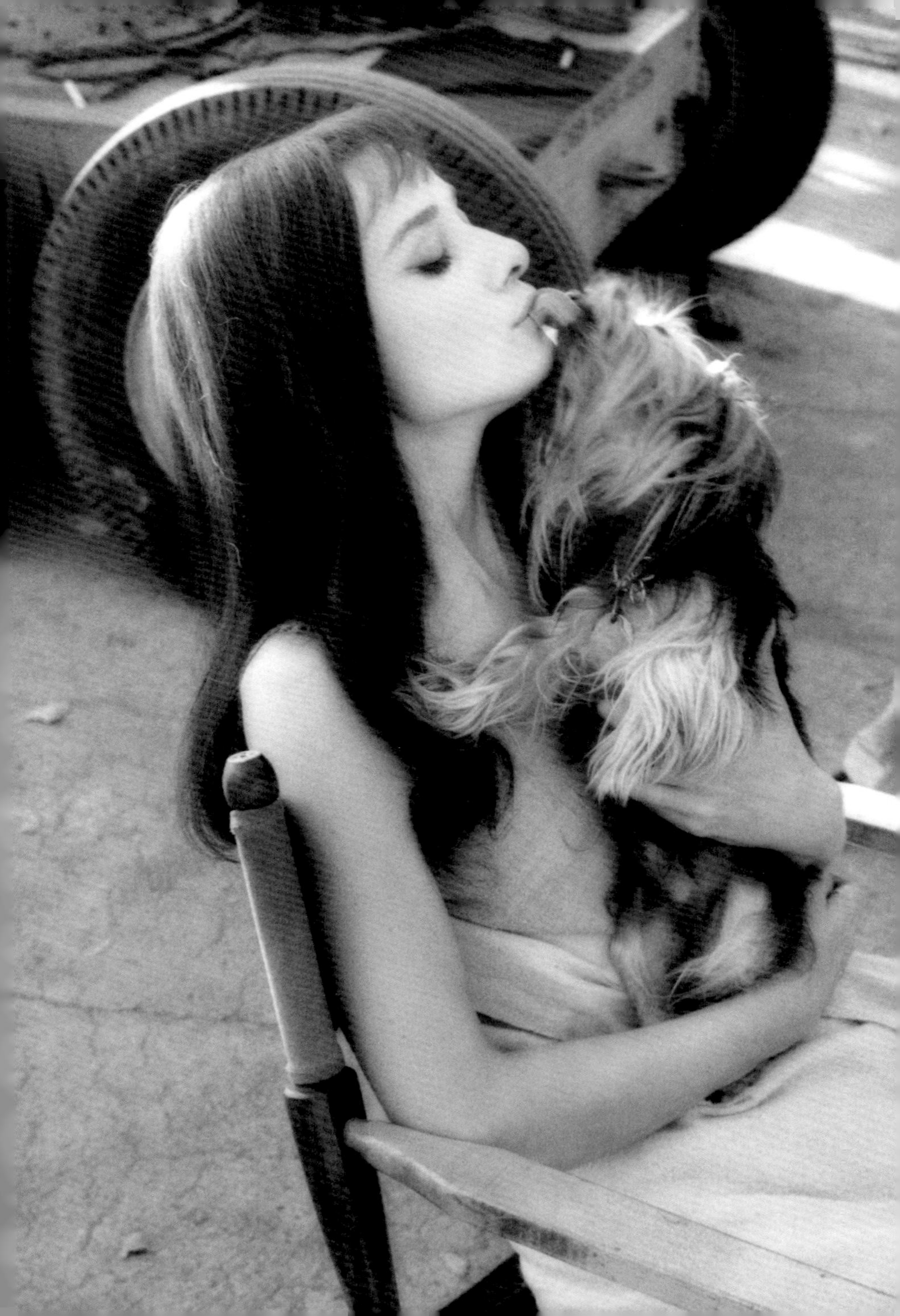

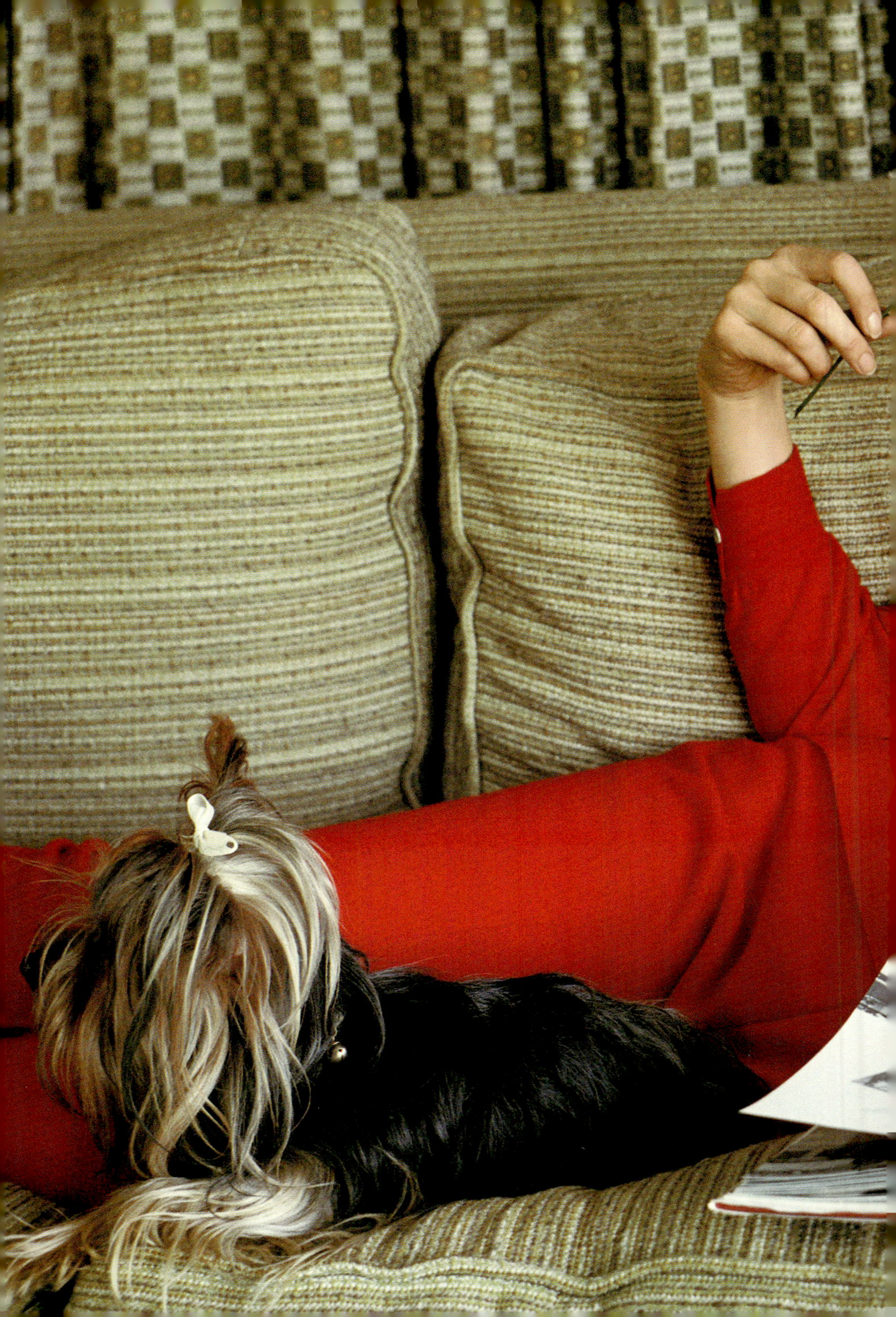

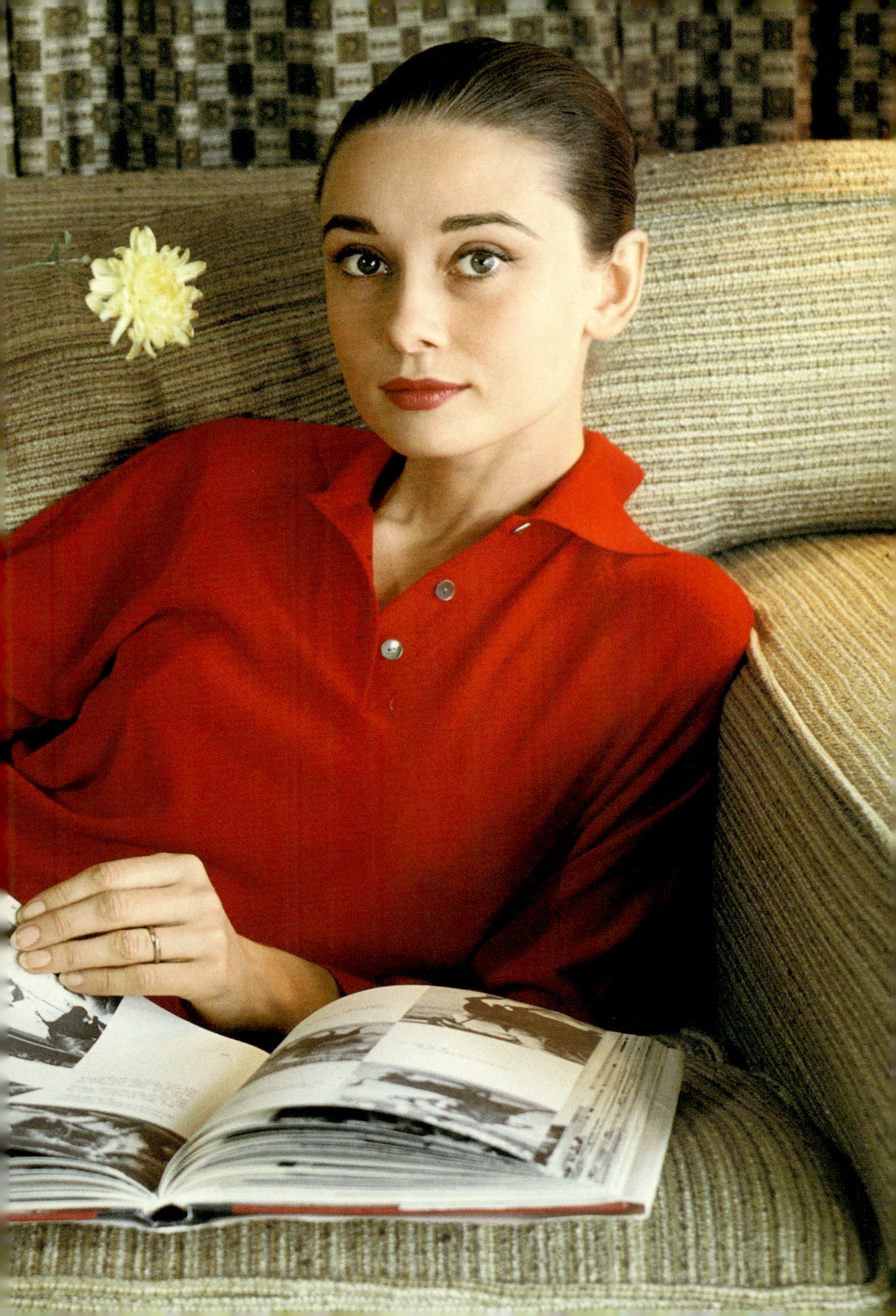

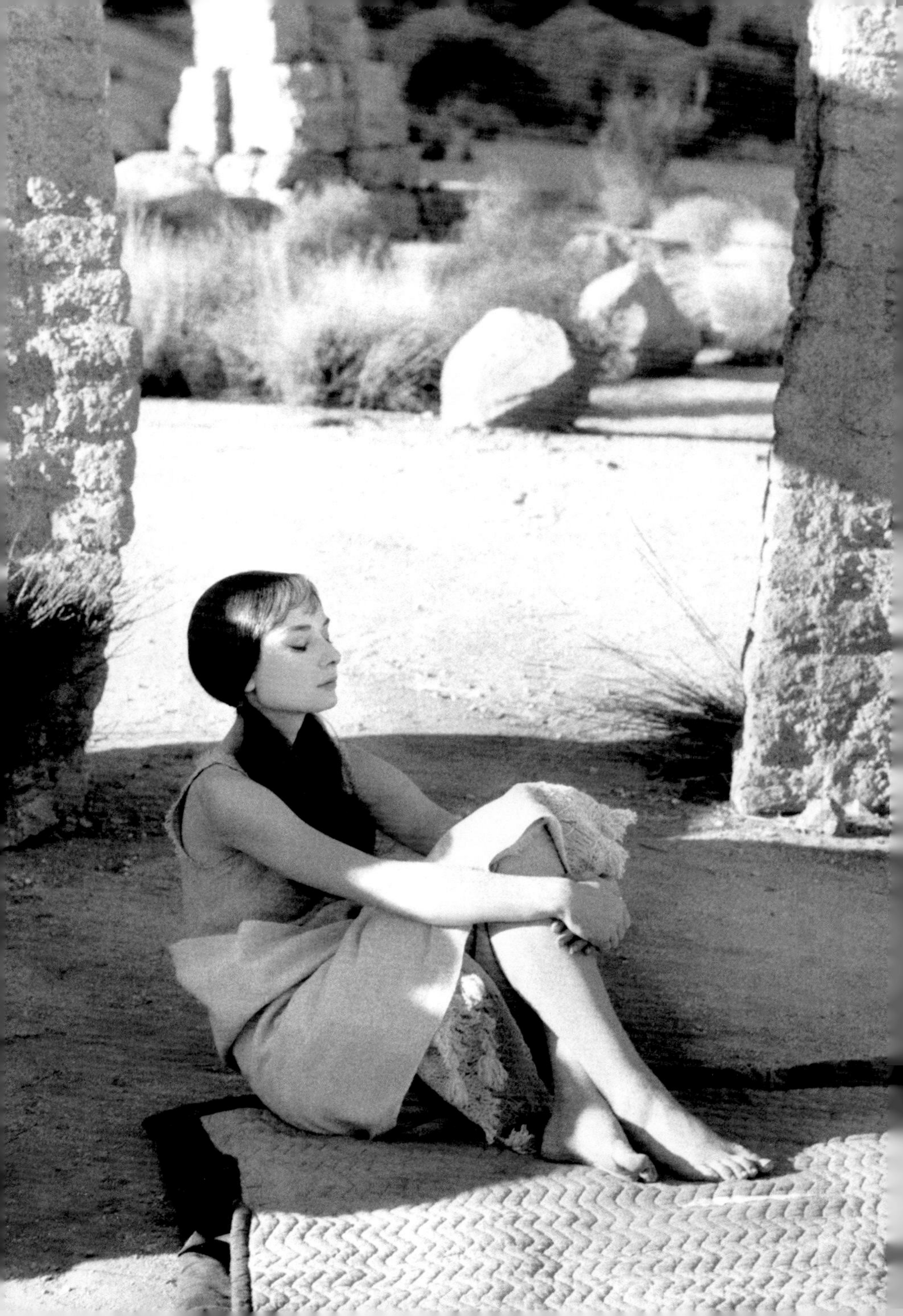

“Uninhibited. For the first time
in my career, I’ve lost my shyness...
Love scenes have always been difficult for me.
But with Mel directing and leading
Tony and me through the emotional passages,
everything’s fallen into place.”

Audrey Hepburn

In her Rima costume and wrapped in a blanket, Audrey takes a moment to collect her thoughts during filming of *Green Mansions*.

Following spread:
In *The Children’s Hour* (1961) a schoolgirl claims that two of her teachers are having a lesbian affair, with tragic consequences. Here the girl looks up at Audrey, who plays the teacher Karen Wright.

THE CHILDREN'S HOUR

1961

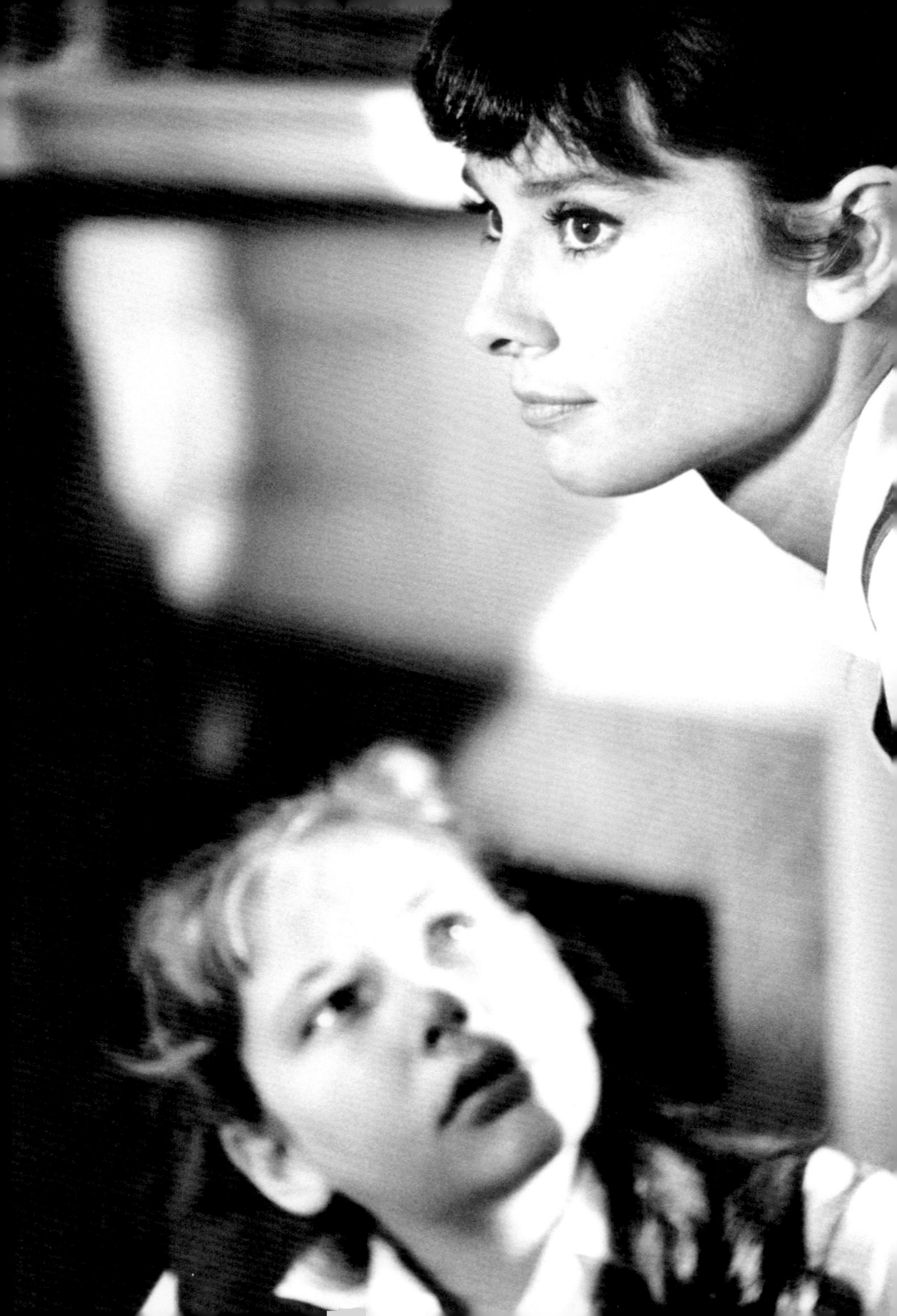

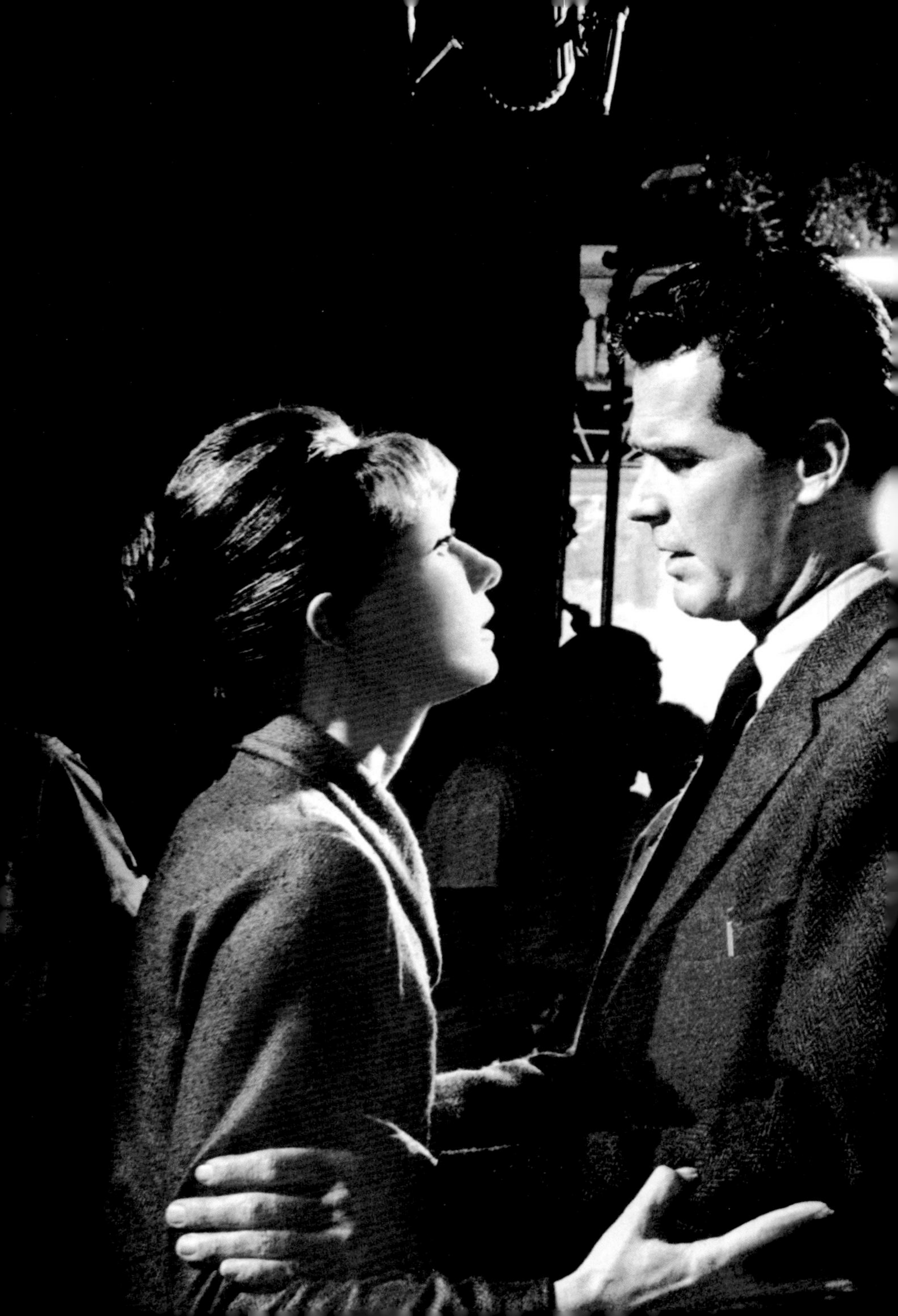

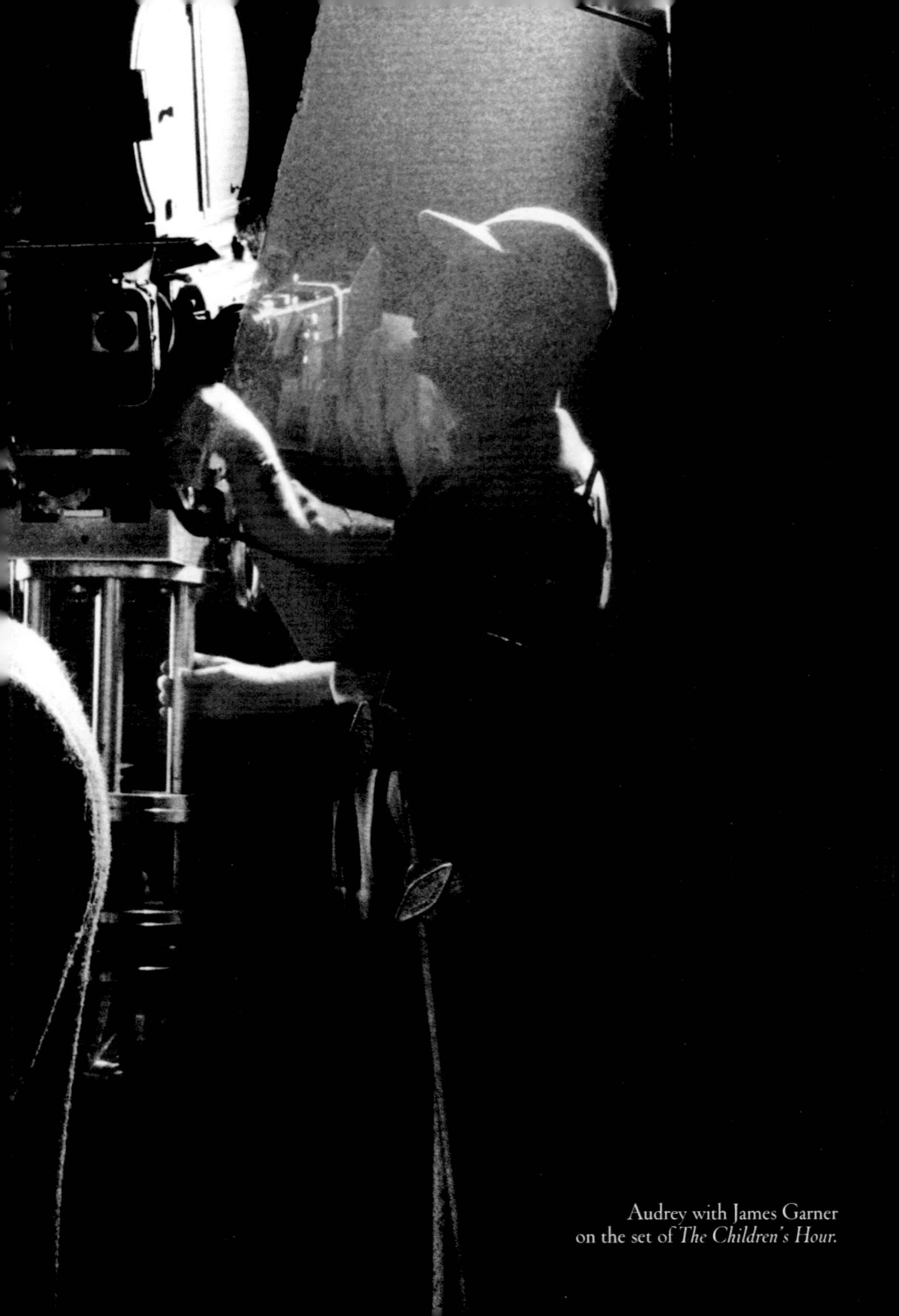

Audrey with James Garner
on the set of *The Children's Hour.*

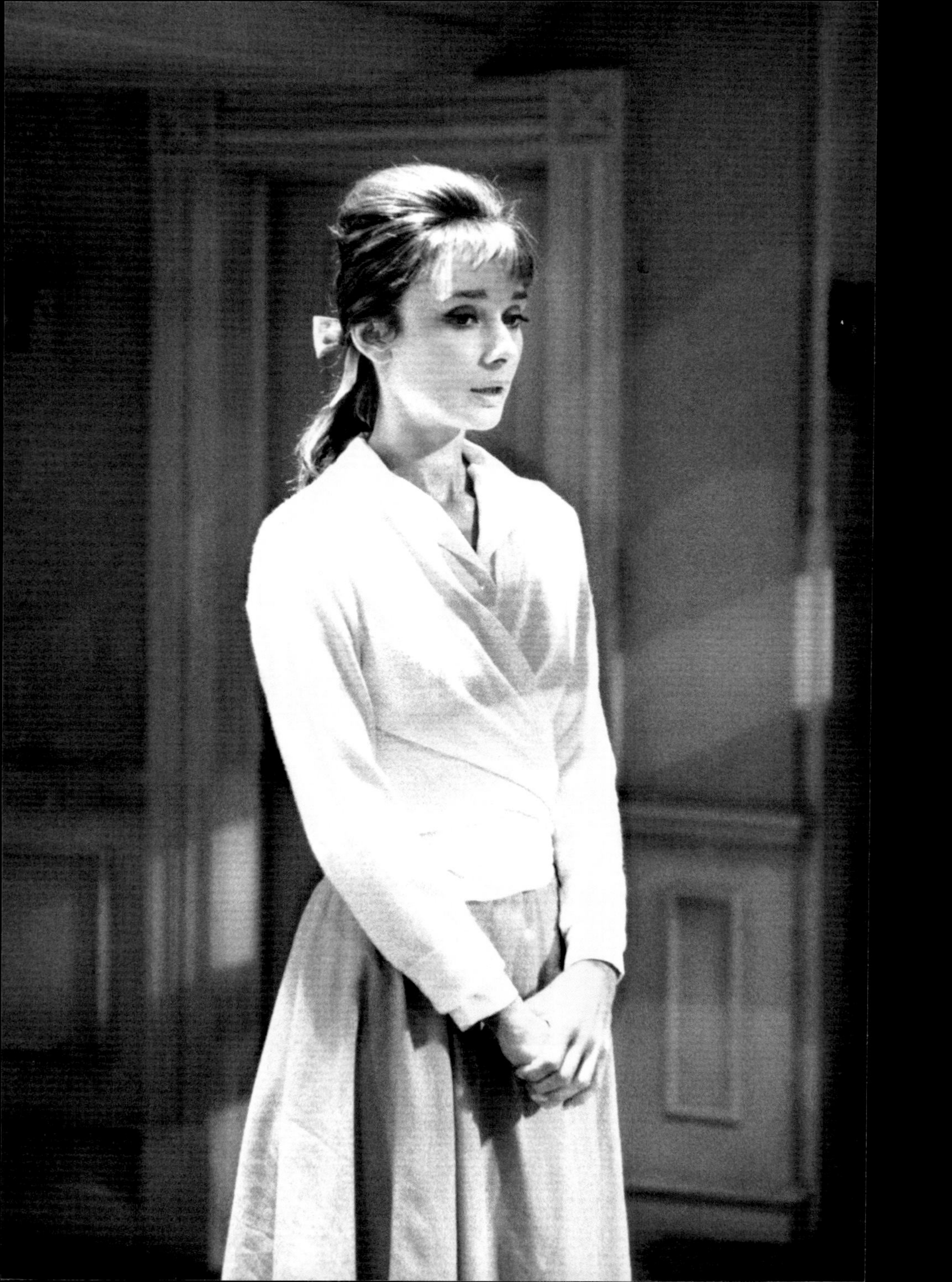

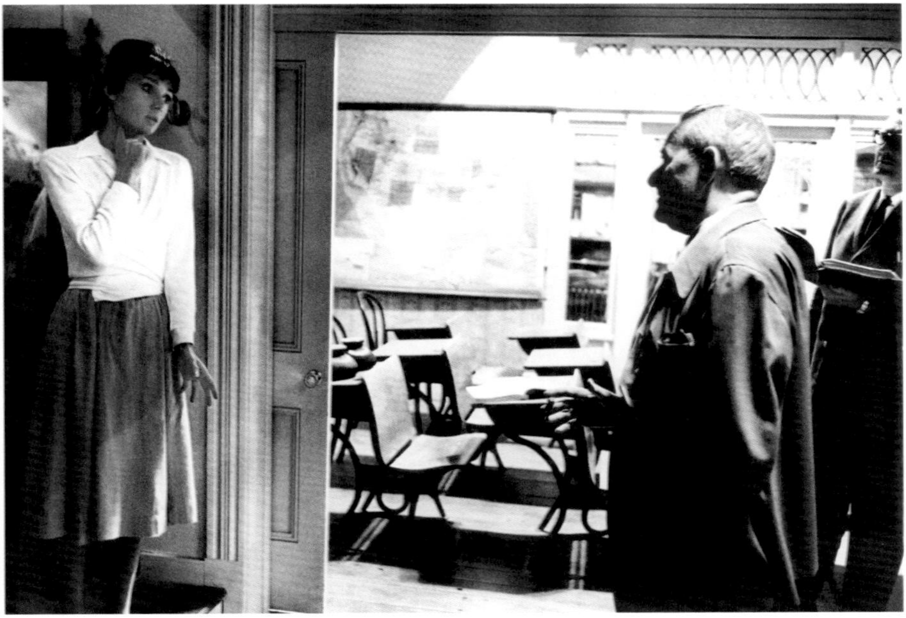

Audrey tries to immerse herself in the role of Karen.

William Wyler (near right) takes a very single-minded and long-winded approach to directing *The Children's Hour.*

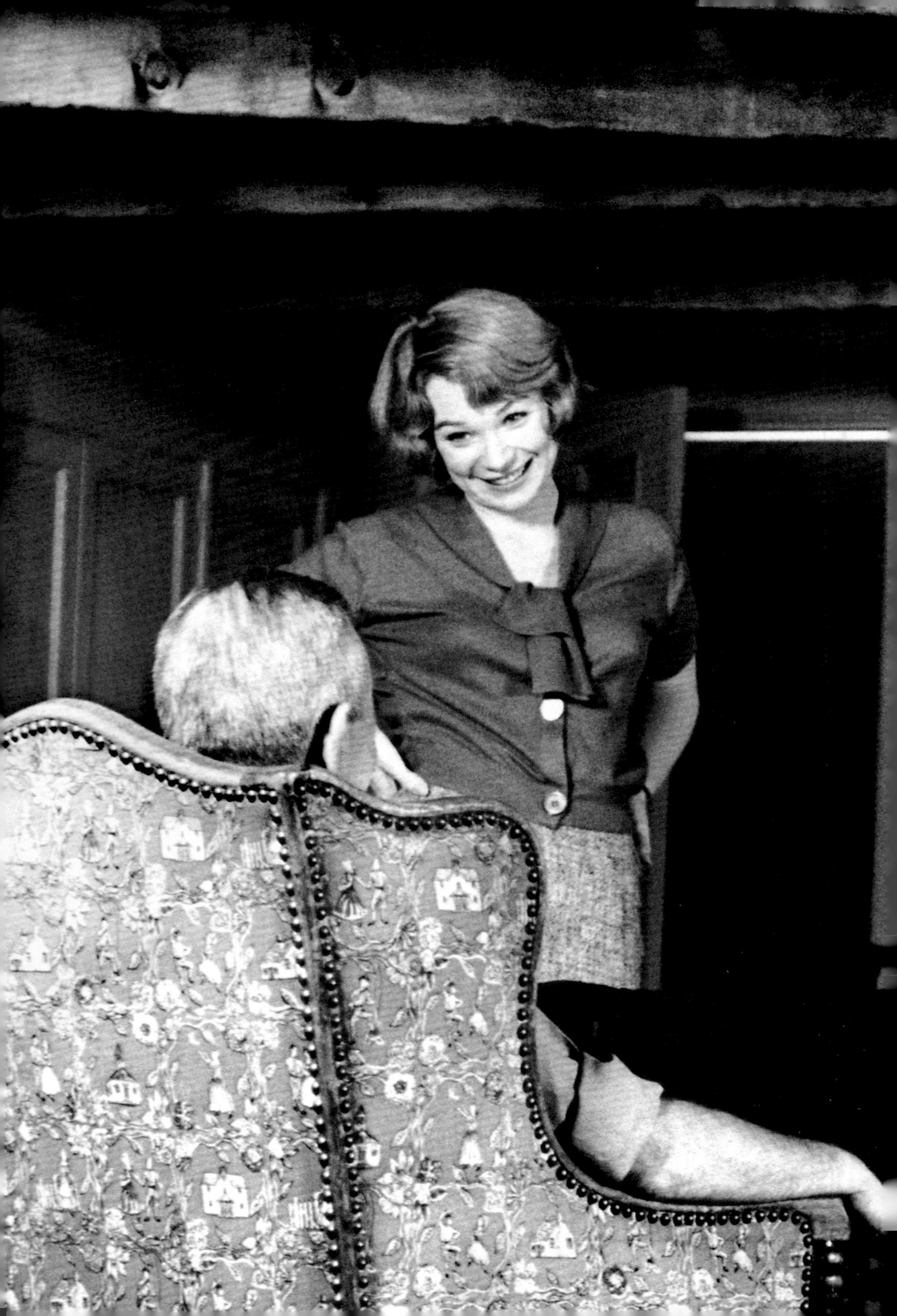

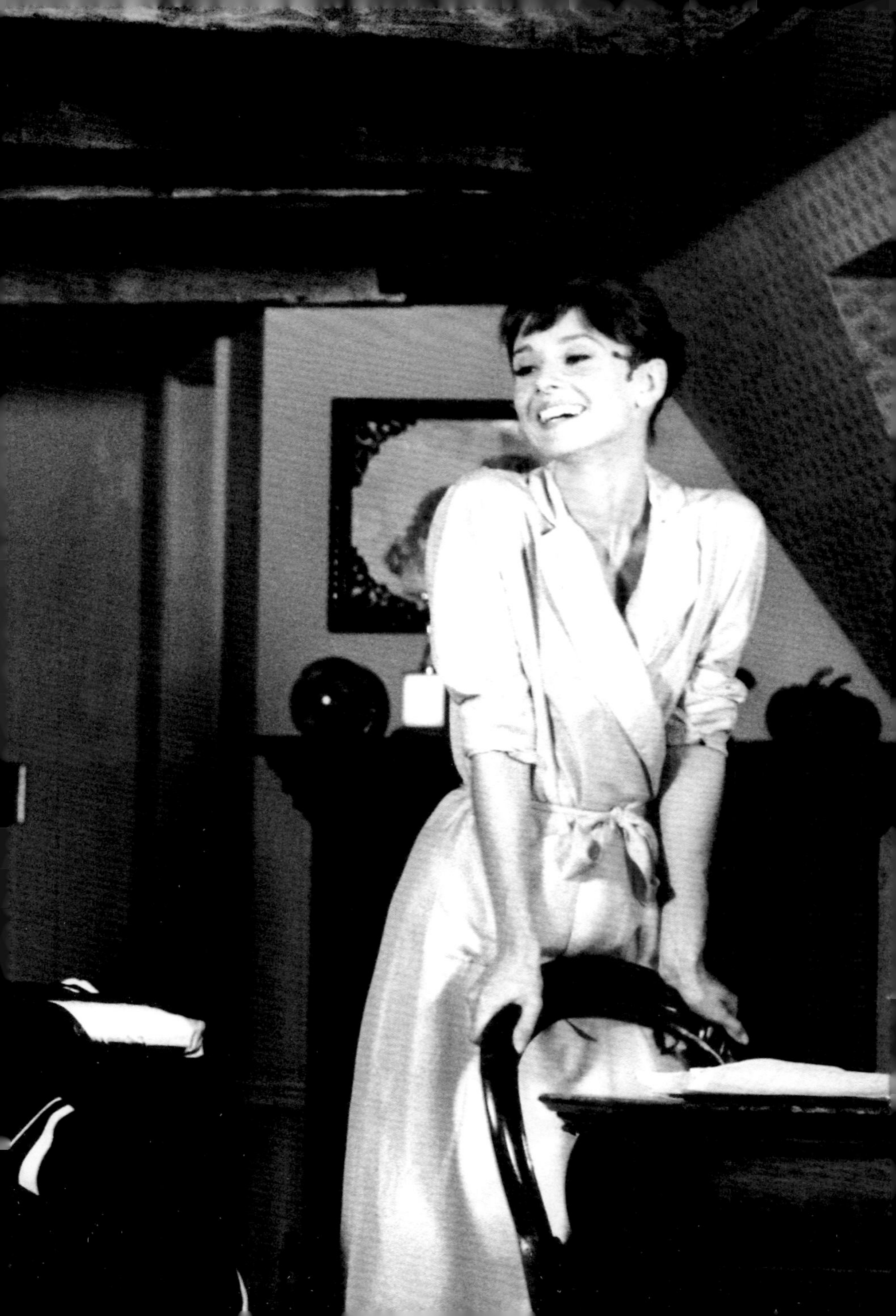

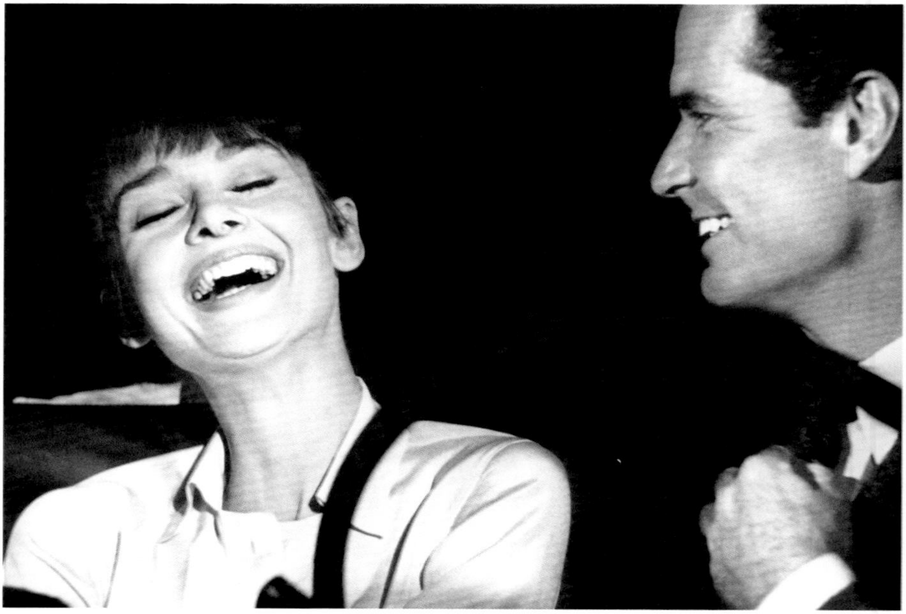

Previous spread:
William Wyler (back to the camera) was said to be an obstinate director; here he brings a smile to the faces of MacLaine and Hepburn.

Above:
James Garner brings laughter to an often somber set.

Opposite:
Audrey fooling around on the set of *The Children's Hour.*

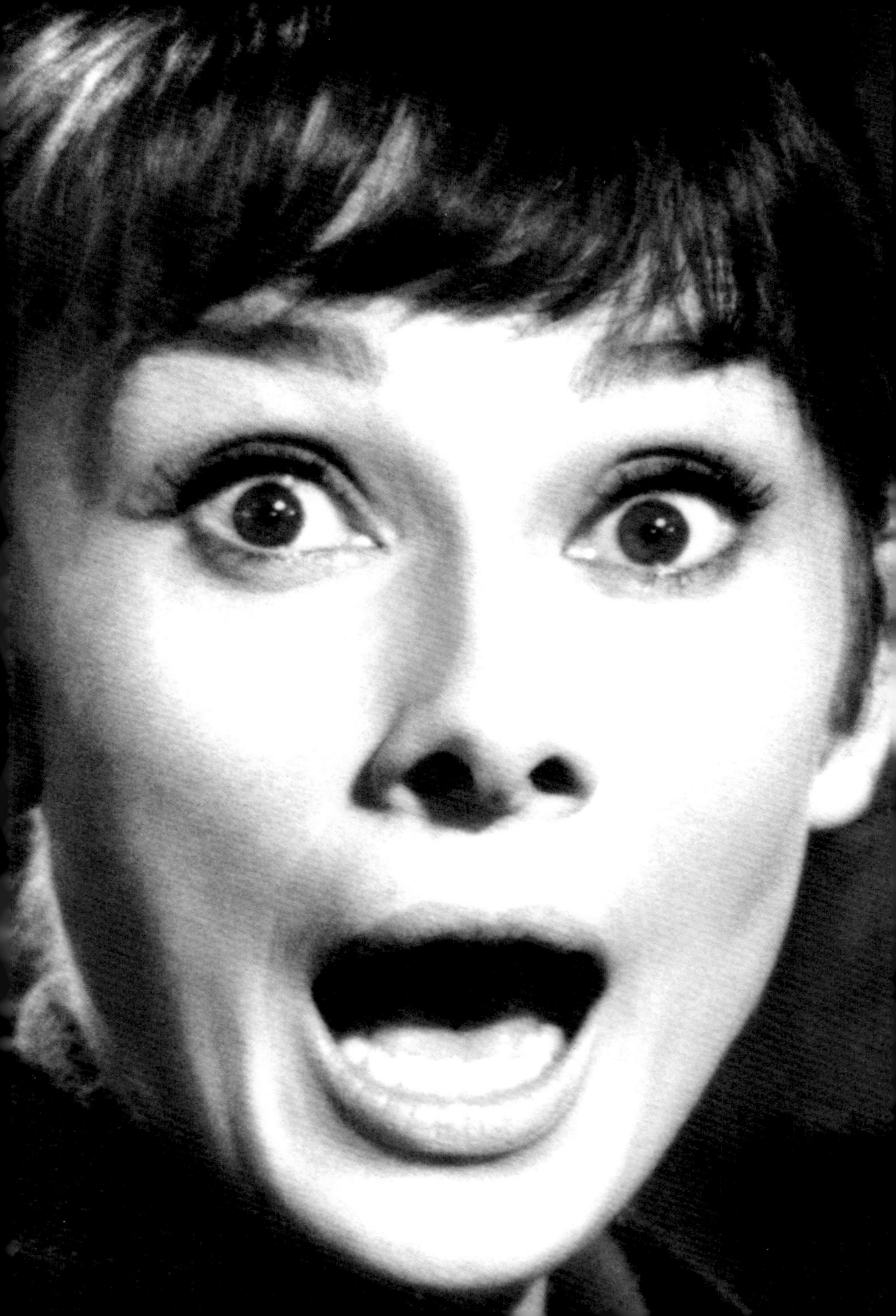

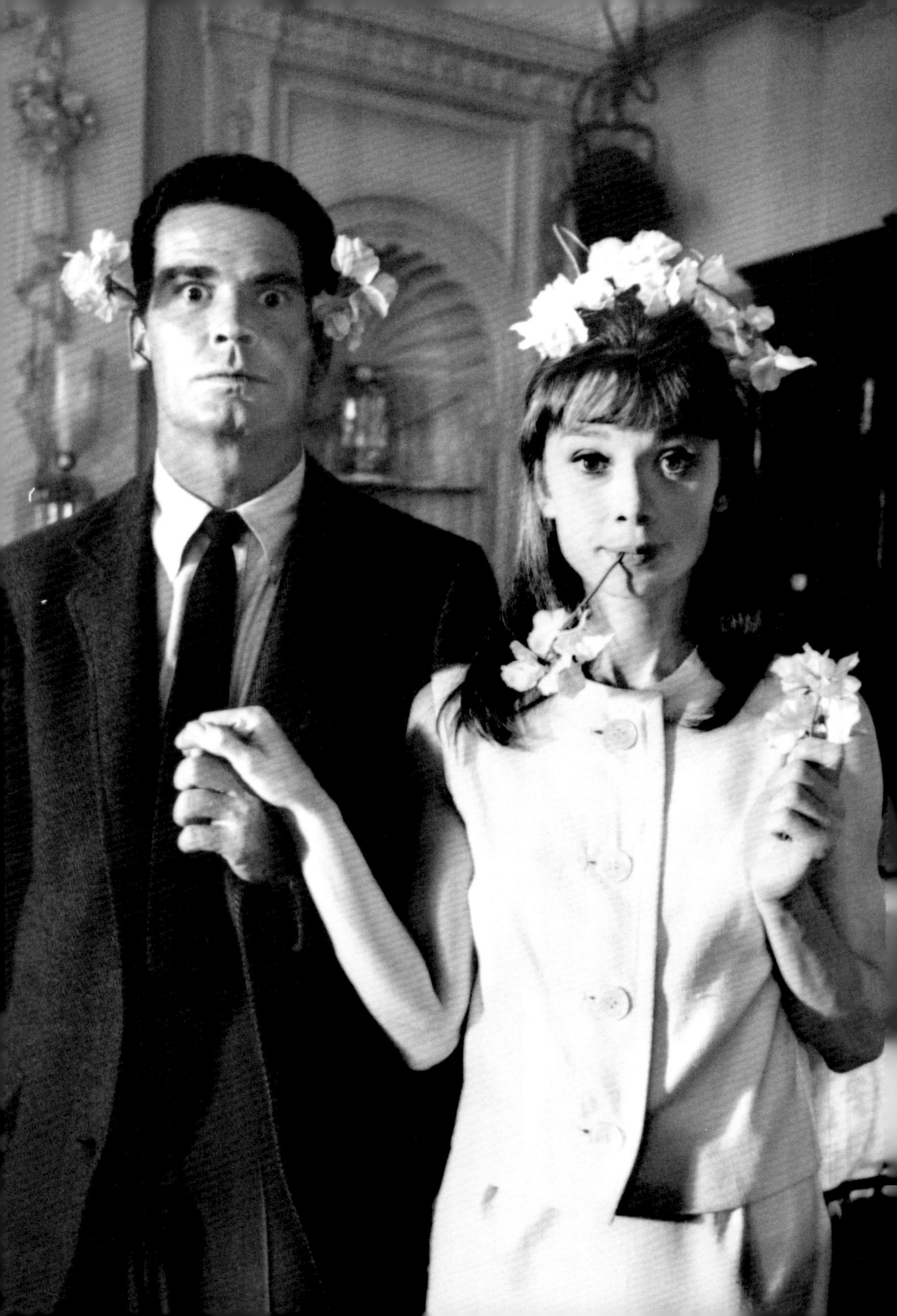

"As a child, I was taught that it was bad
manners to bring attention to yourself,
and to never, ever make a spectacle of yourself.
...All of which I've earned a living doing."

Audrey Hepburn

Garner and Hepburn lark around at the wedding
that would never take place after Mary Tilford has made her allegations.

Following spread:
At home with the Willoughbys: Audrey's son Sean leads
Willoughby's son Christopher in a crawling race.

AT HOME

1961

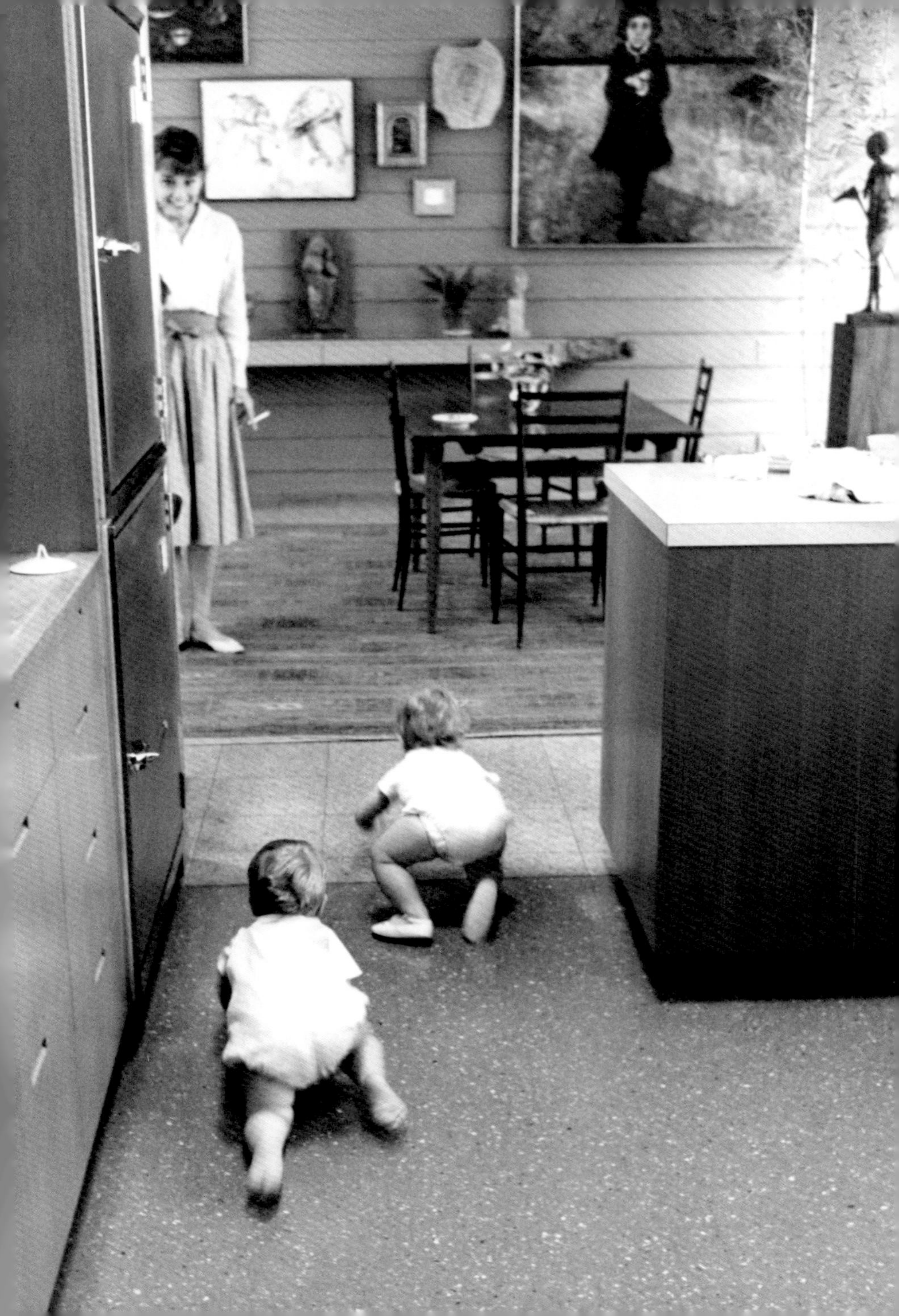

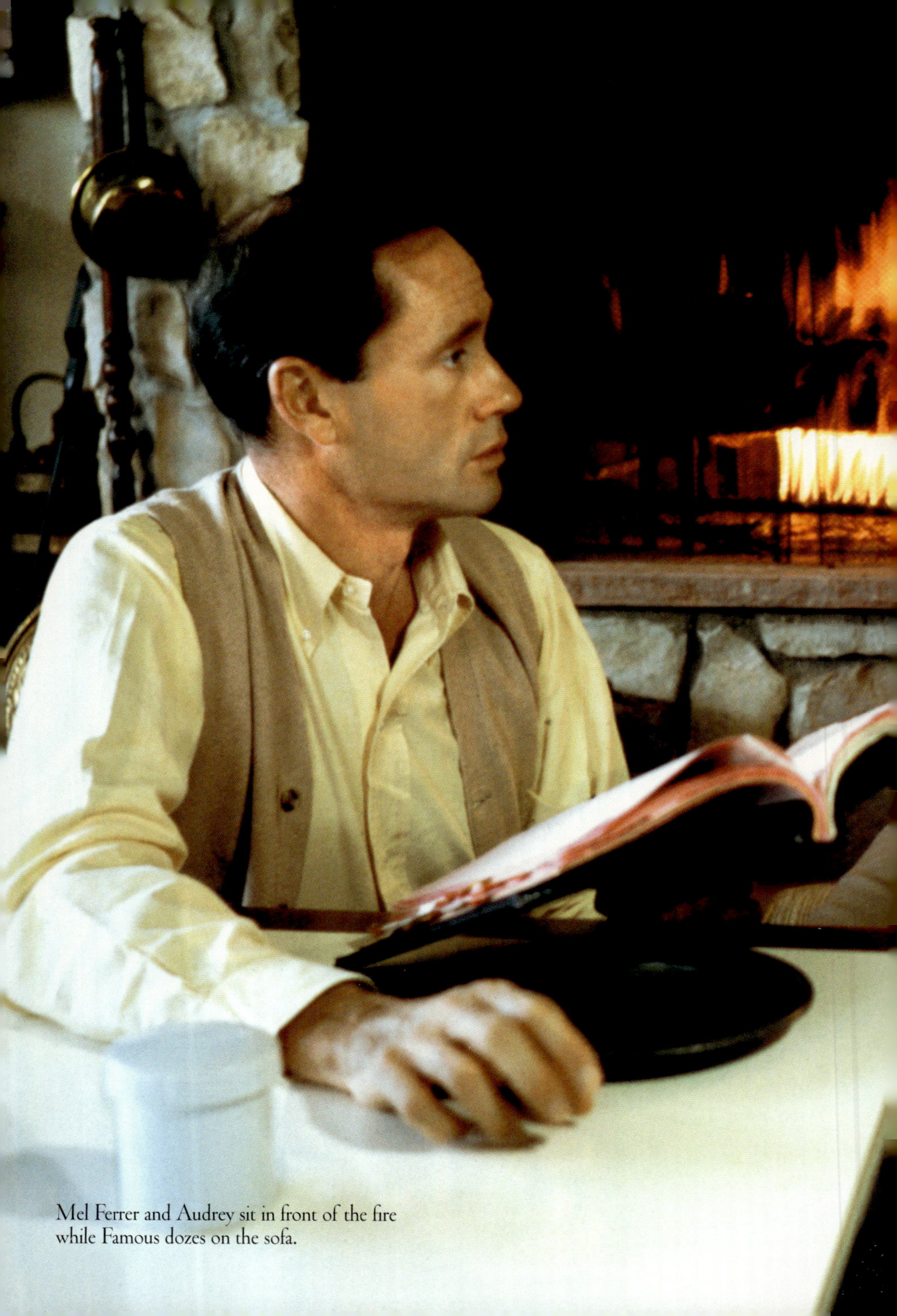

Mel Ferrer and Audrey sit in front of the fire while Famous dozes on the sofa.

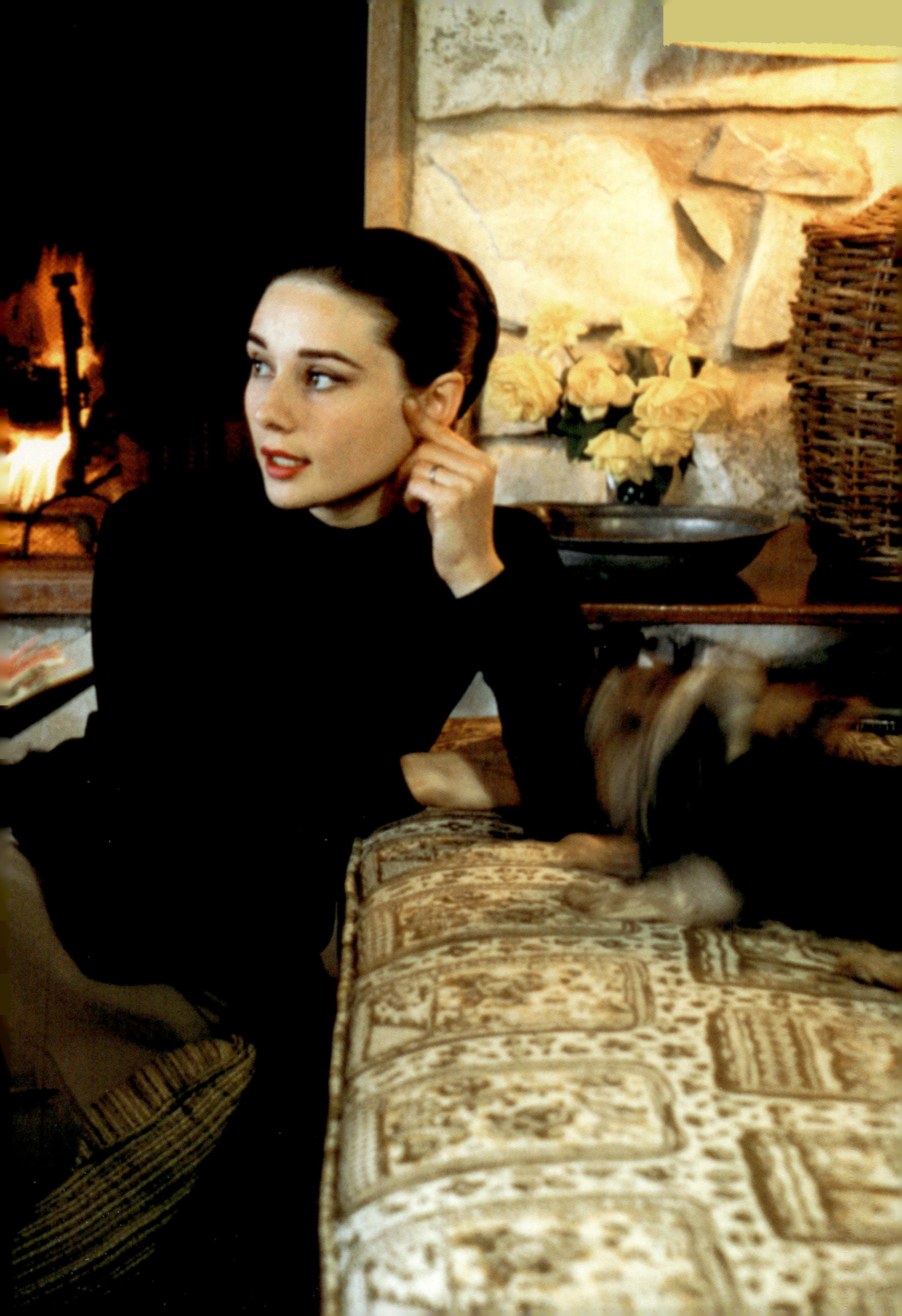

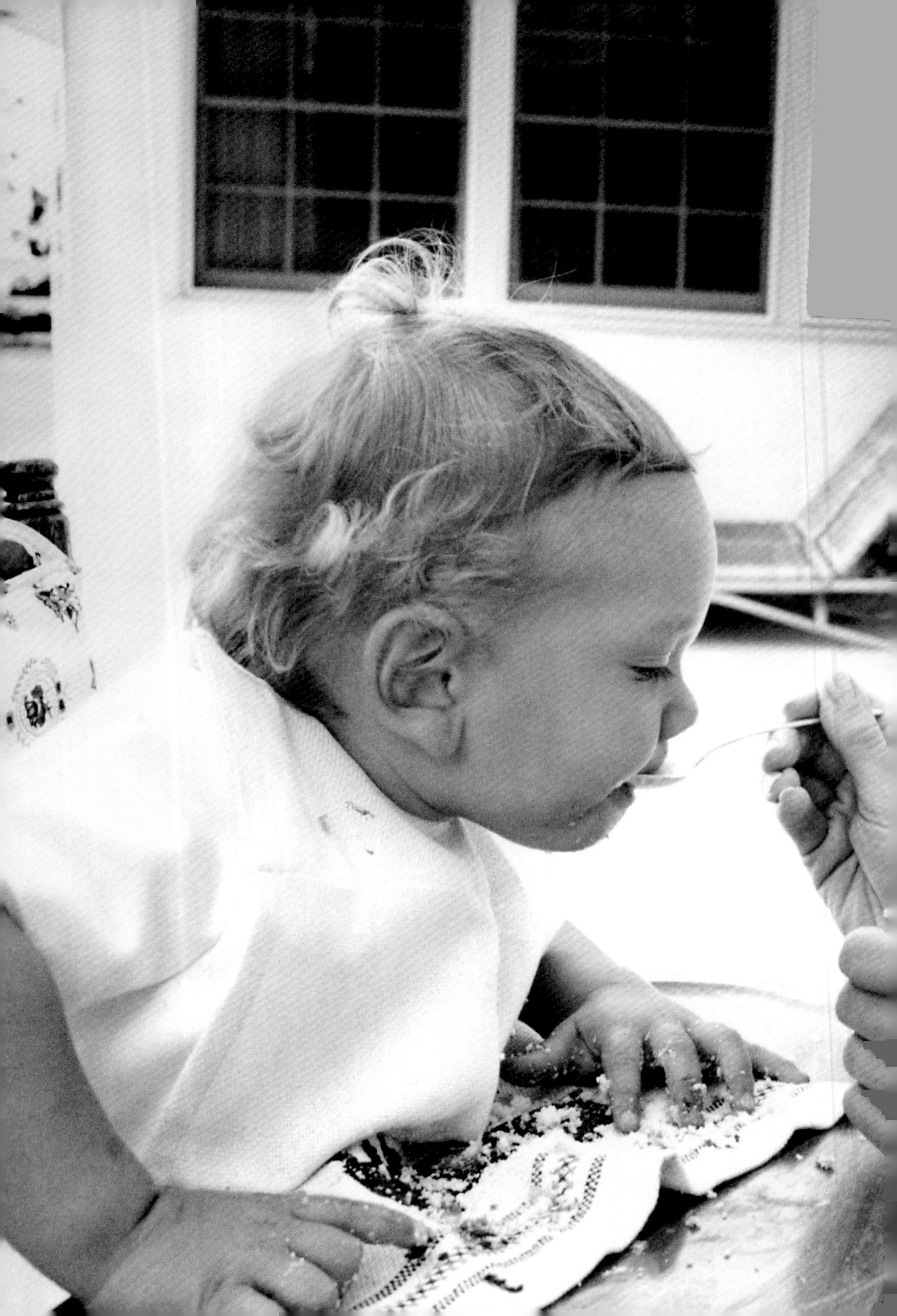

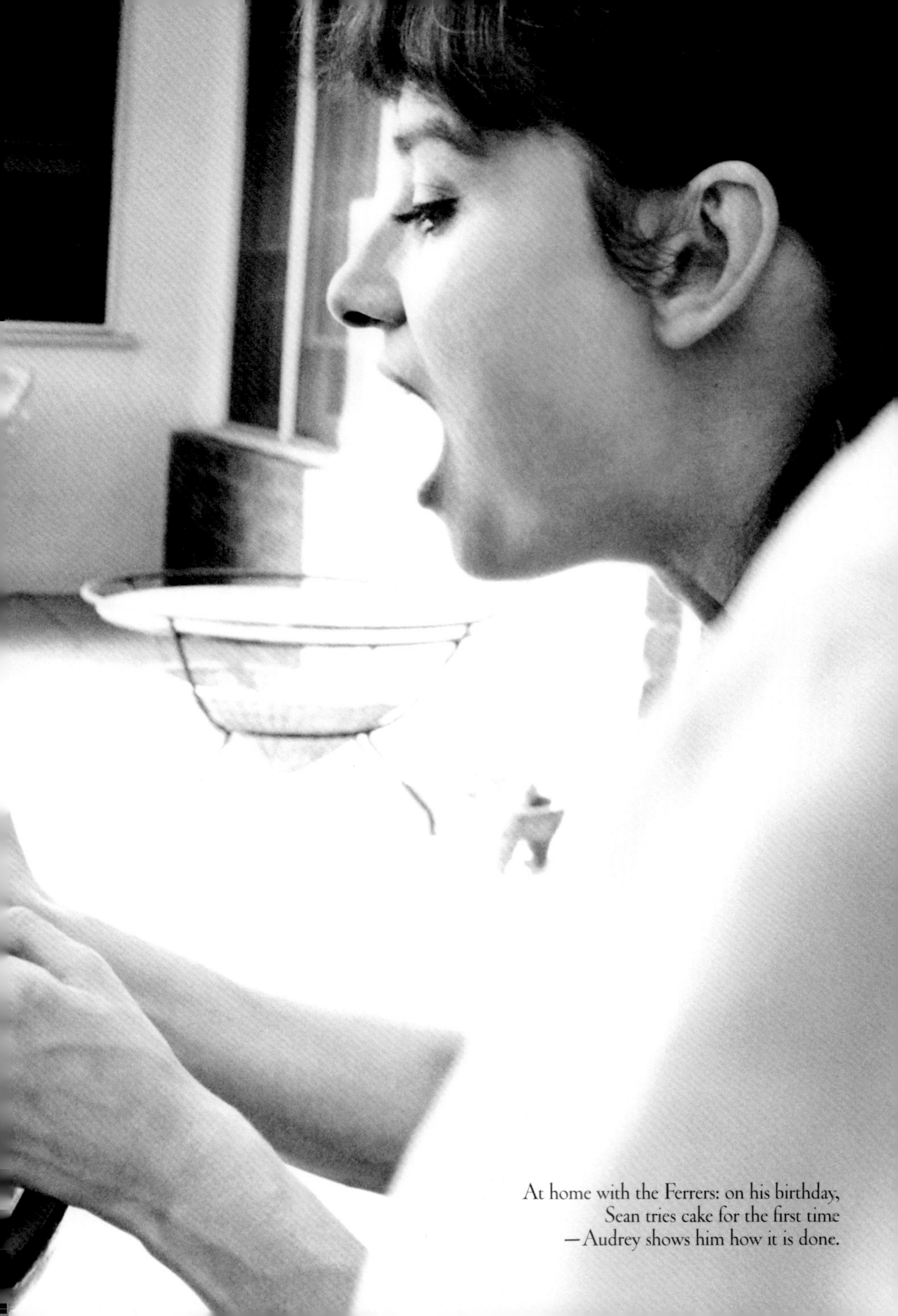

At home with the Ferrers: on his birthday,
Sean tries cake for the first time
—Audrey shows him how it is done.

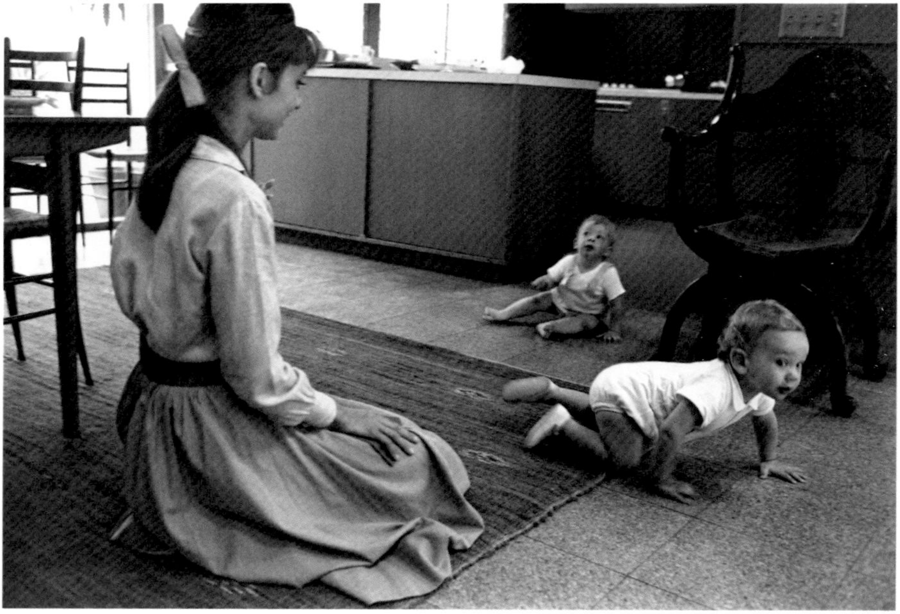

Audrey watches as Sean and Christopher explore the Willoughbys' kitchen.

Audrey and Willoughby's wife, Dorothy, help their sons take some of their first steps.

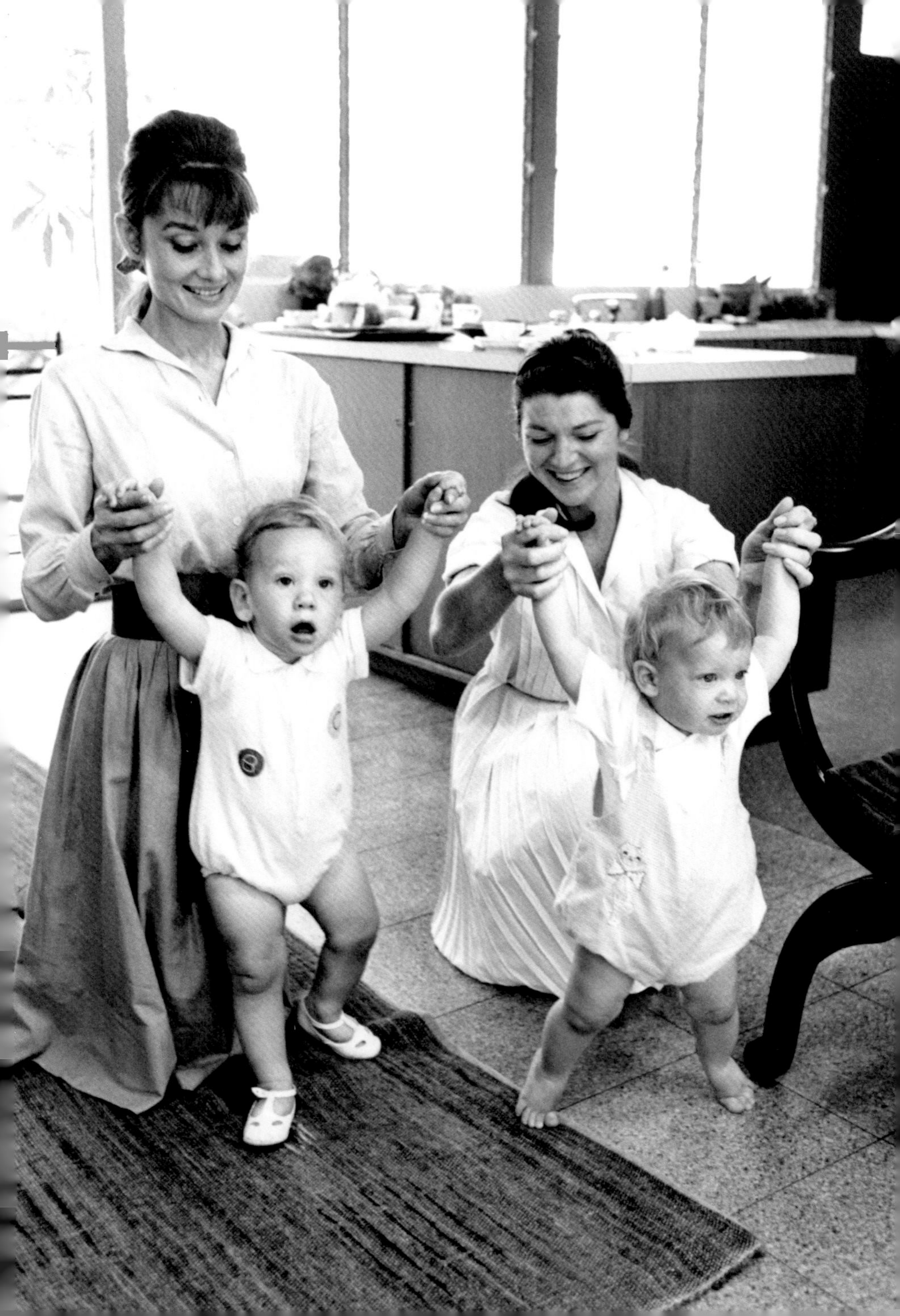

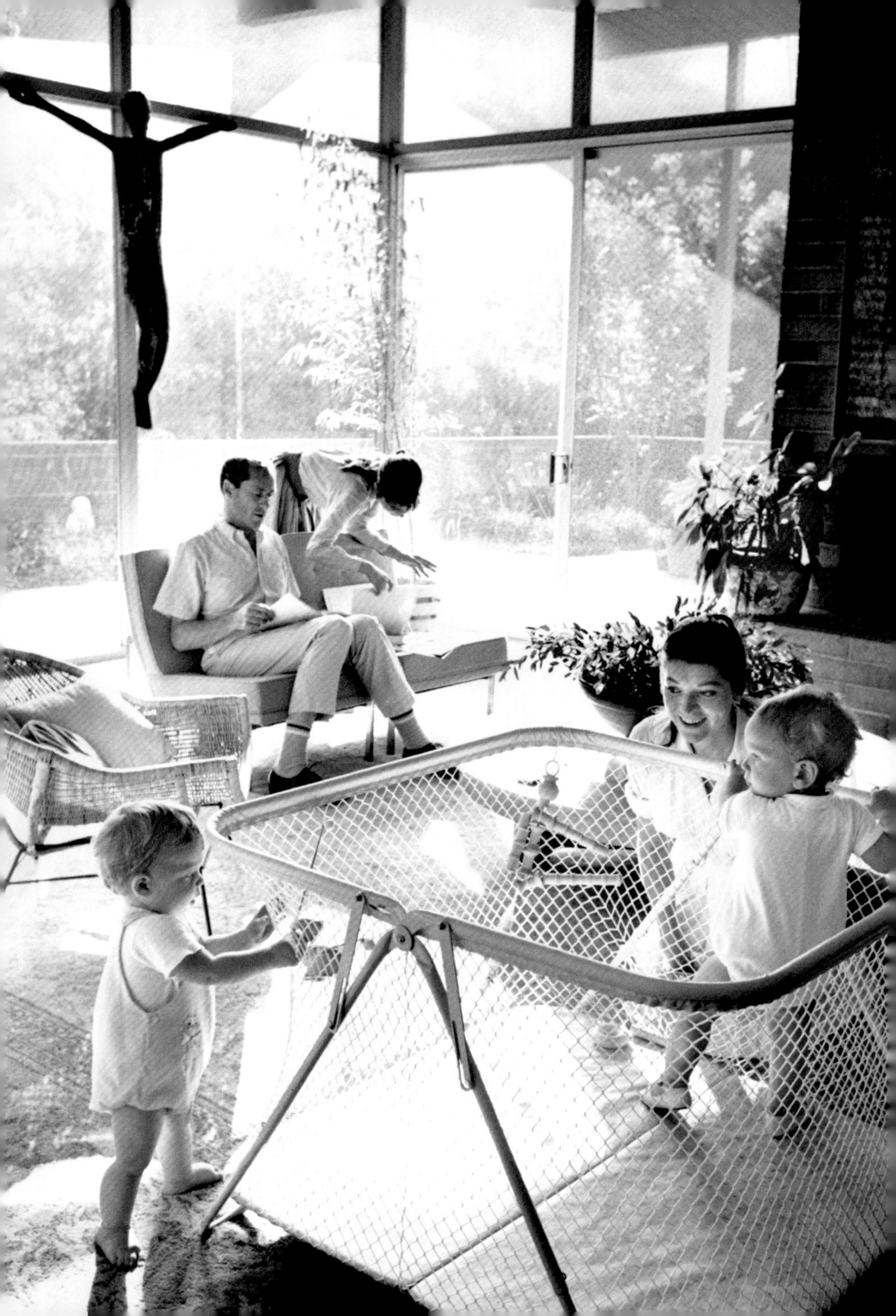

"Whether Audrey was in jeans and a bandana or all dolled up for the Oscars—she was so beautiful that you couldn't bear it."

André Previn

From left: Christopher, Mel, Audrey, Dorothy, and Sean at the Willoughbys' sunlit home.

PARIS WHEN IT SIZZLES

1962

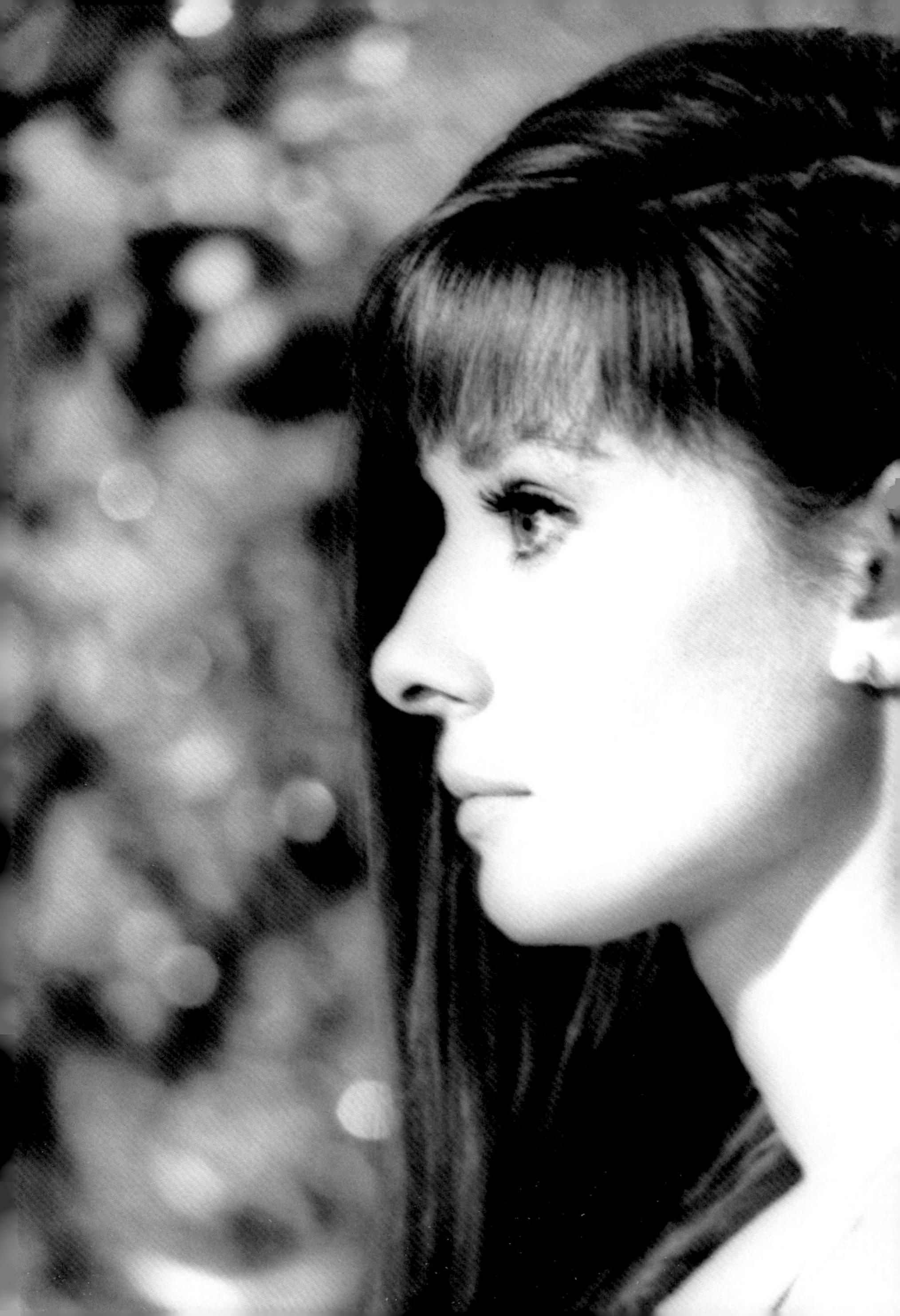

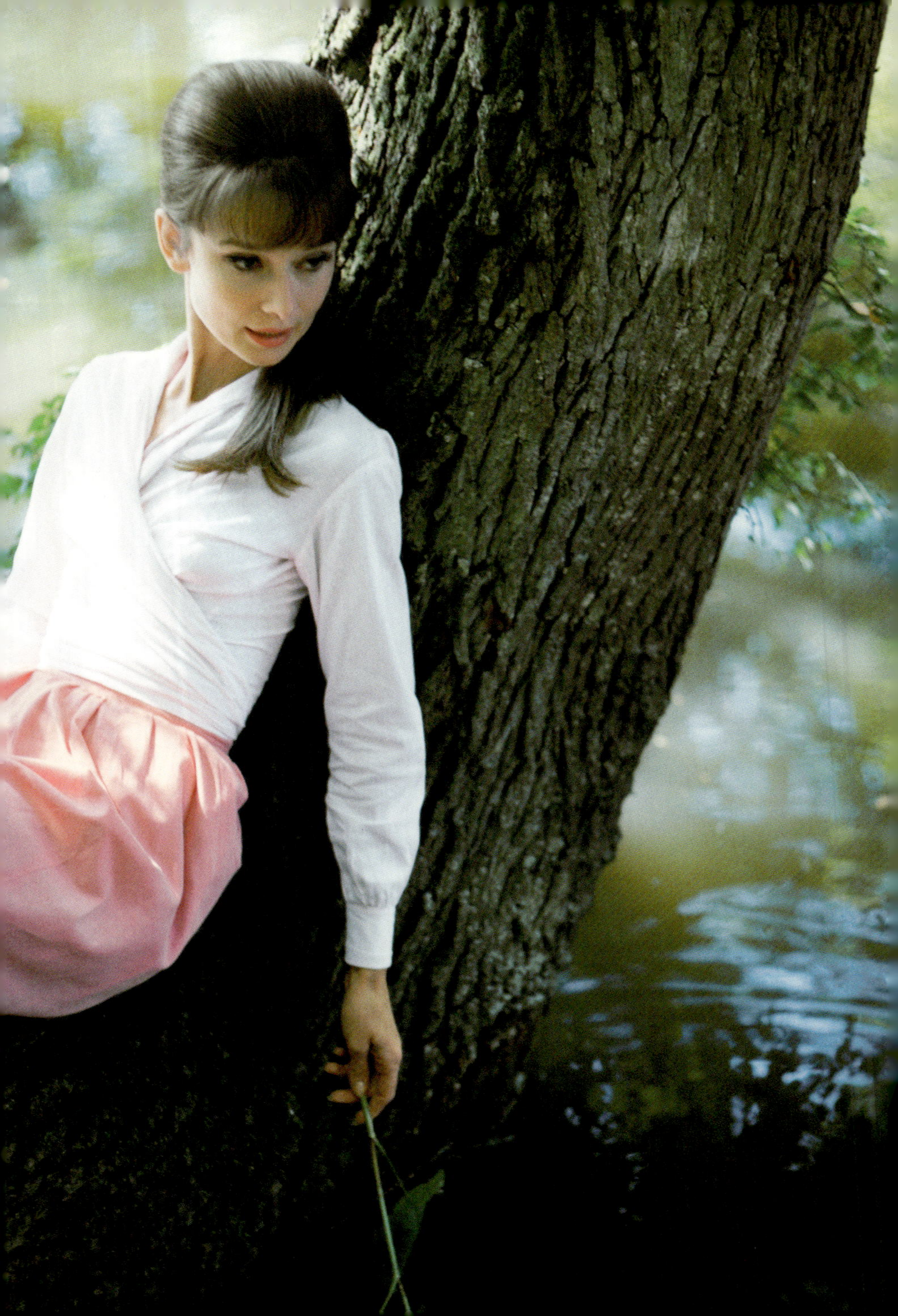

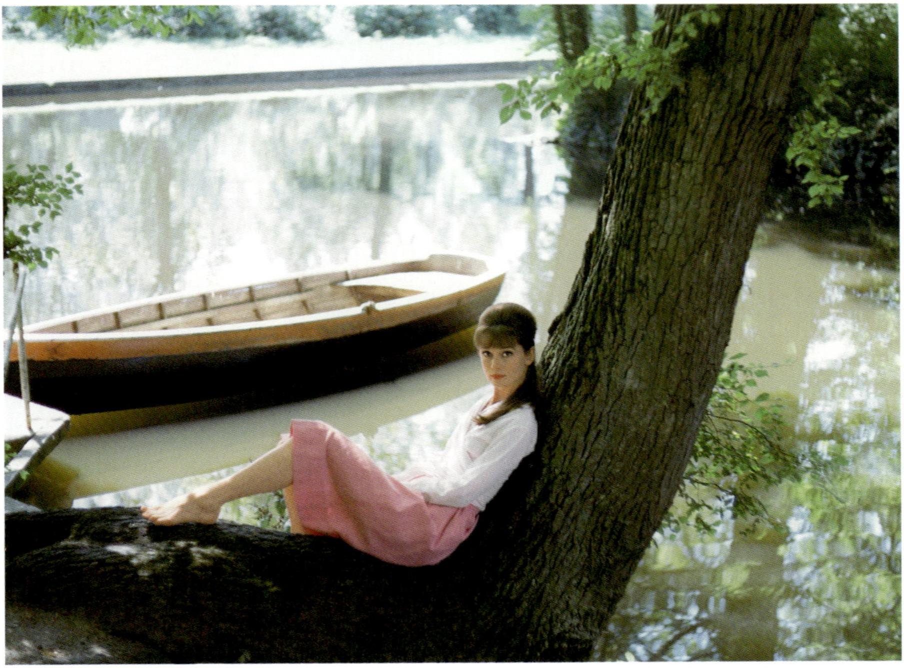

Previous spread:
On the set of *Paris When It Sizzles:* Audrey wears her long hair down.

This spread:
Audrey poses in the garden of the villa the Ferrers have rented for the duration of the shooting. The palatial abode has its own lake with swans.

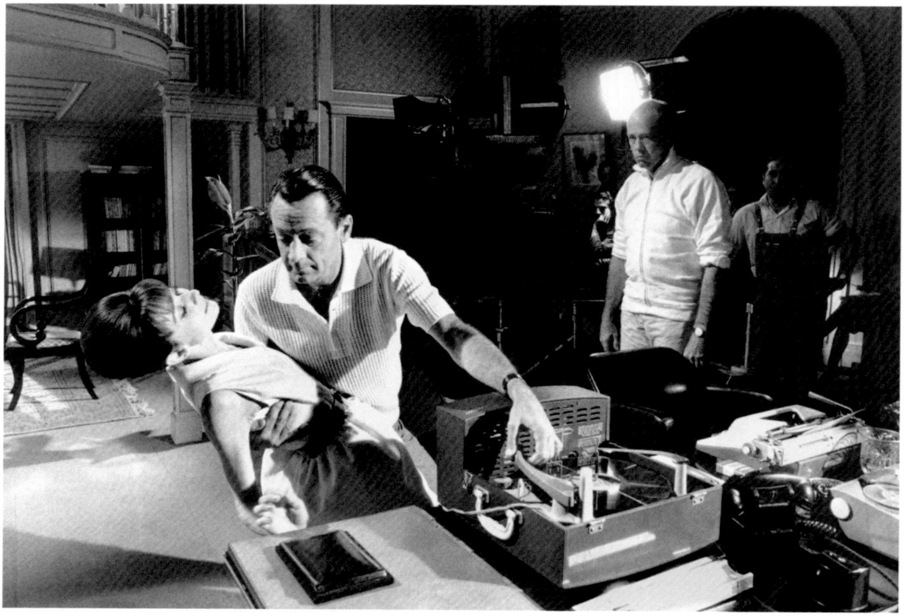

Dick Quine showed Bill Holden how he should hold Audrey before shooting this scene—now he watches the actors intently.

Audrey giggles as she waits for her cue to enter the scene as Gabrielle Simpson in *Paris When It Sizzles* when she encounters Bill Holden as Richard Benson for the first time.

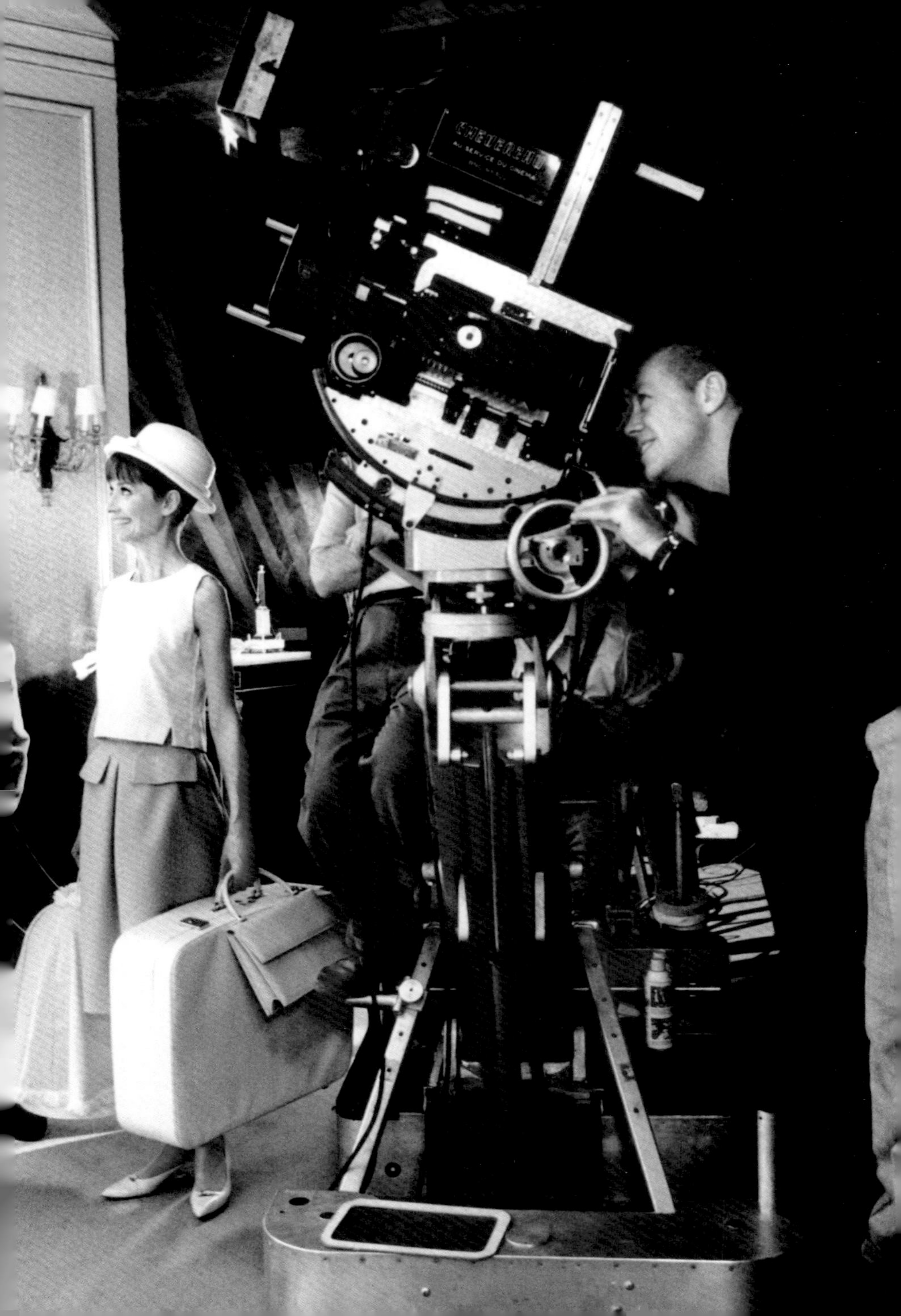
AU SERVICE DU CINÉMA

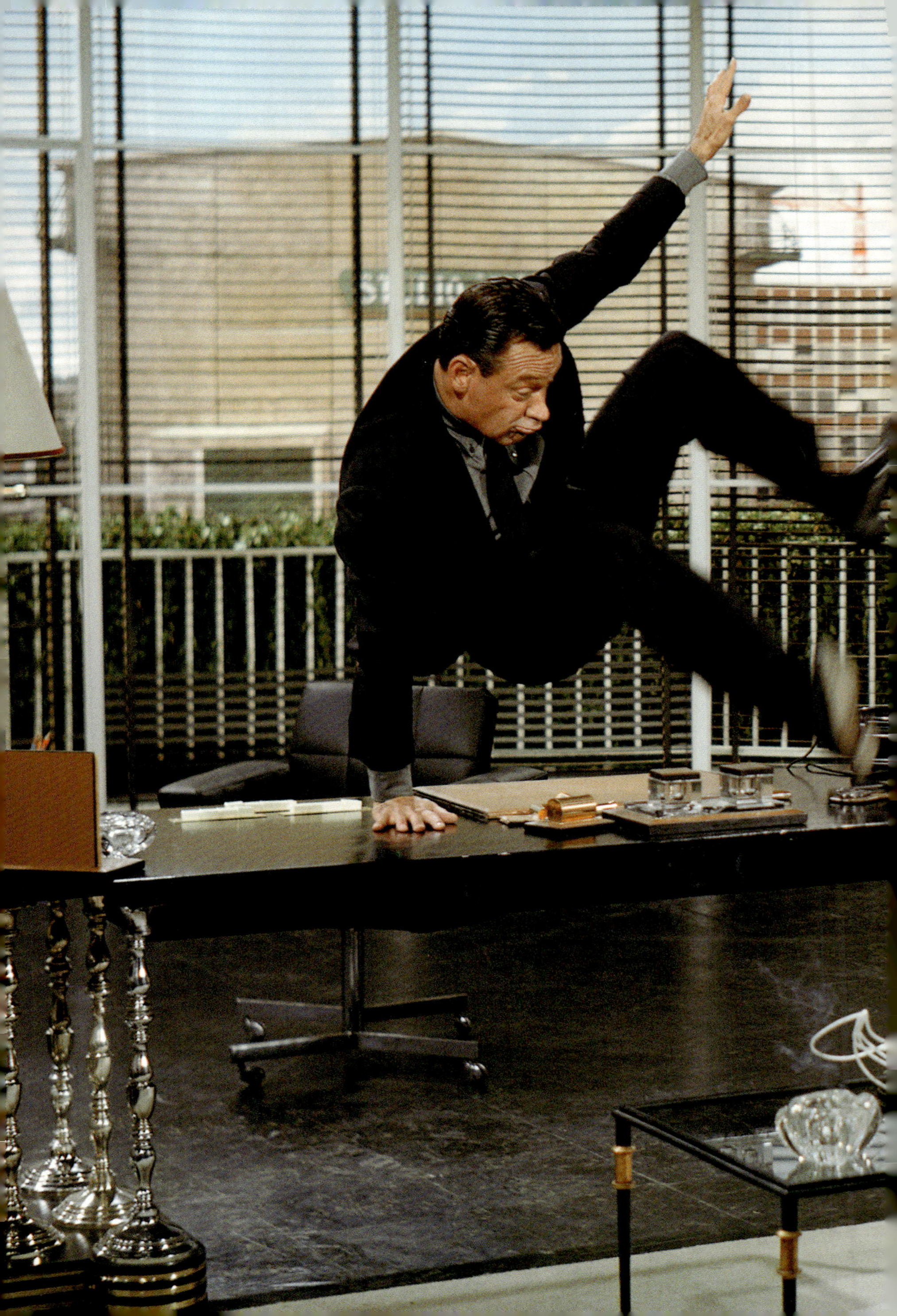

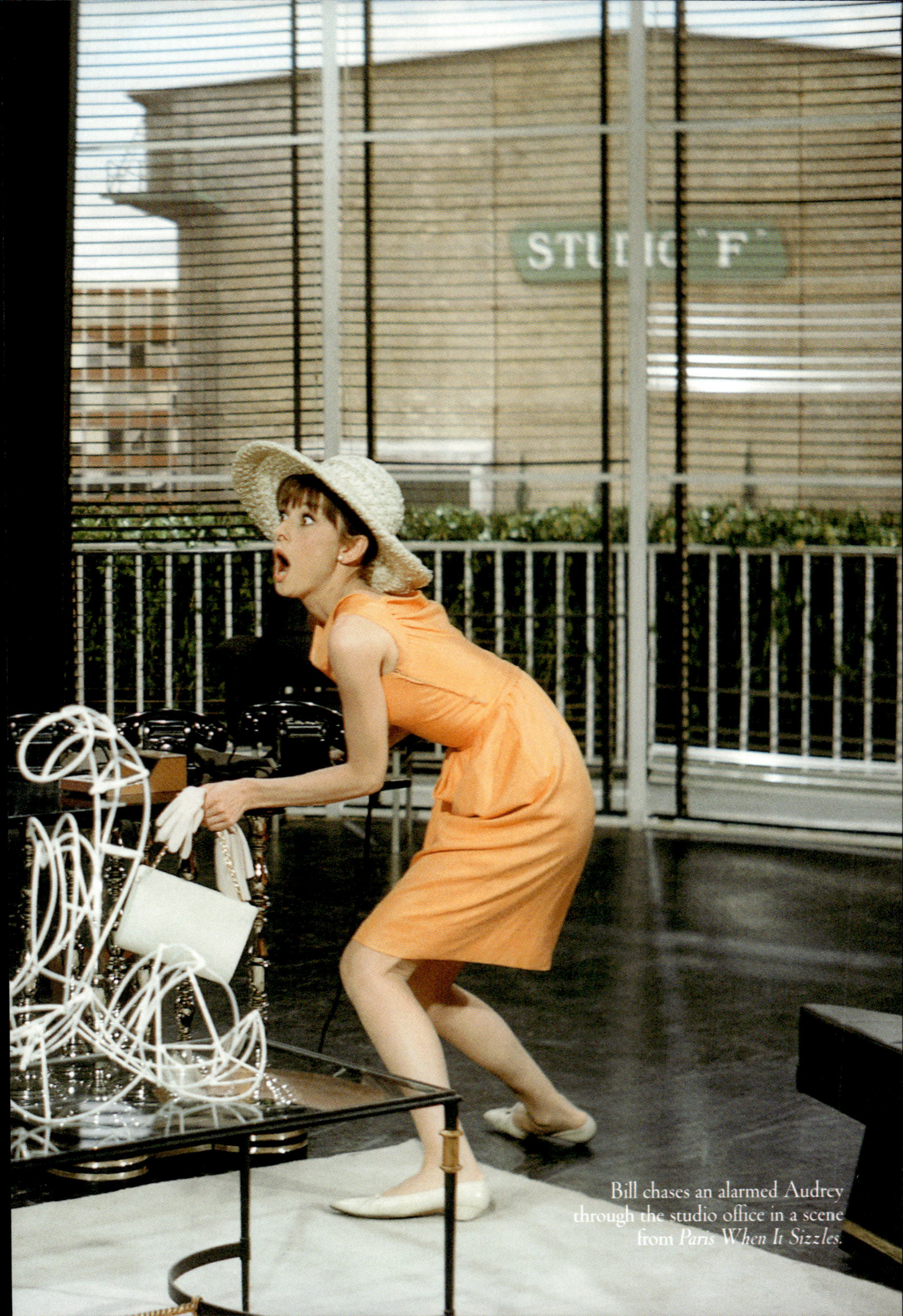

Bill chases an alarmed Audrey through the studio office in a scene from *Paris When It Sizzles.*

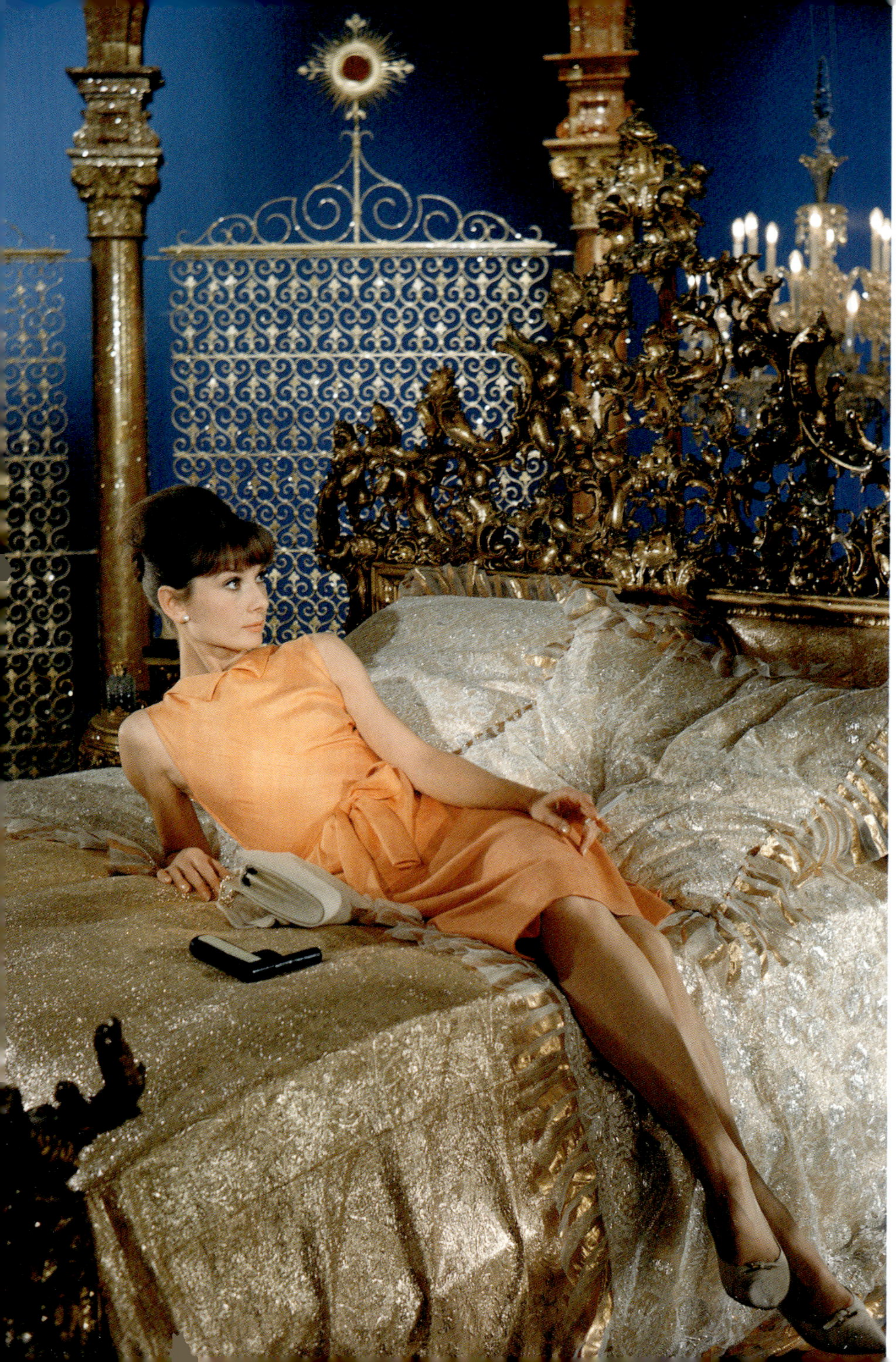

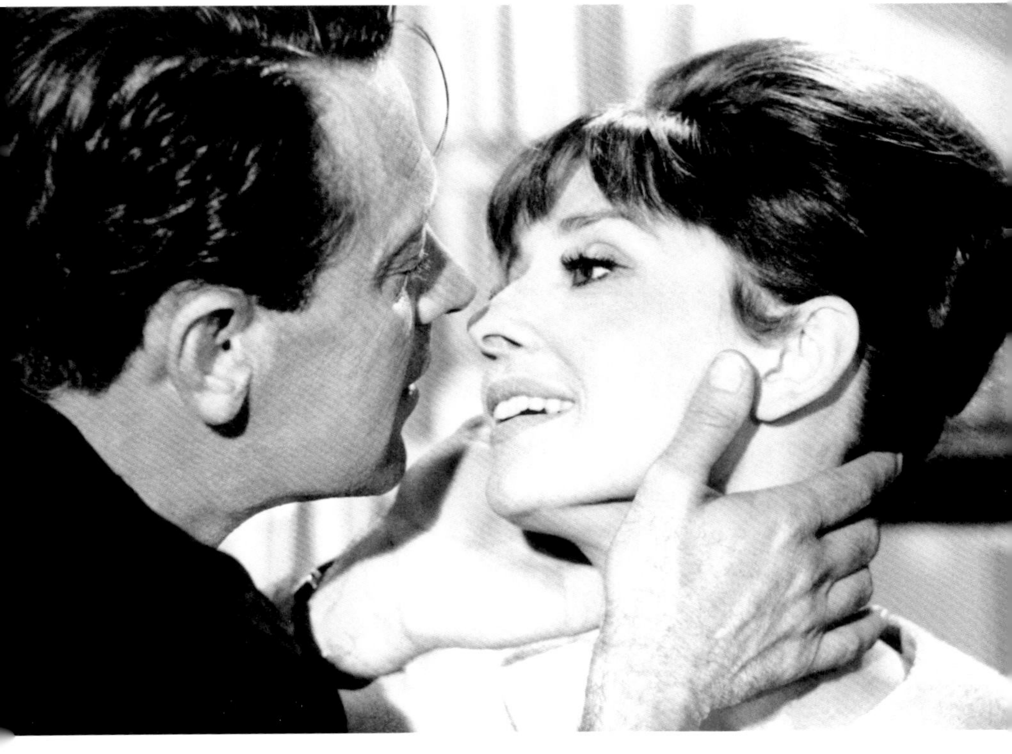

Wearing a beautiful dress designed for her by Givenchy, Audrey reclines on a grandiose bed in *Paris When It Sizzles.*

Bill Holden is clearly infatuated with Audrey.

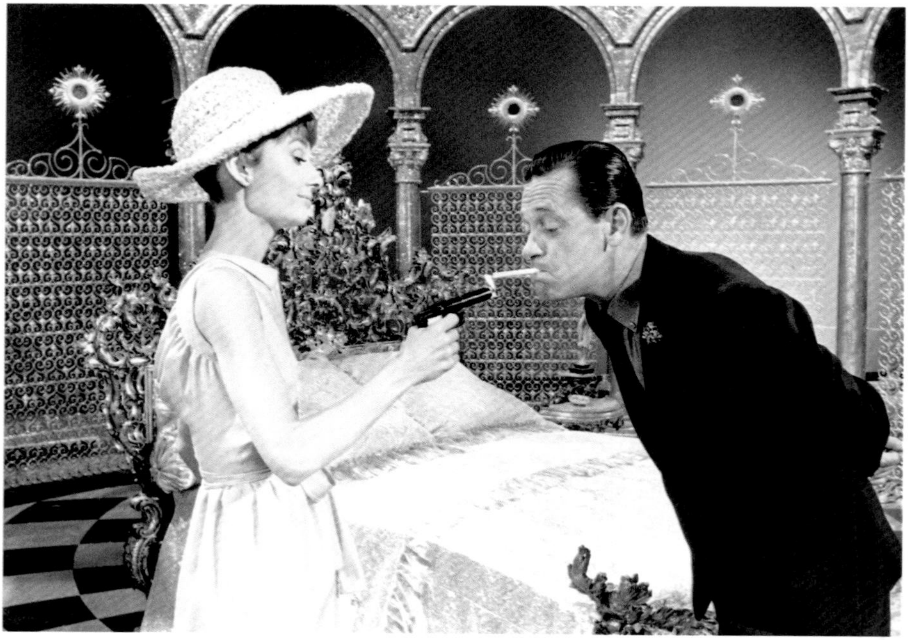

In one of the "improvised" scenes in *Paris When It Sizzles*,
Audrey points her pistol at Bill... and lights his cigarette.

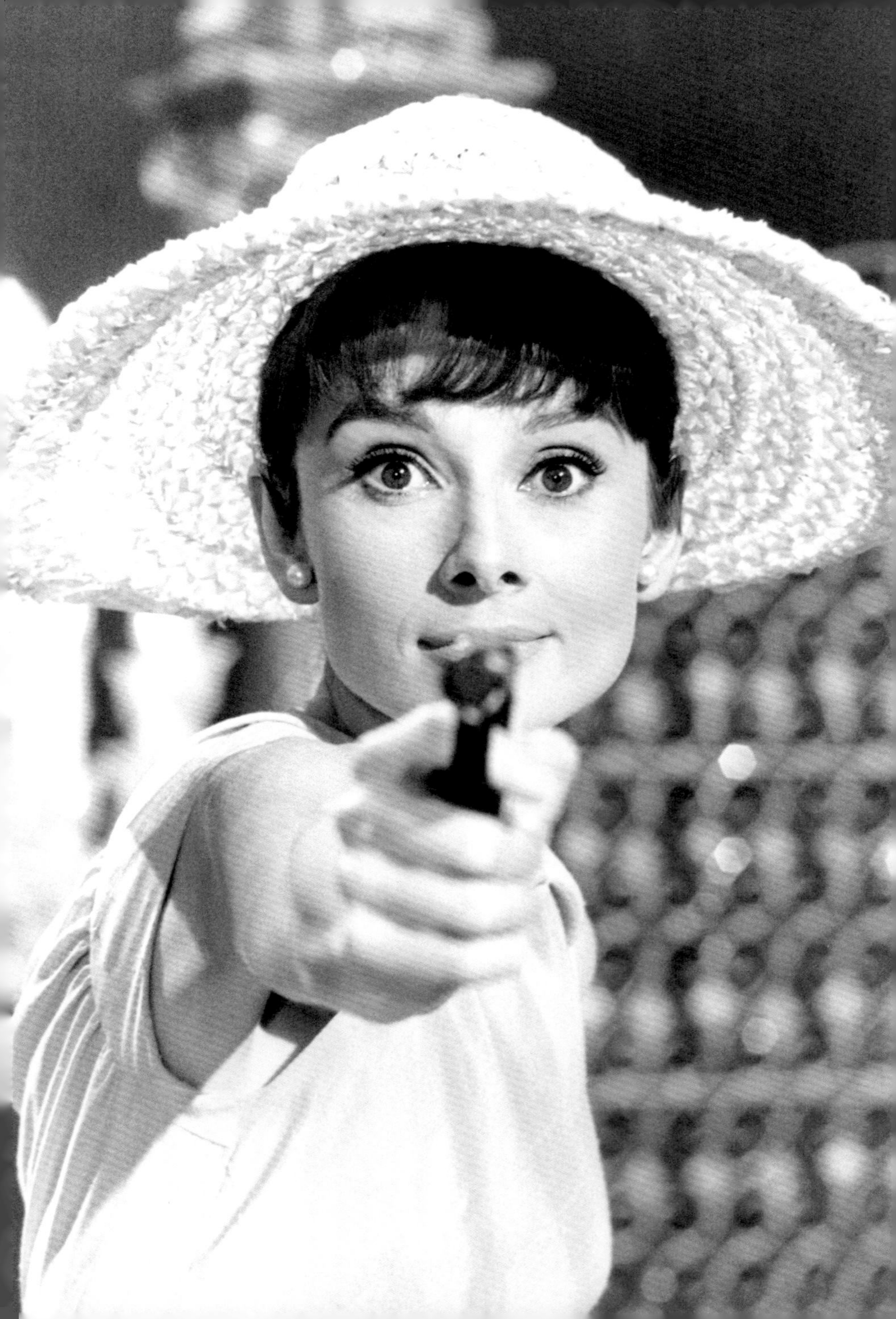

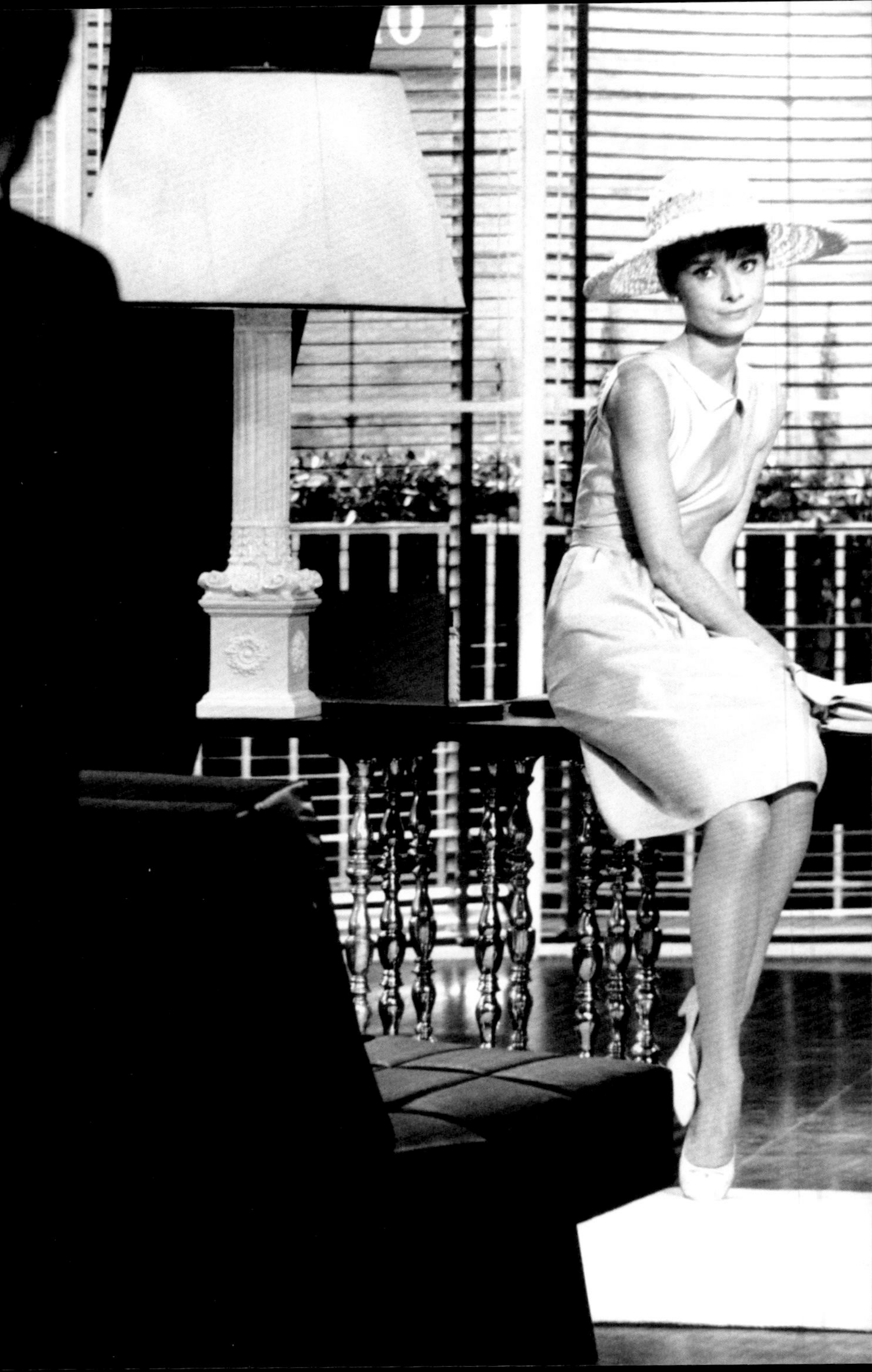

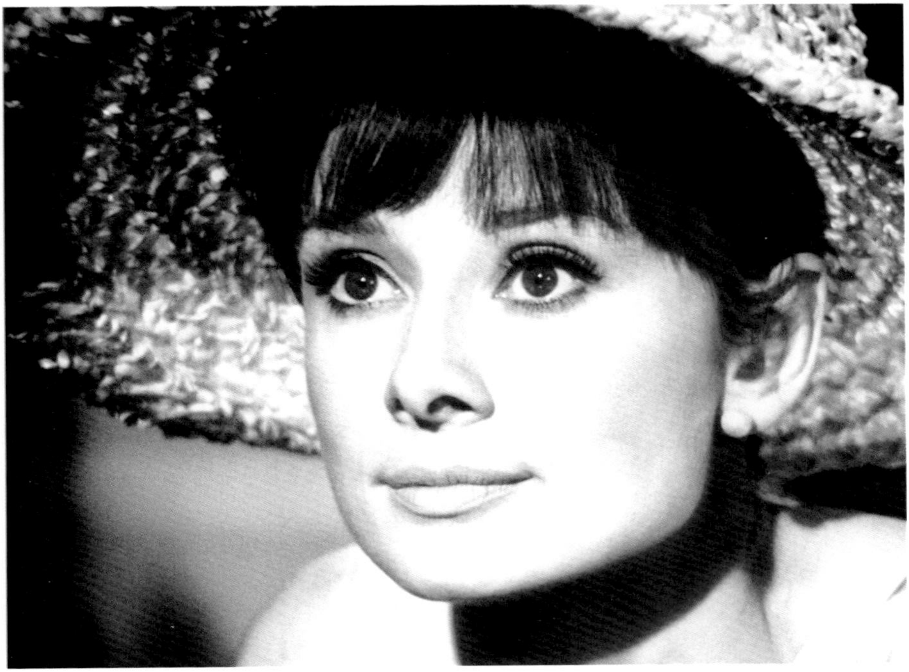

Wearing her Givenchy dress and a straw hat, Audrey sits on the desk in Bill's office.

Audrey looked dazzling during the shooting.

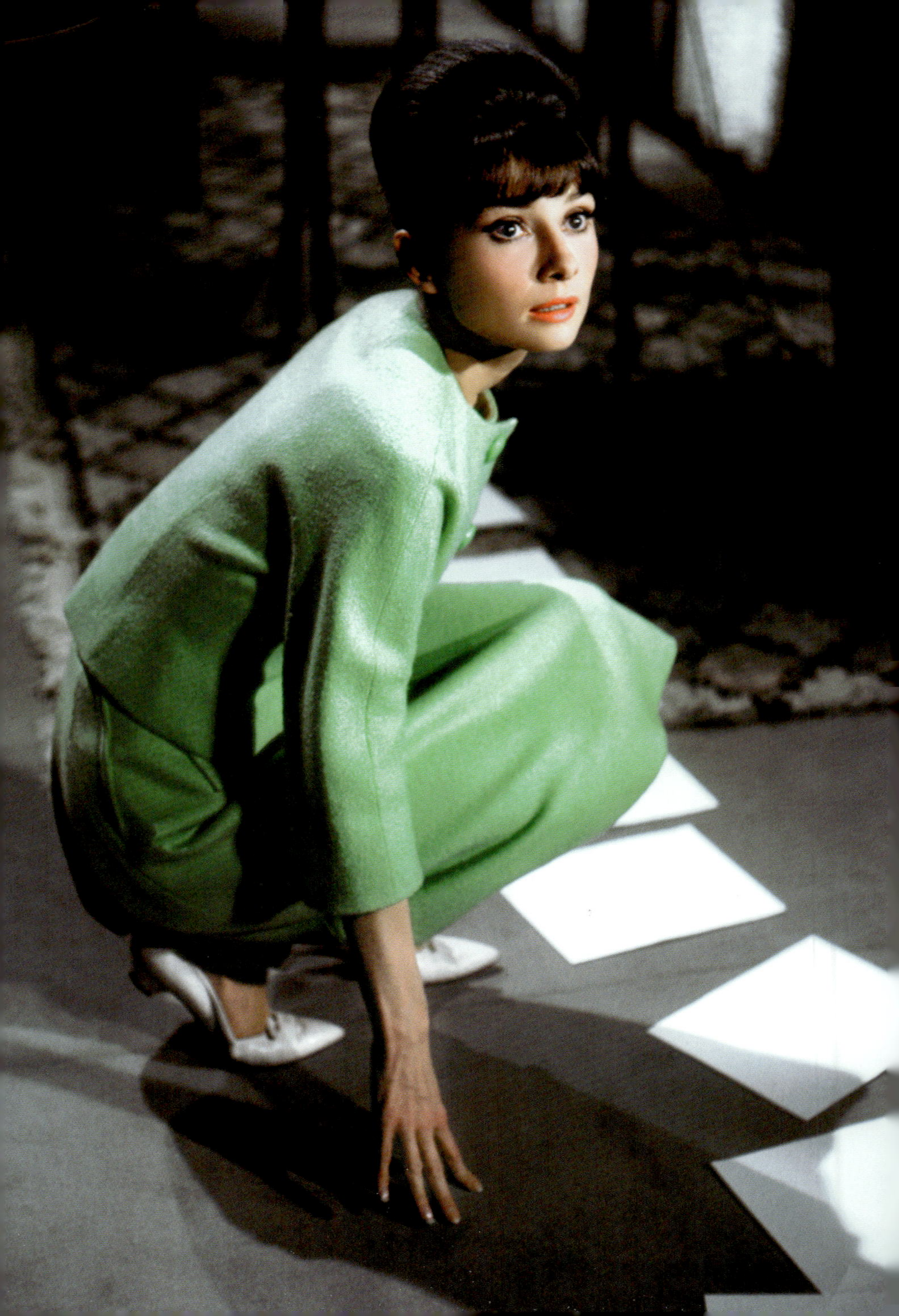

Audrey wears another beautiful Givenchy outfit,
this one in emerald green.

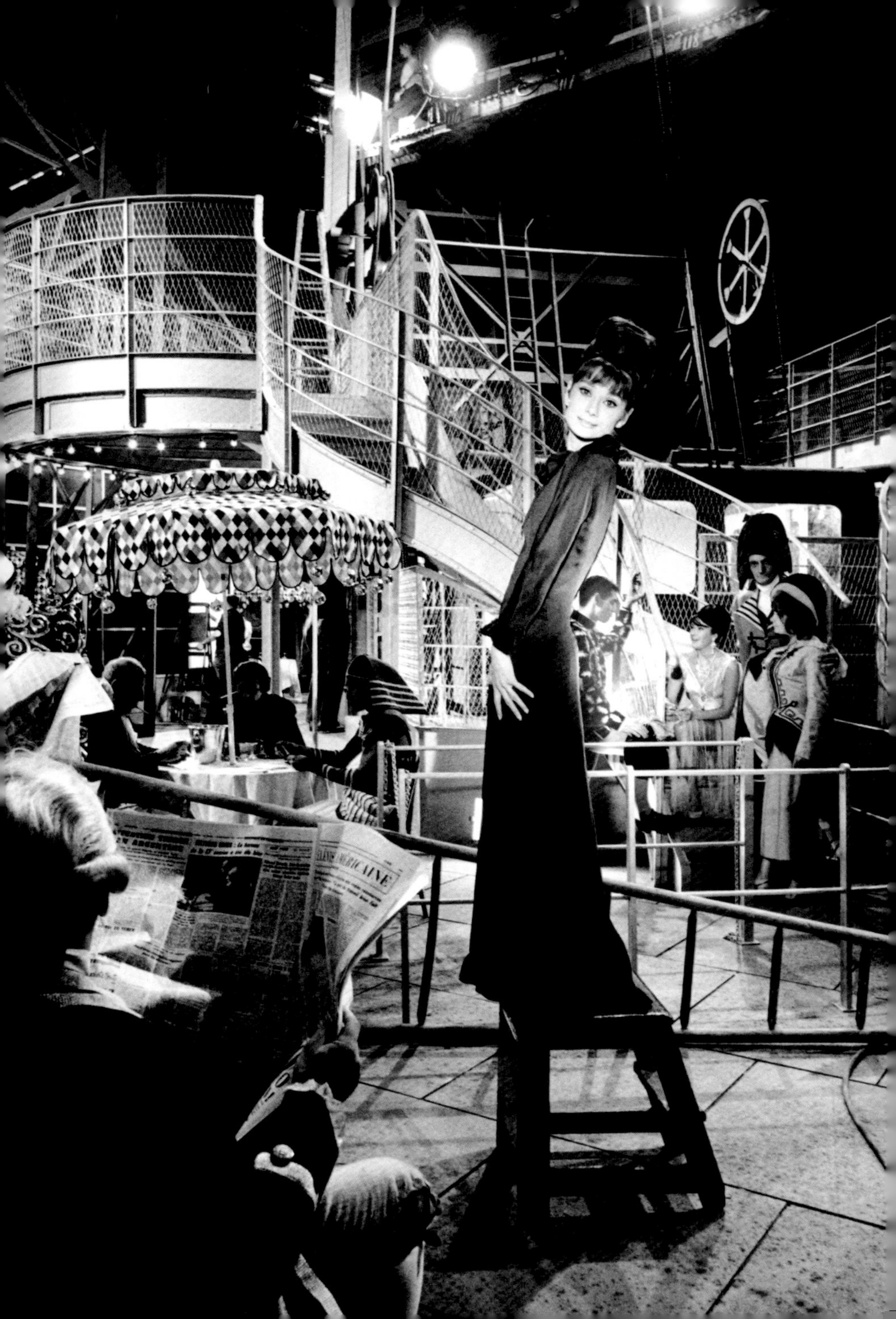

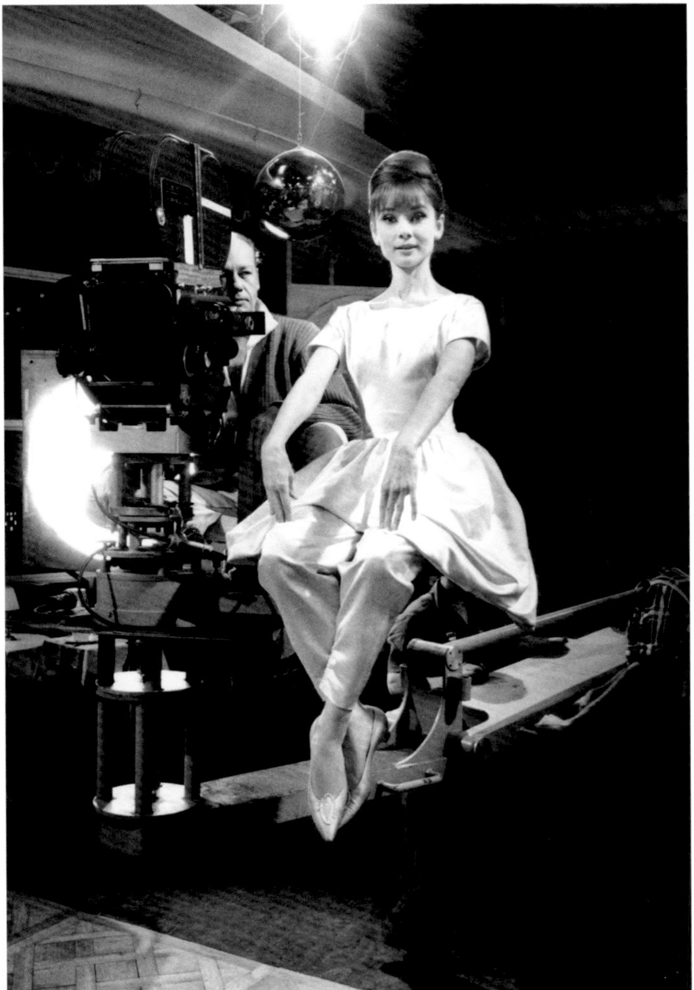

On the set of *Paris When It Sizzles.*

Audrey poses on a camera jib while director Richard Quine looks on.

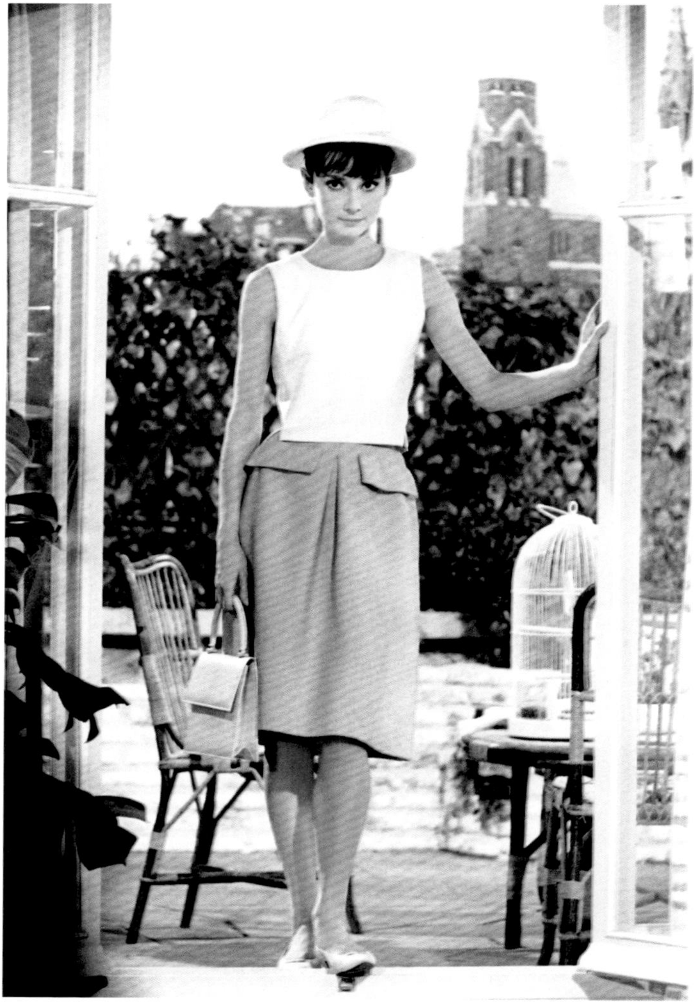

Audrey oozes seductive charm at the French windows
on the set of *Paris When It Sizzles.*

A yellow canary sings for a stylish Ms. Hepburn.

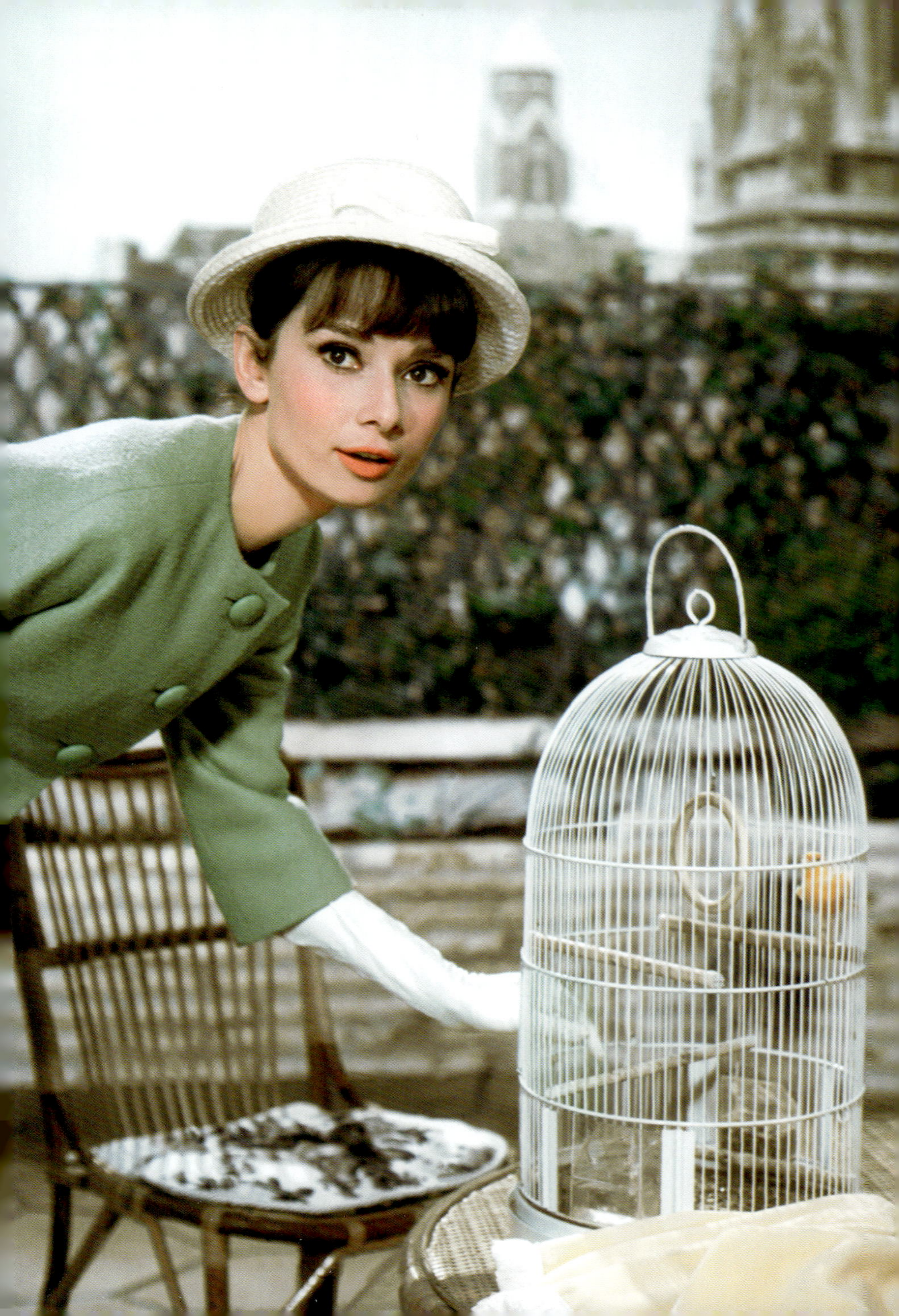

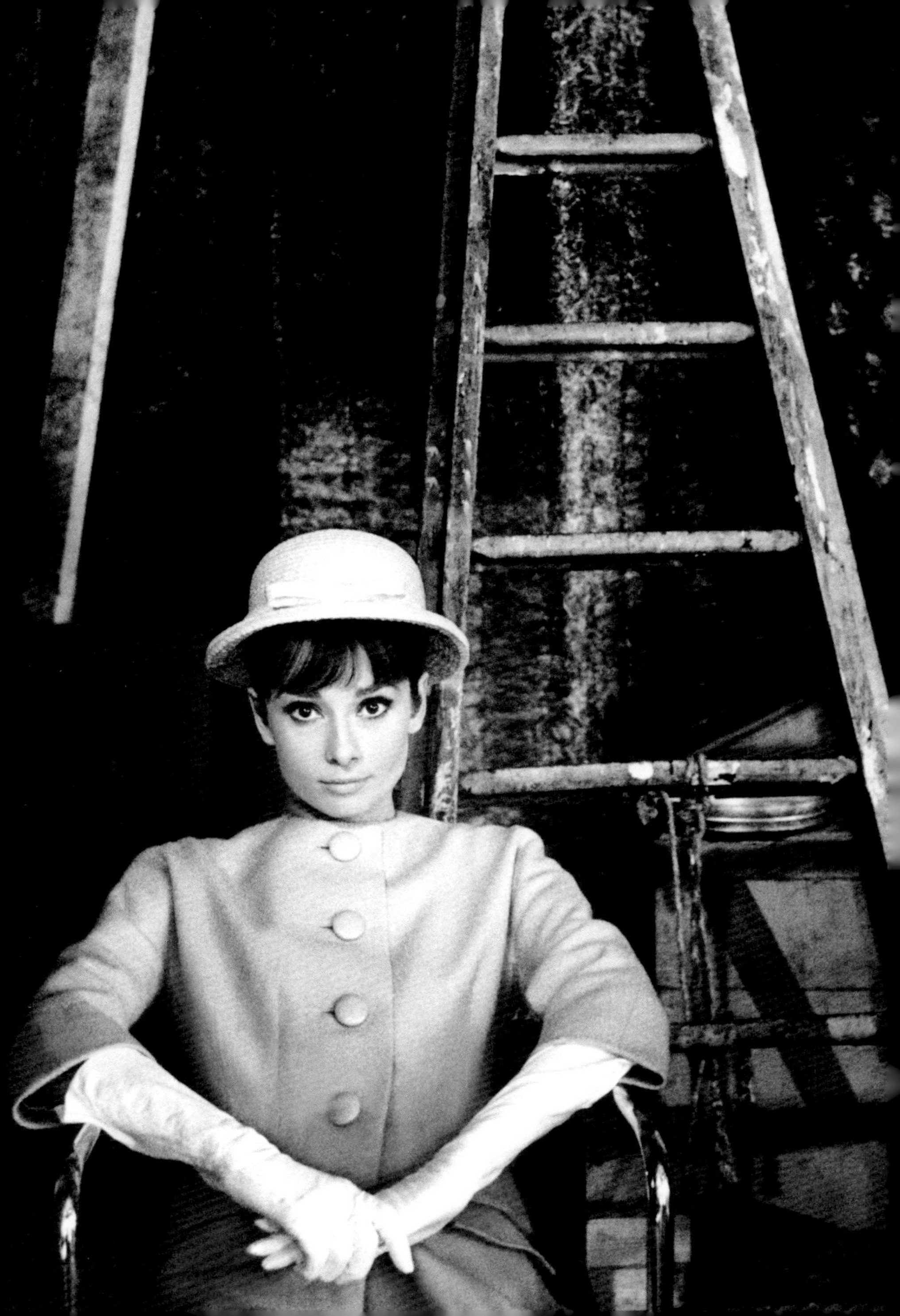

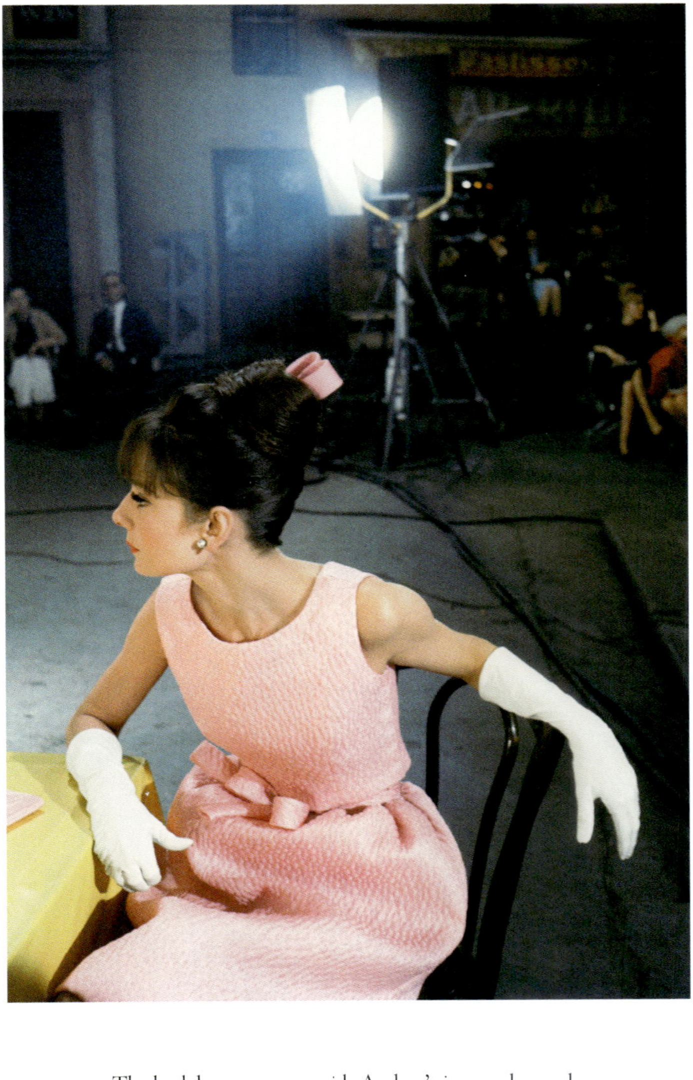

The backdrop contrasts with Audrey's immaculate style.

Audrey wears a pink dress with matching ribbon and elegant white gloves.

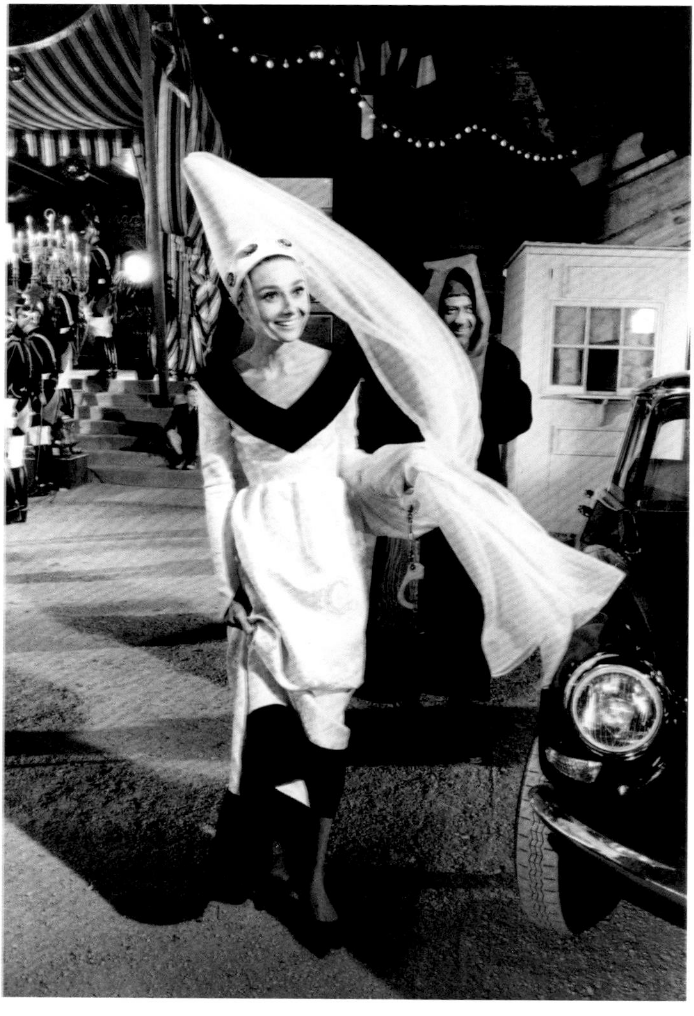

Arriving for the last scene, which is set at the Eiffel Tower.

Even the uniformed Republican Guard are beguiled by Audrey
as she waits for shooting to resume.

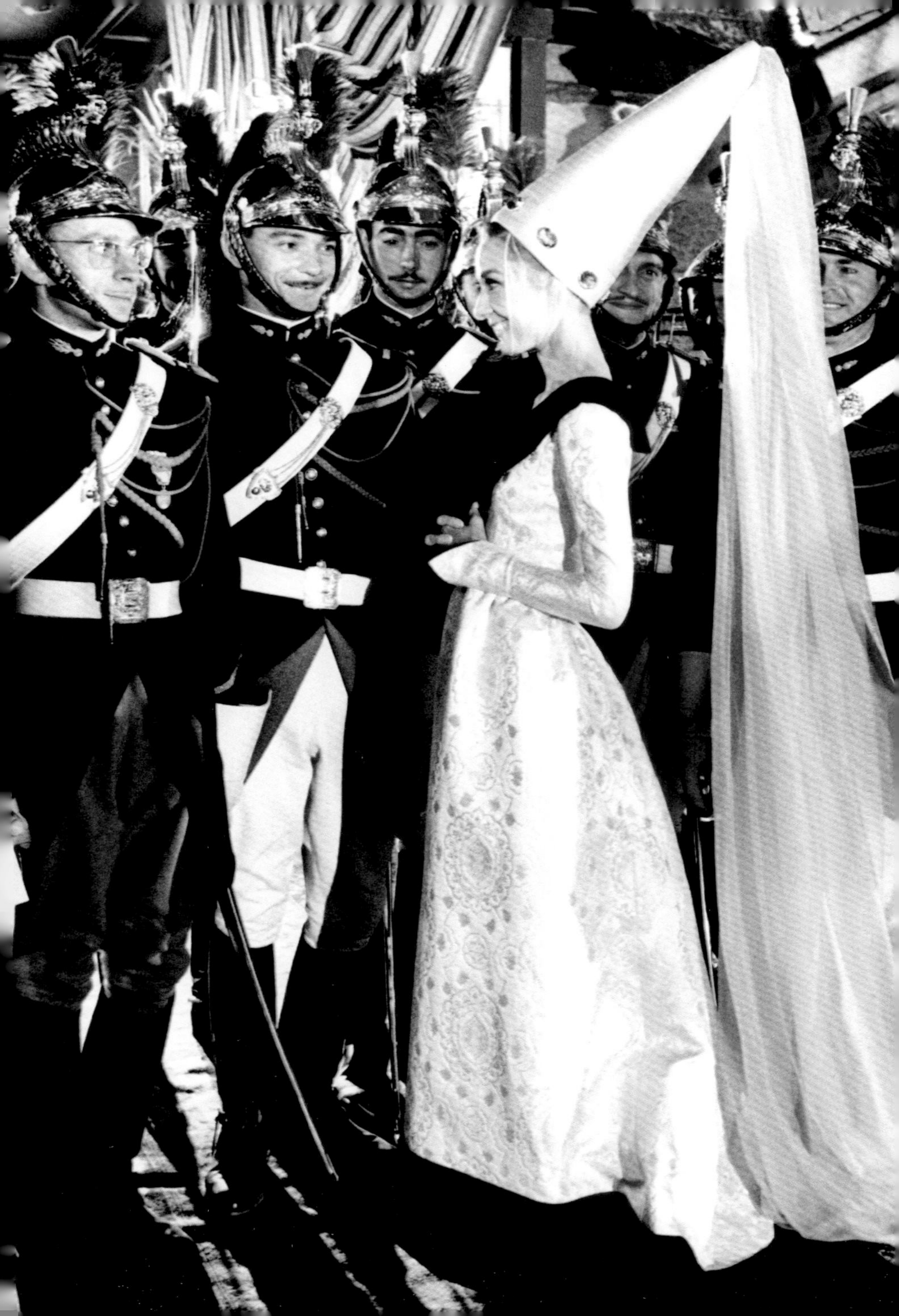

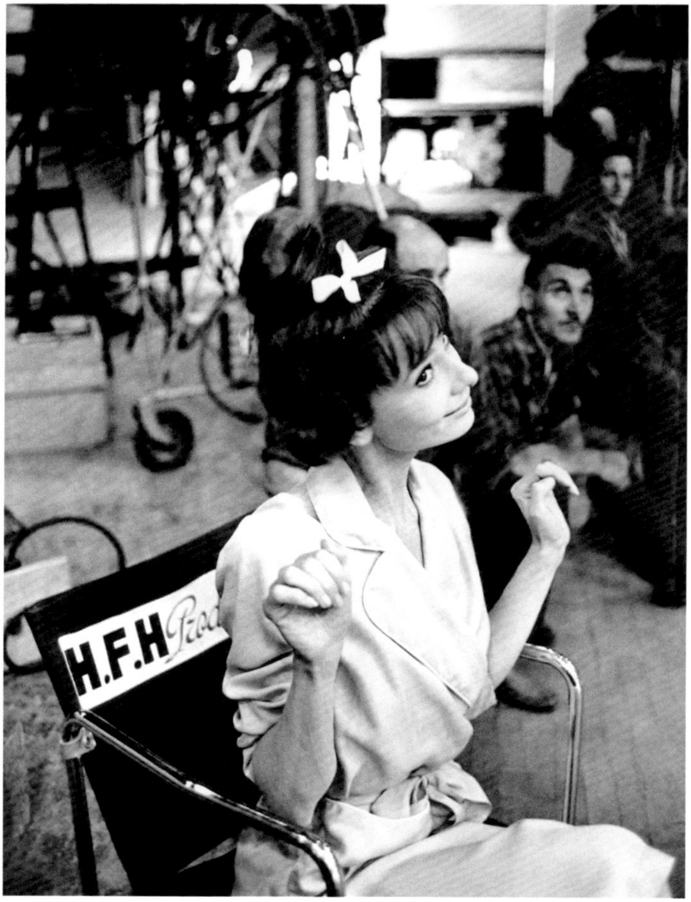

Audrey sits up and begs, aping her Yorkshire terrier, Famous.

A chilly shoot on the Eiffel Tower.

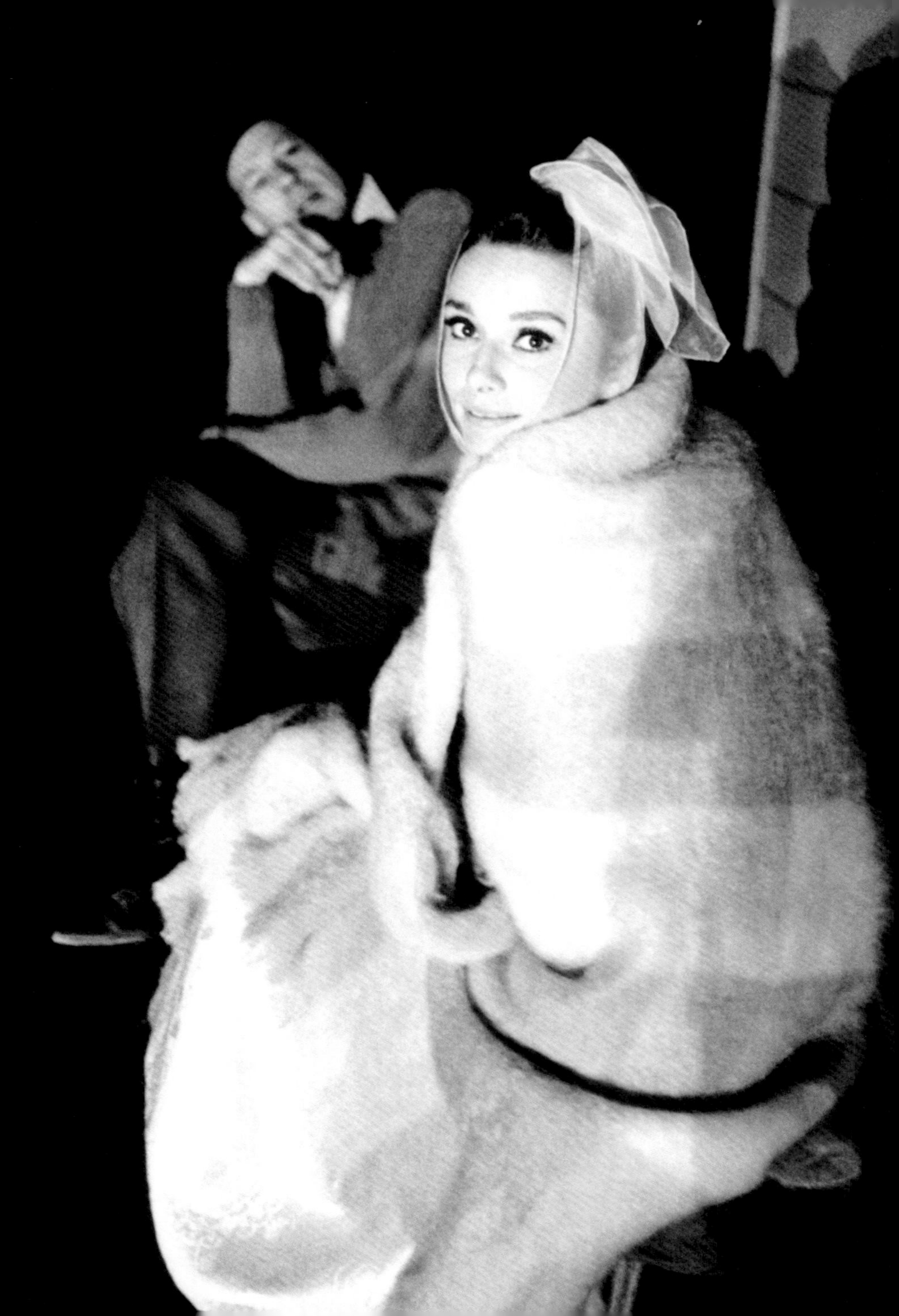

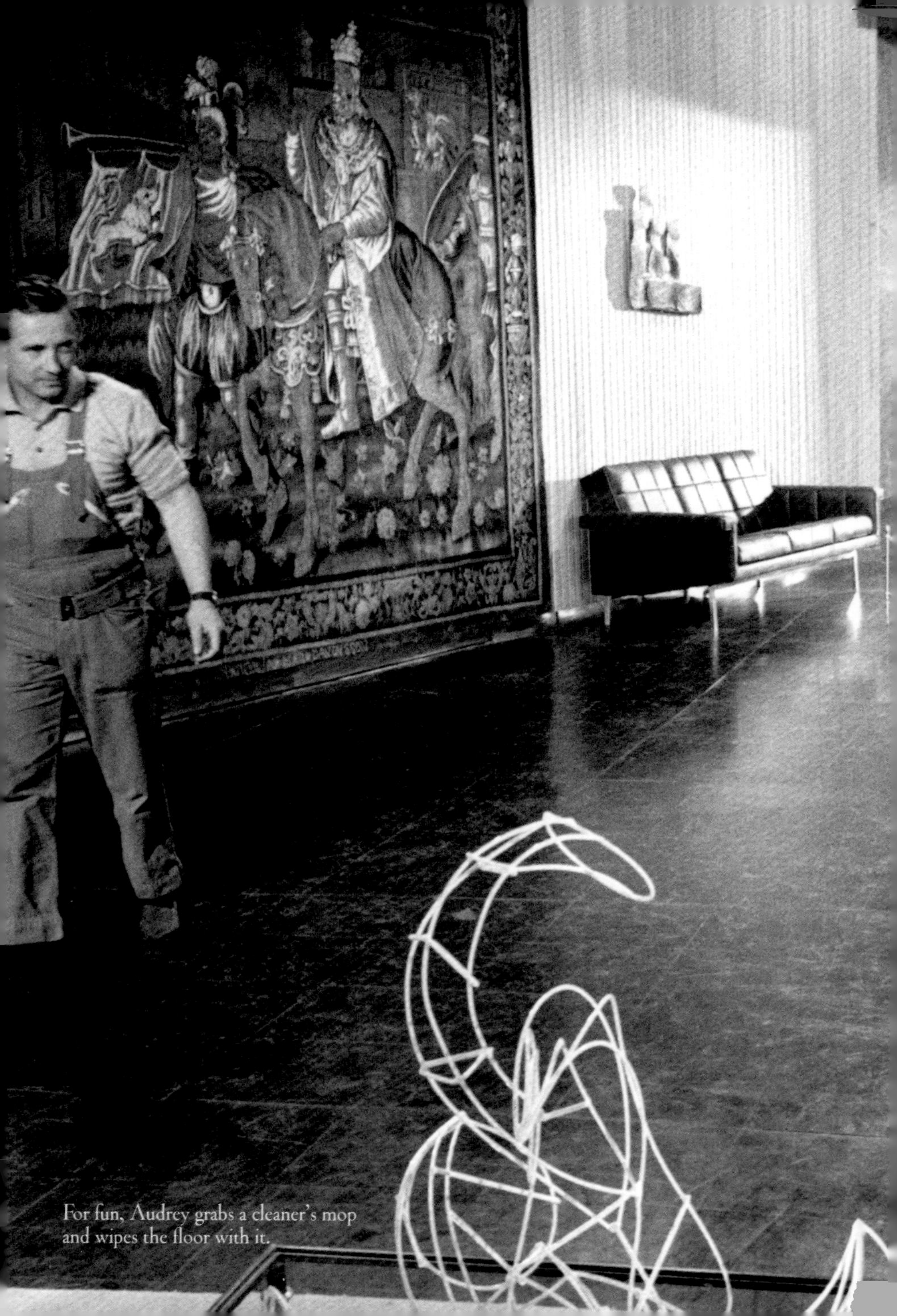

For fun, Audrey grabs a cleaner's mop
and wipes the floor with it.

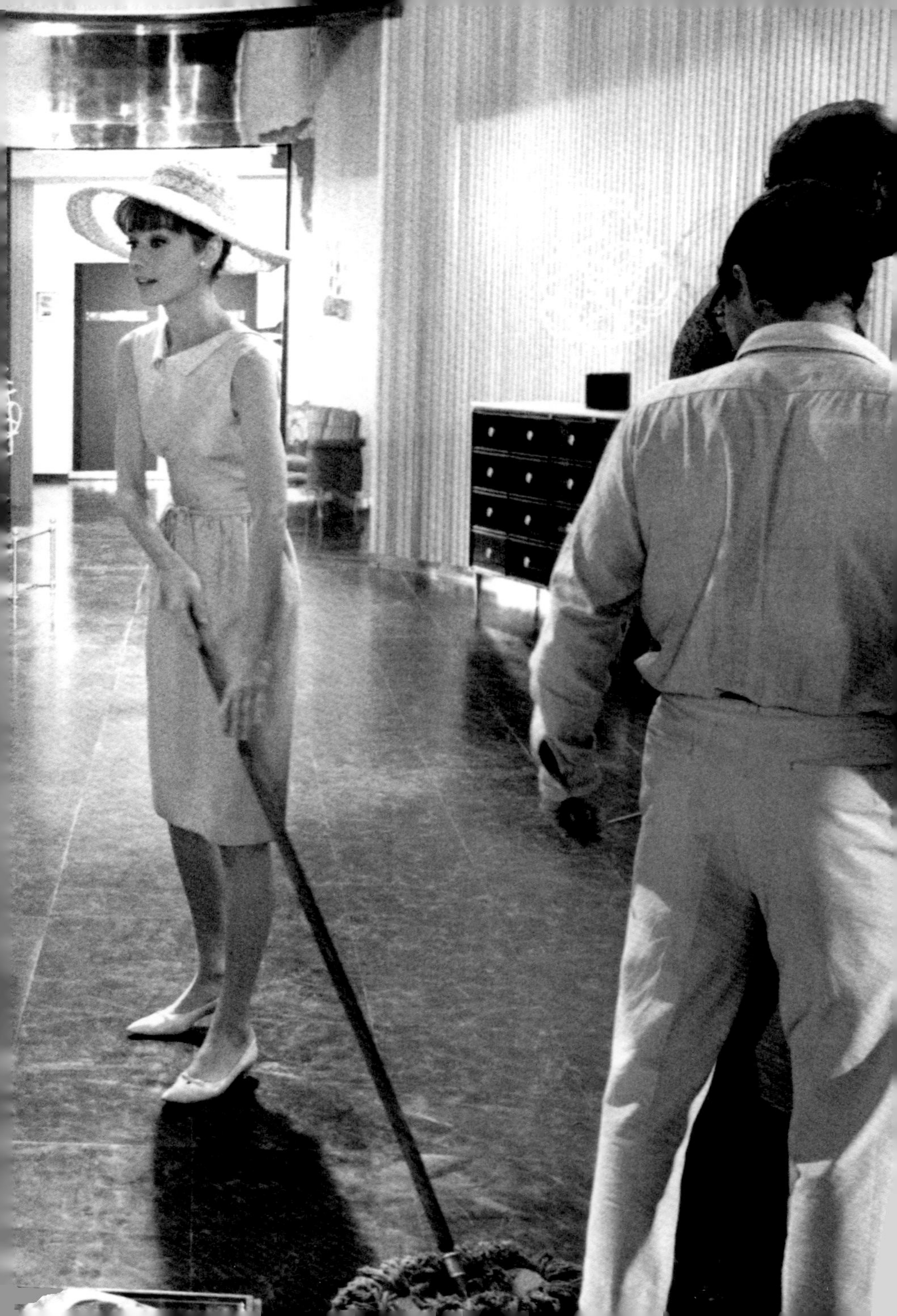

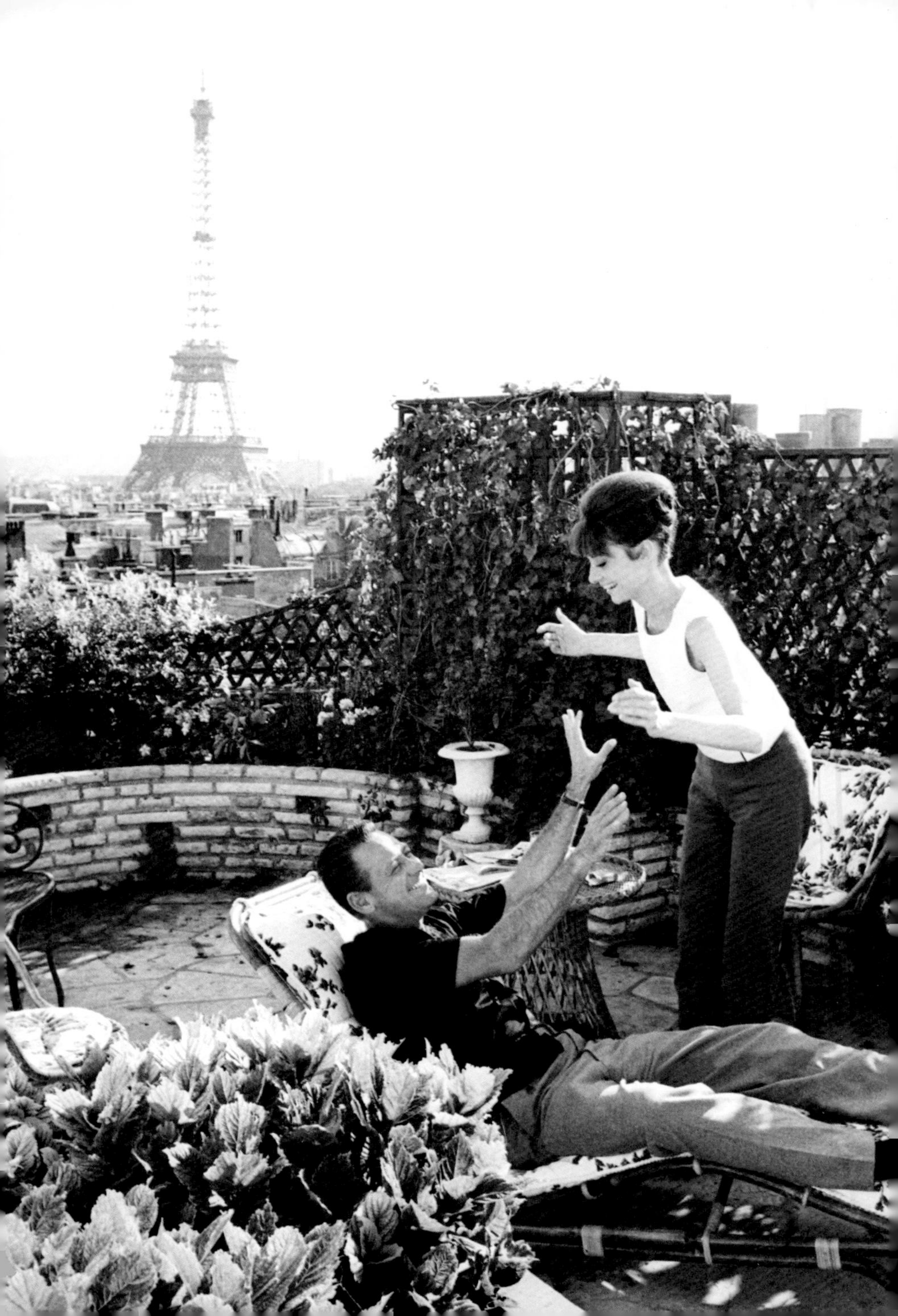

"She was an enchantress,
inspiring love and beauty.
And fairies never quite disappear
altogether."

Hubert de Givenchy

Bill and Audrey about to fall
into each other's arms on a Parisian terrace.

Following spread:
Audrey plays Eliza Doolittle in *My Fair Lady,* 1963.

MY FAIR LADY

1963

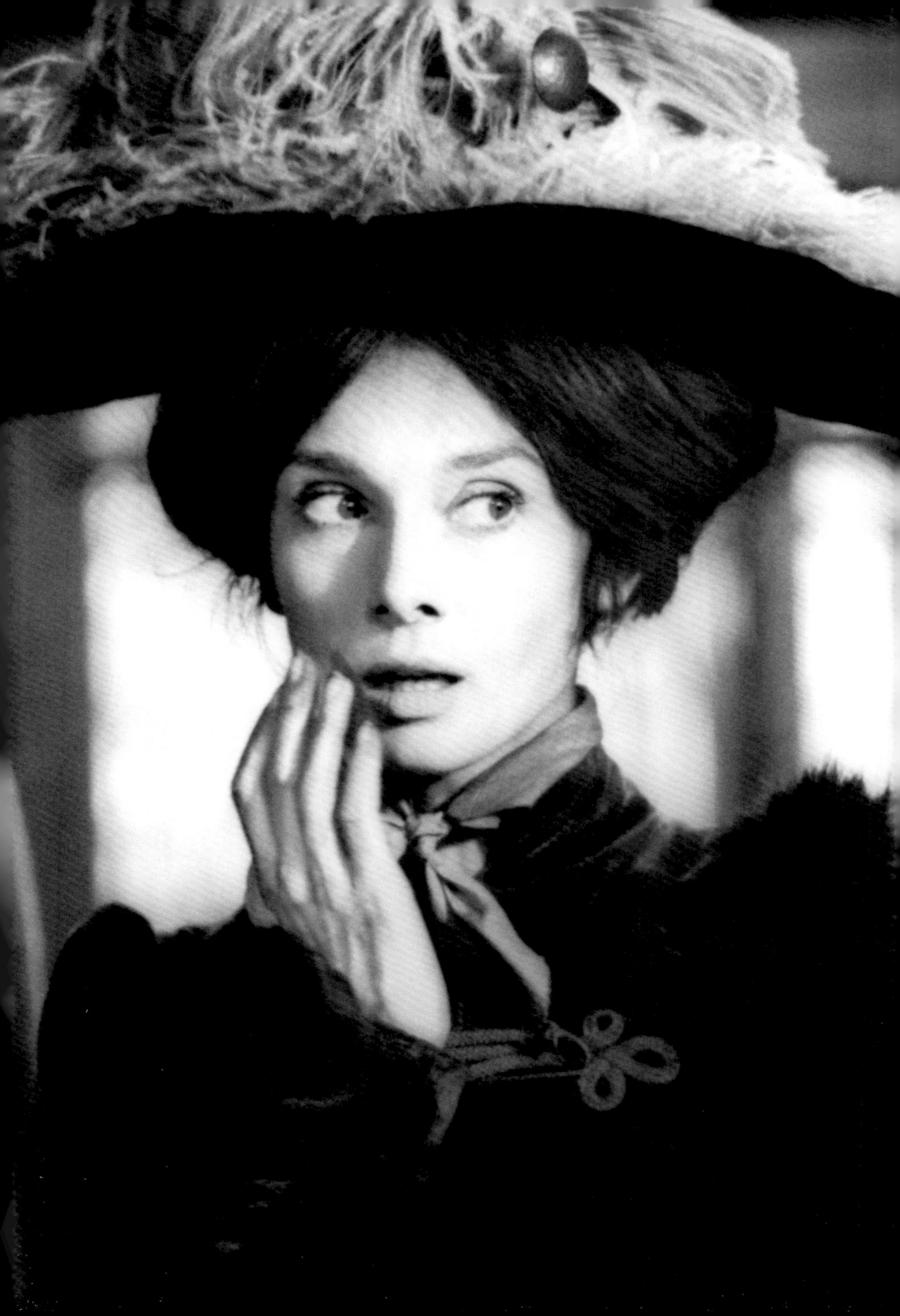

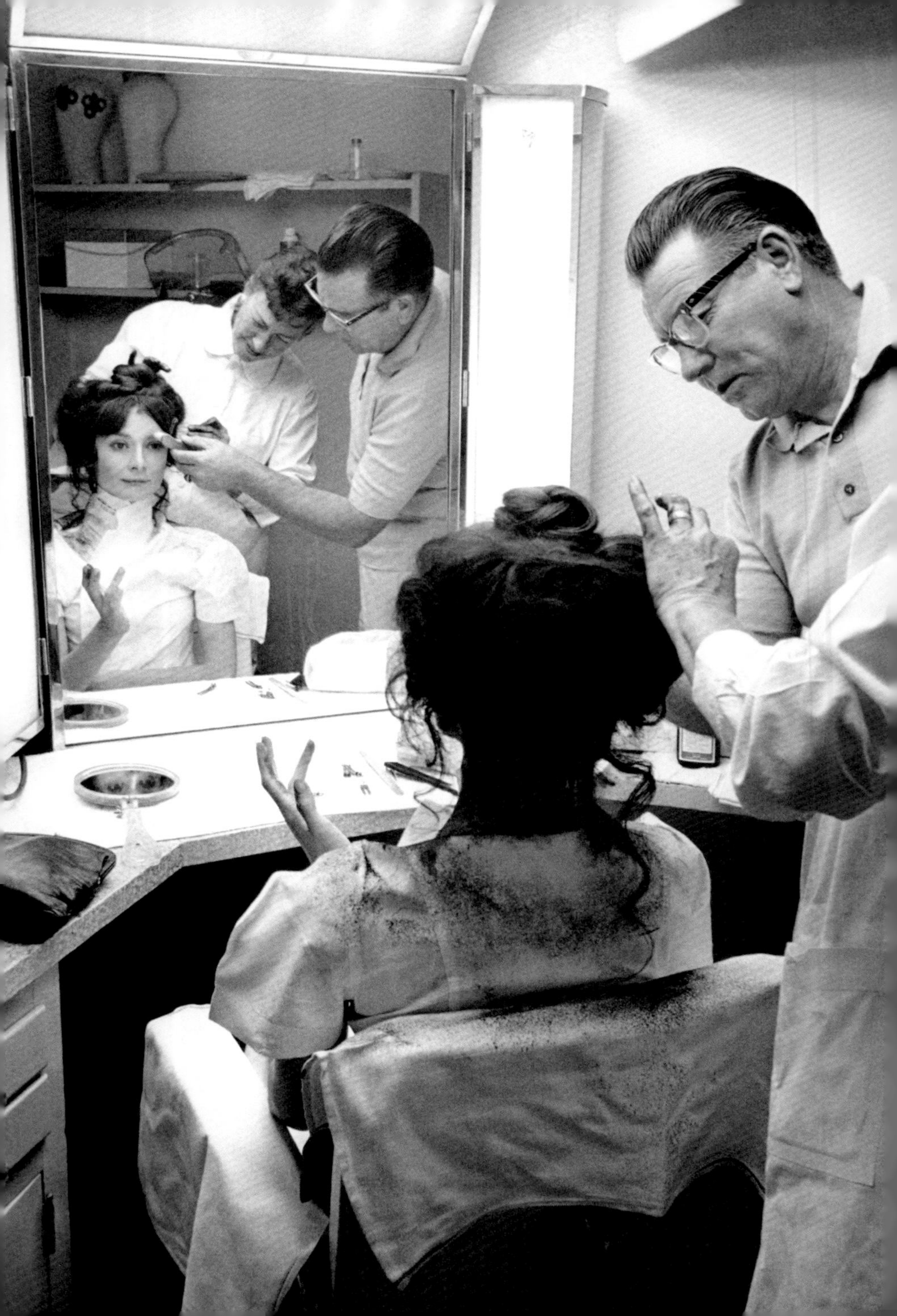

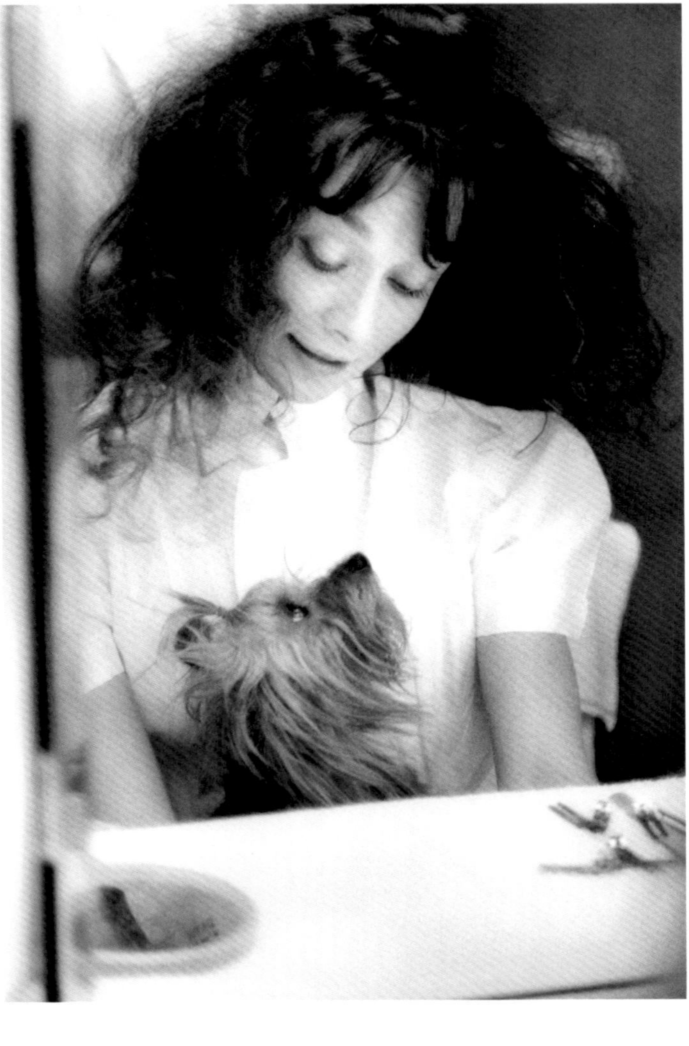

Frank McCoy and Dean Cole transform Audrey into the common flower girl Eliza Doolittle.

Audrey chatting to her new Yorkshire terrier, Assam.

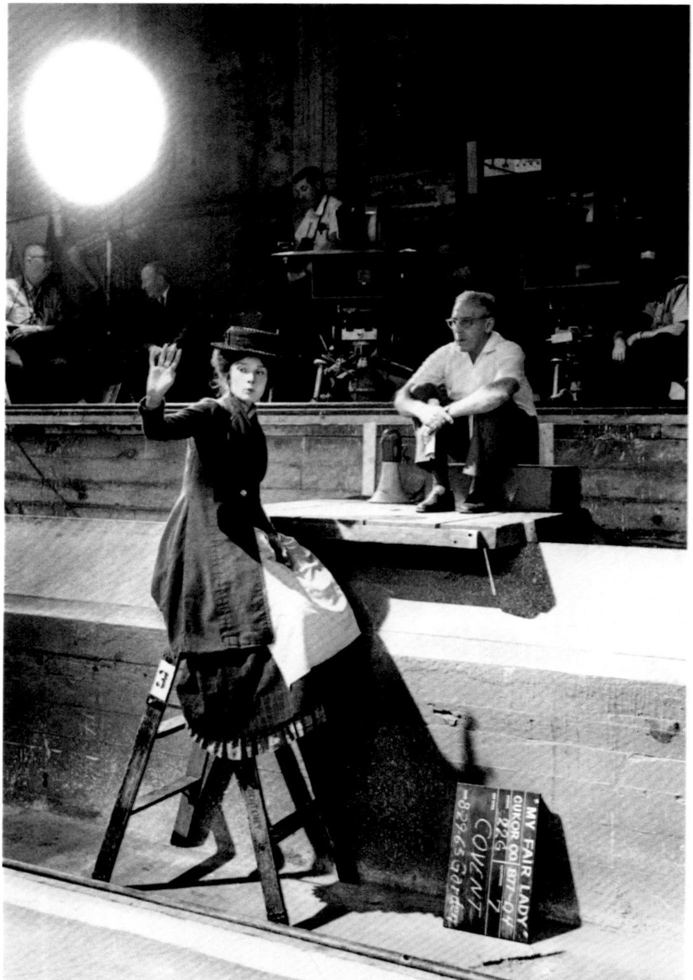

Audrey climbs up a ladder to discuss with
director George Cukor how she should move in the next scene.

The first day of shooting as Eliza Doolittle.

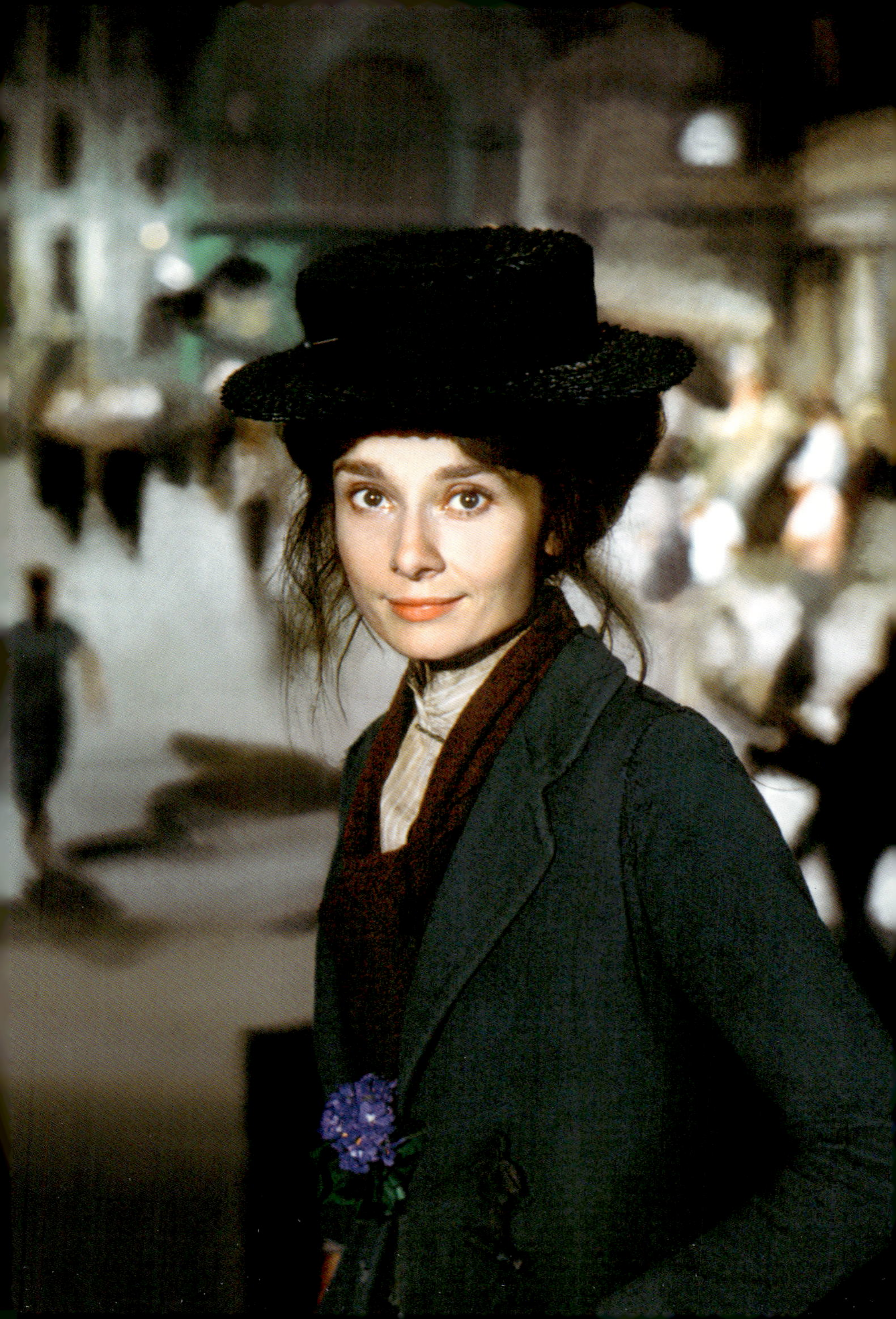

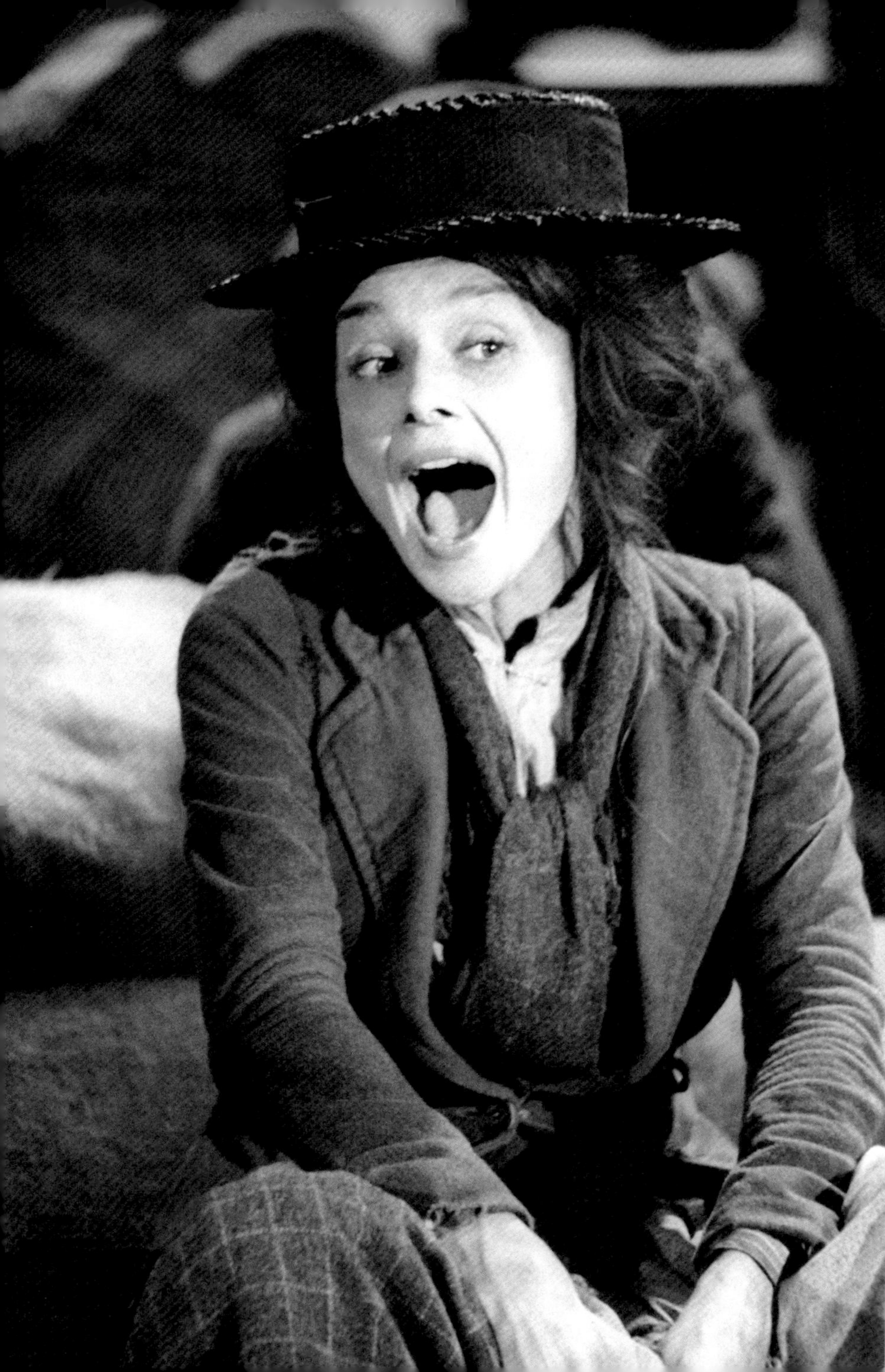

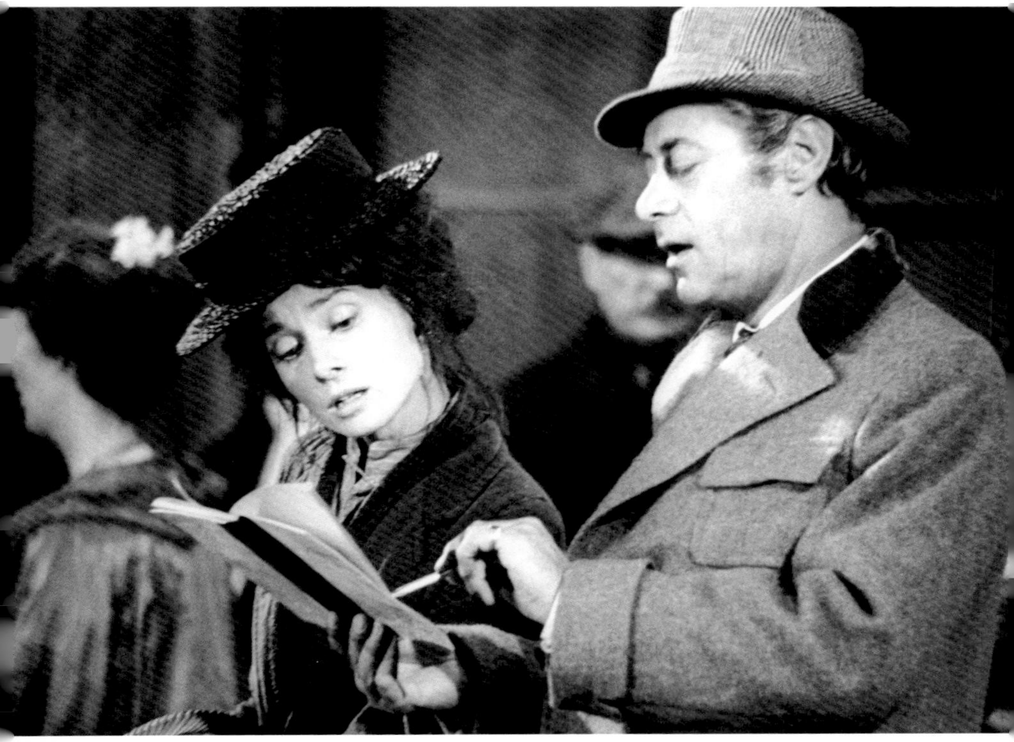

"Oh wouldn't it be loverly?": Eliza dreams of a better life.

Eliza encounters Professor Henry Higgins, played by Rex Harrison.

Audrey spent the whole day's
shoot soaked to the skin.

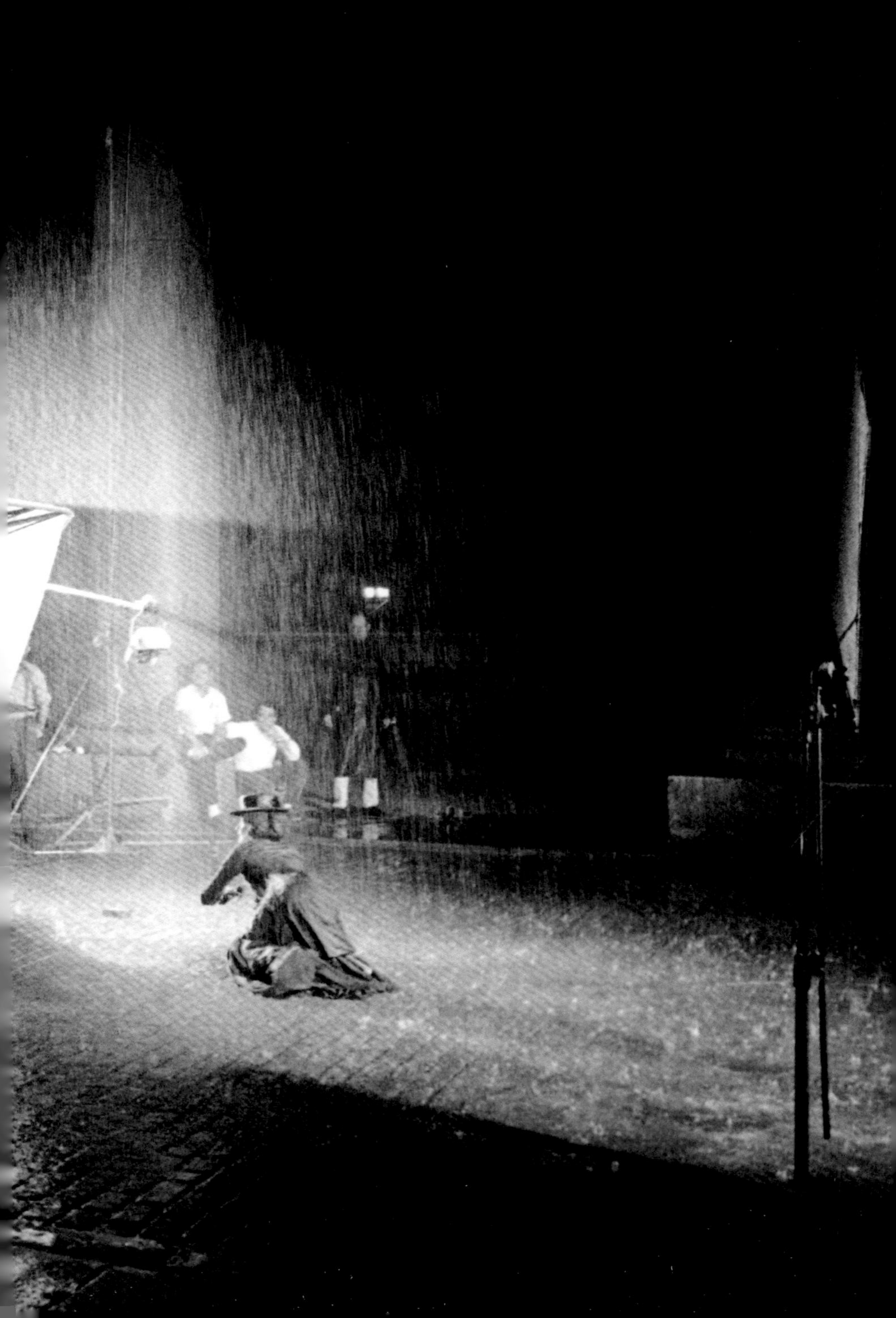

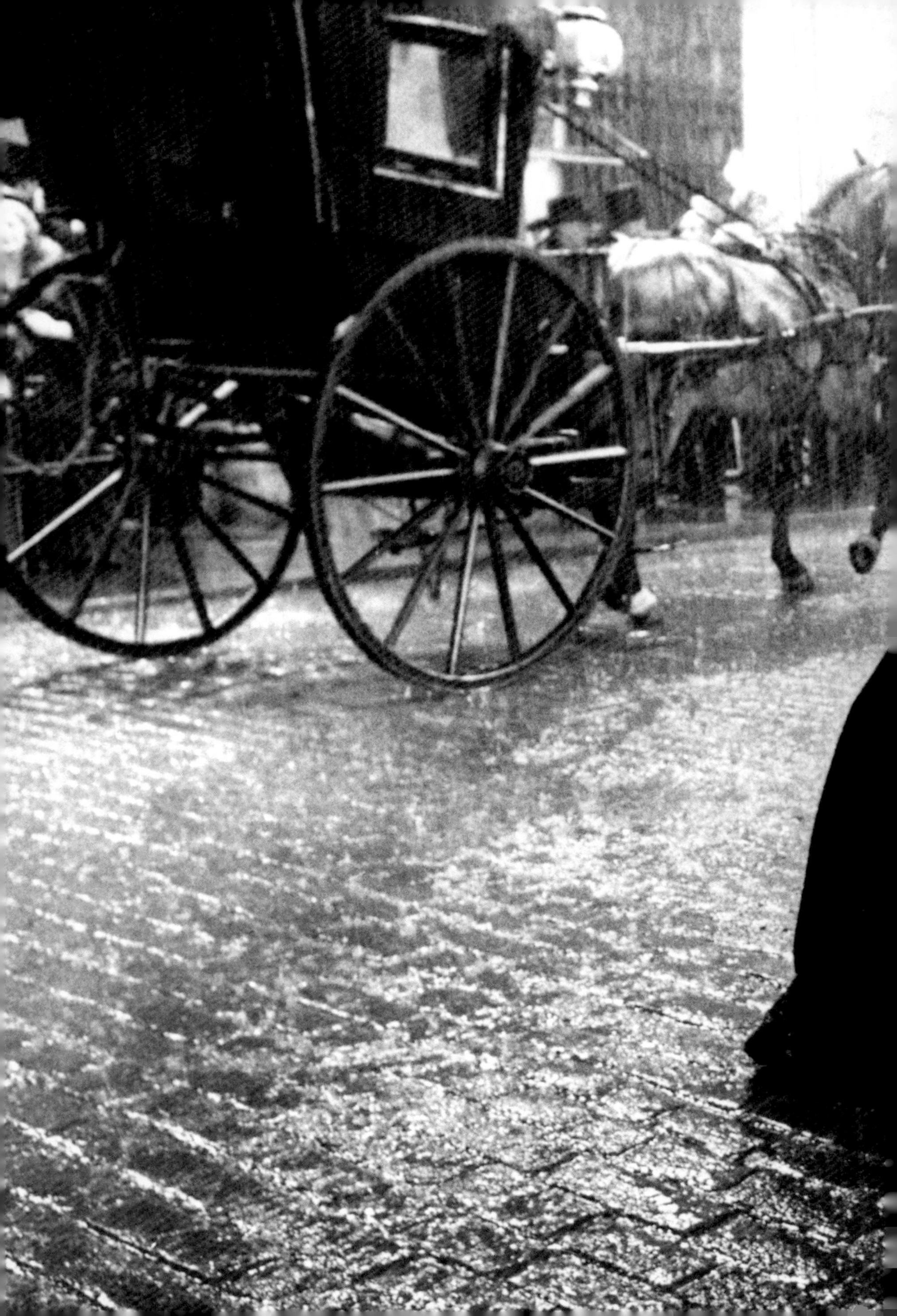

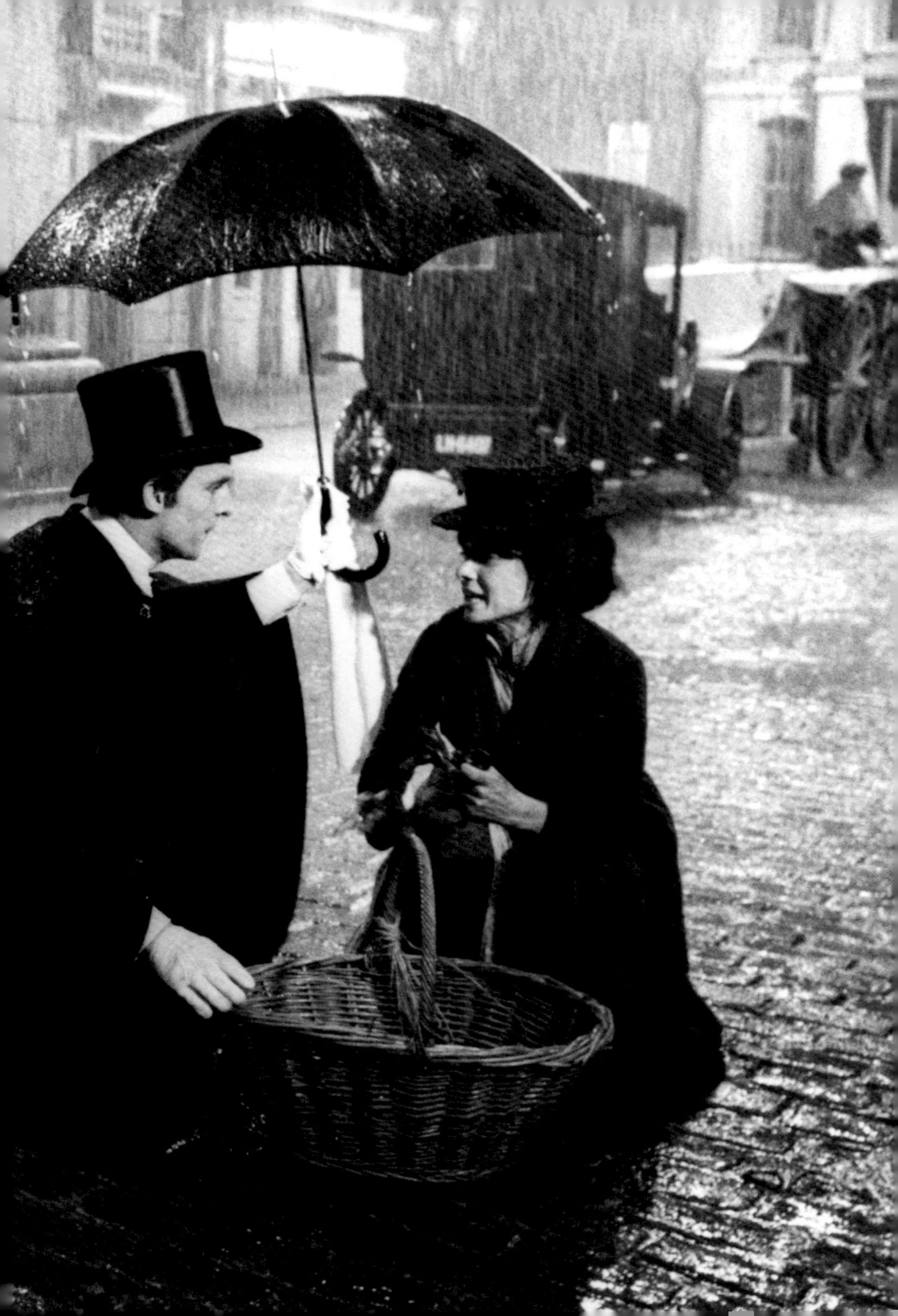

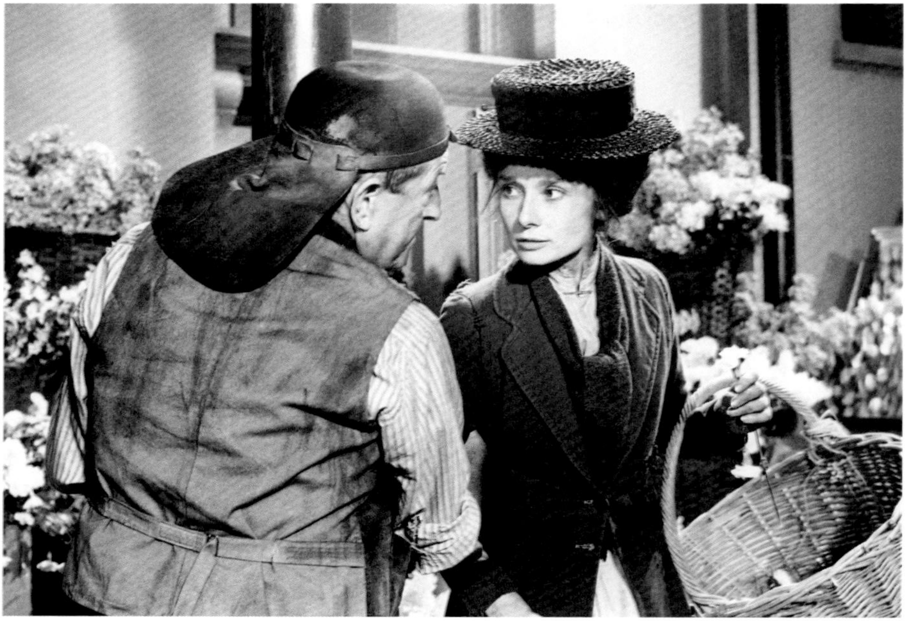

Previous spread:
Warner Bros. recreated London's Covent Garden for the set. Here, Jeremy Brett as Freddy Eynsford-Hill collides with Eliza, sending her flowers tumbling to the floor.

Above:
Eliza with her father, the dustman Alfred P. Doolittle, played by Stanley Holloway.

Opposite:
Audrey enjoys a cigarette break during filming.

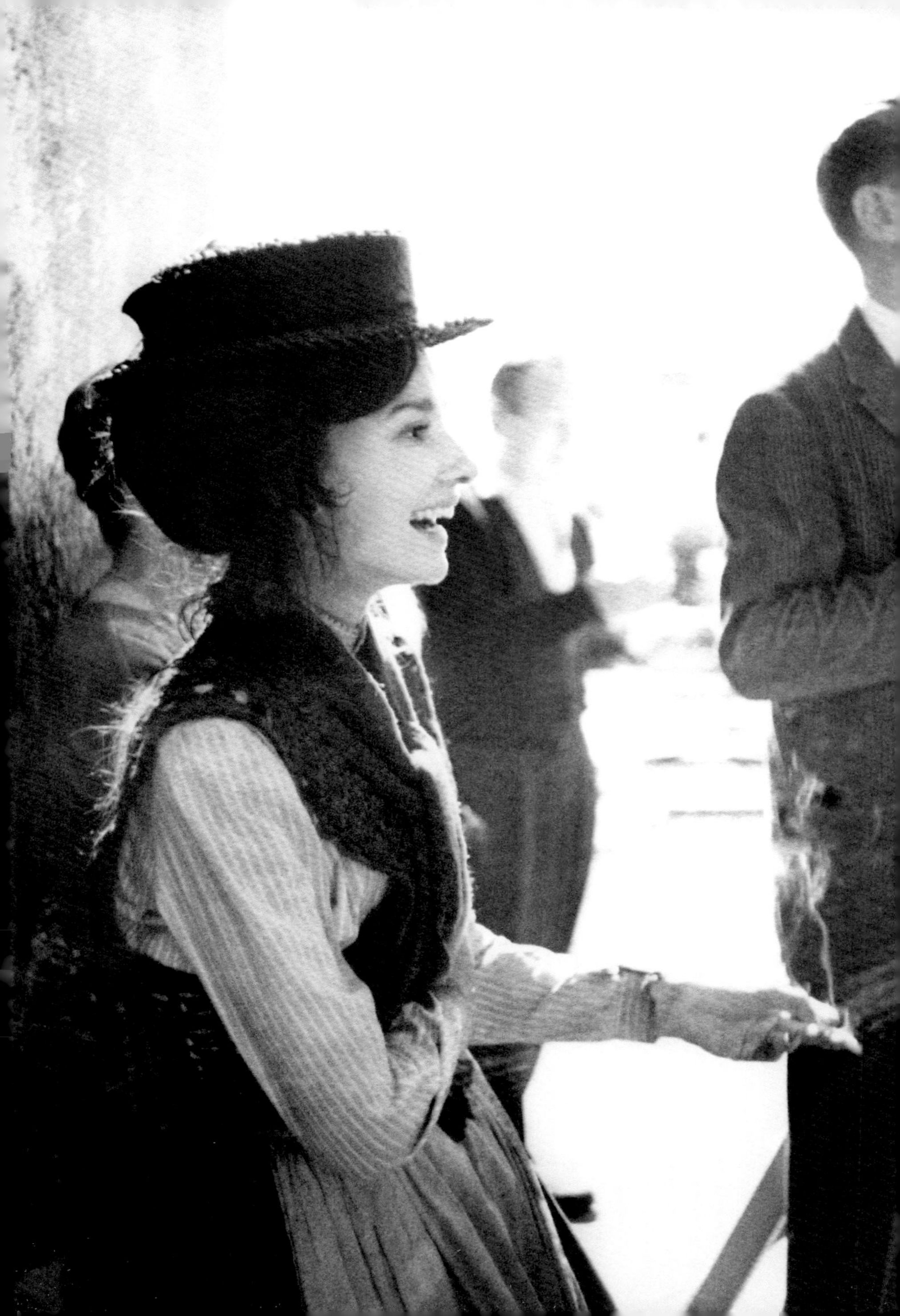

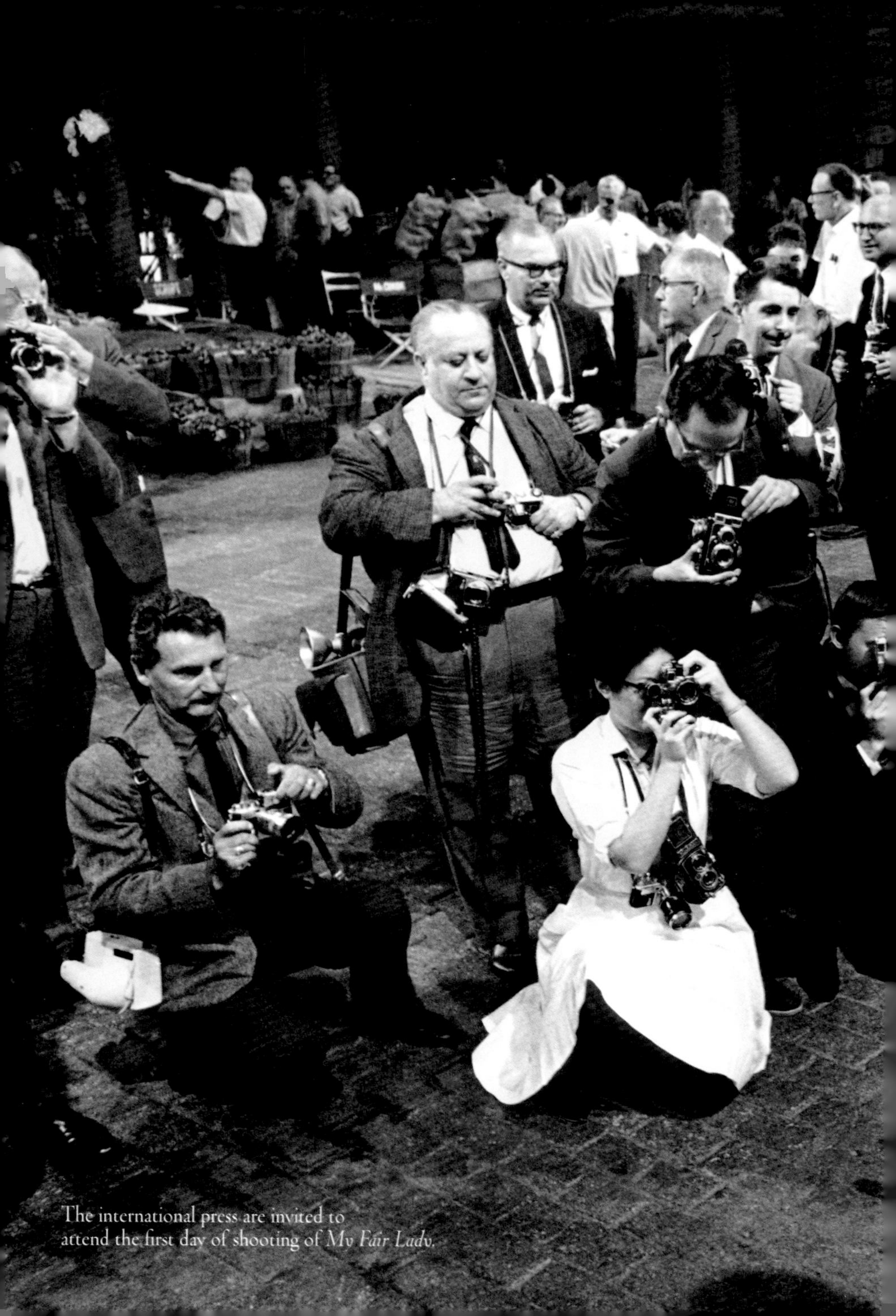

The international press are invited to attend the first day of shooting of *My Fair Lady*.

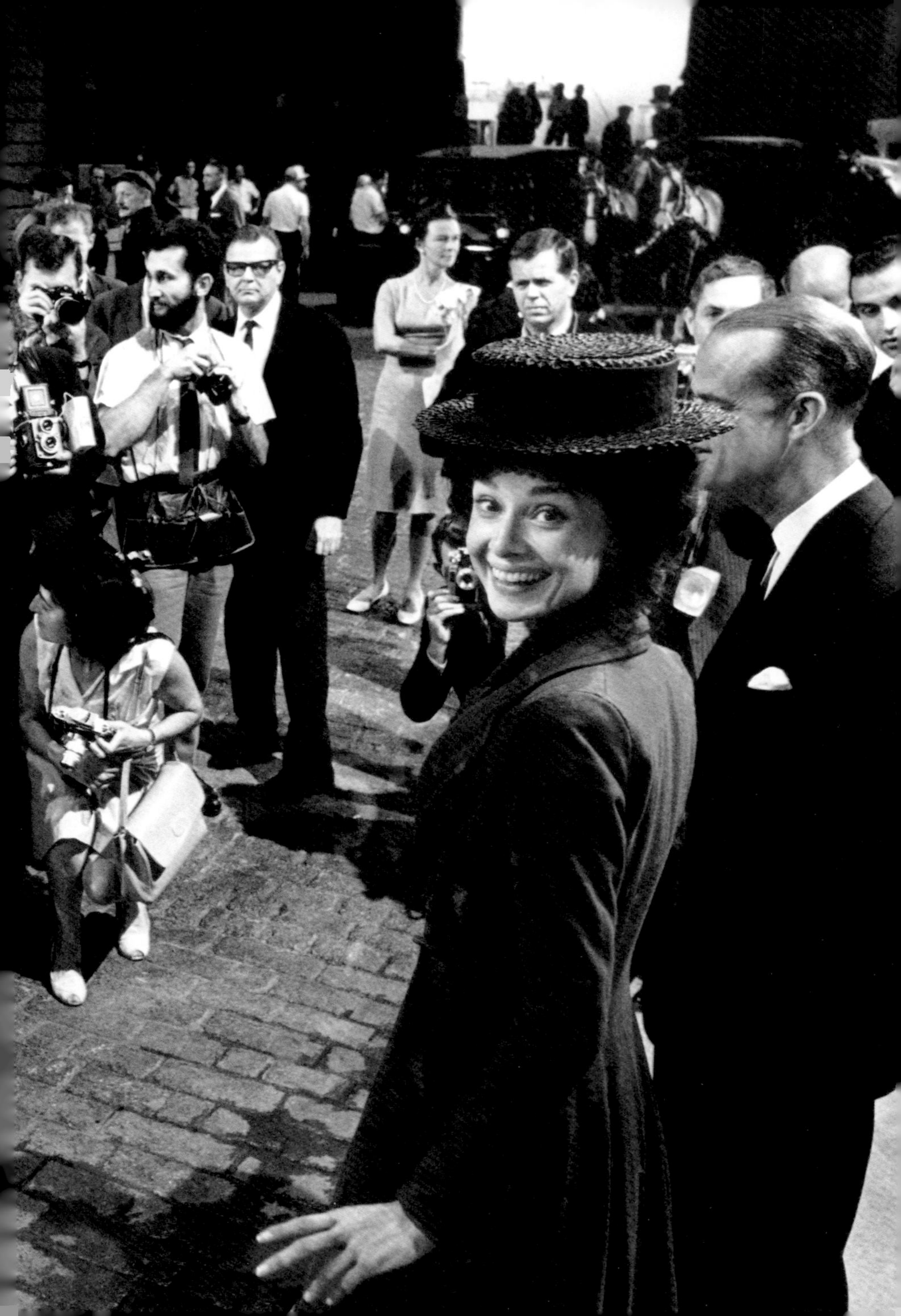

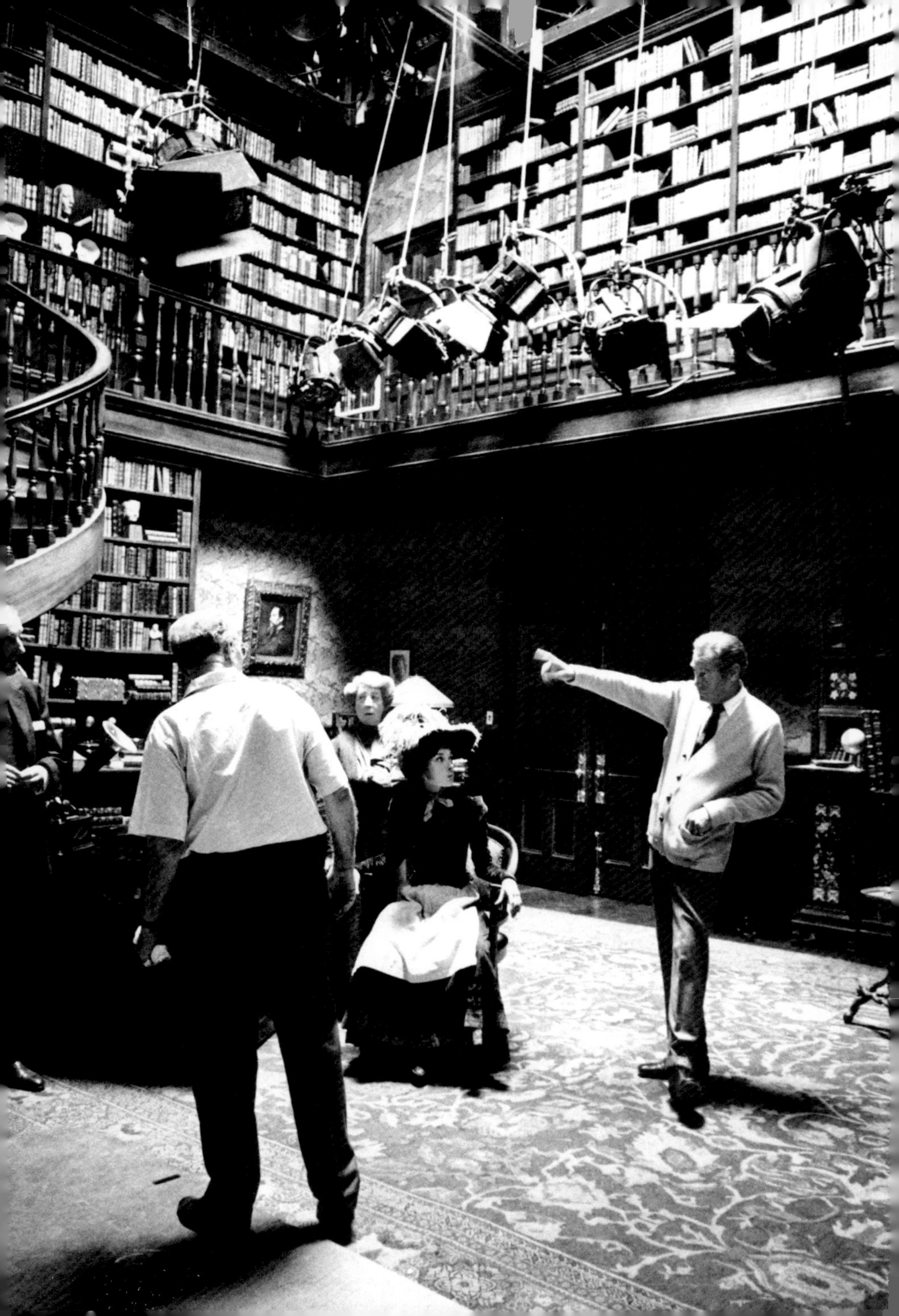

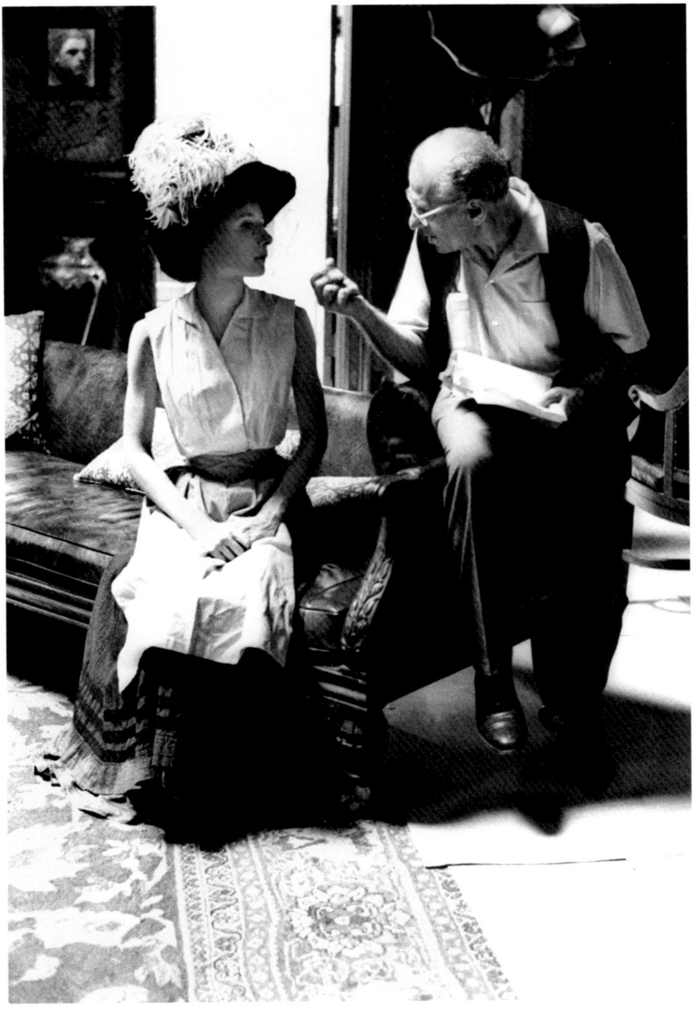

Opposite:
George Cukor watches as Audrey and Rex Harrison rehearse a scene.

Above and following spread:
Cukor is giving a line reading to Audrey.

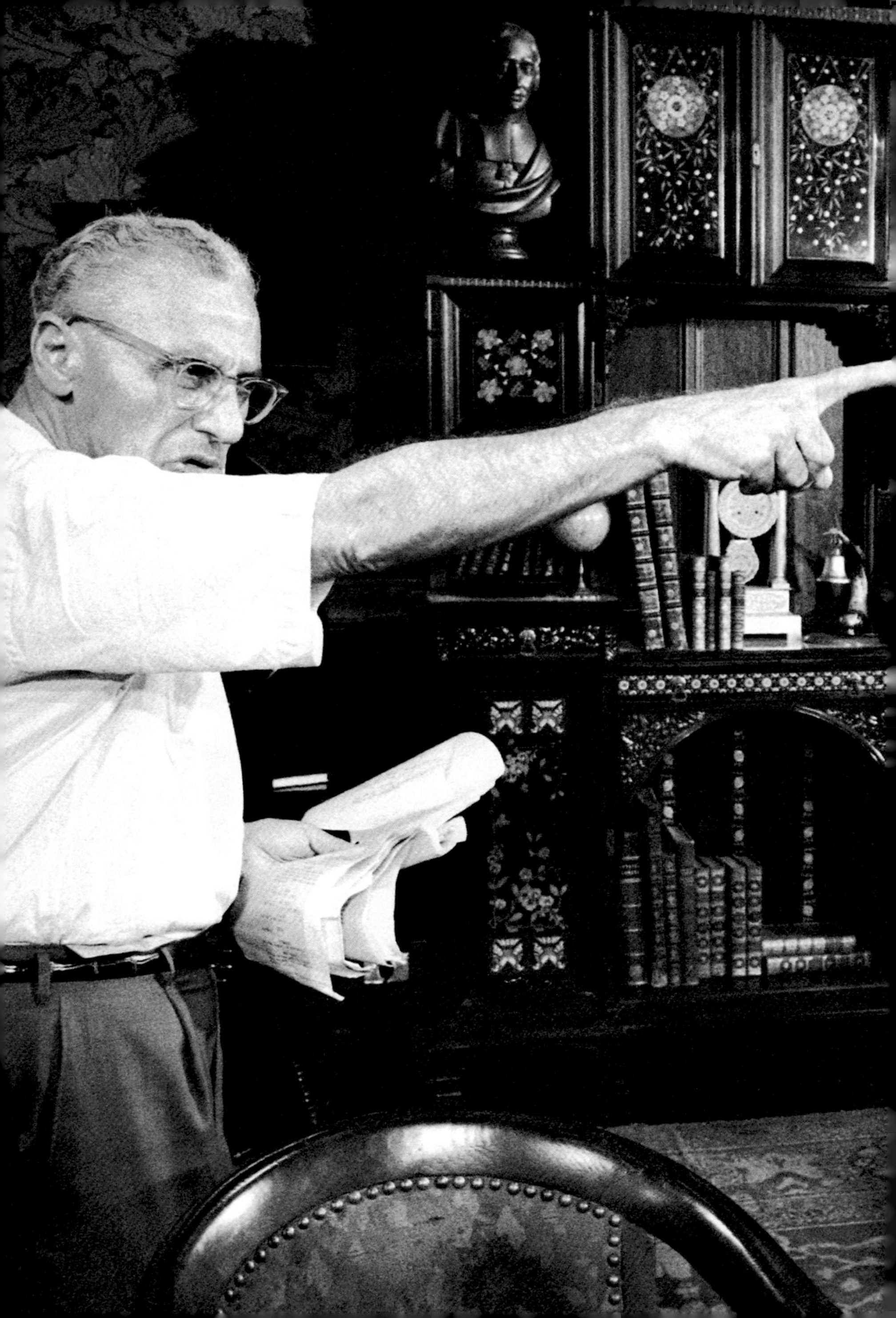

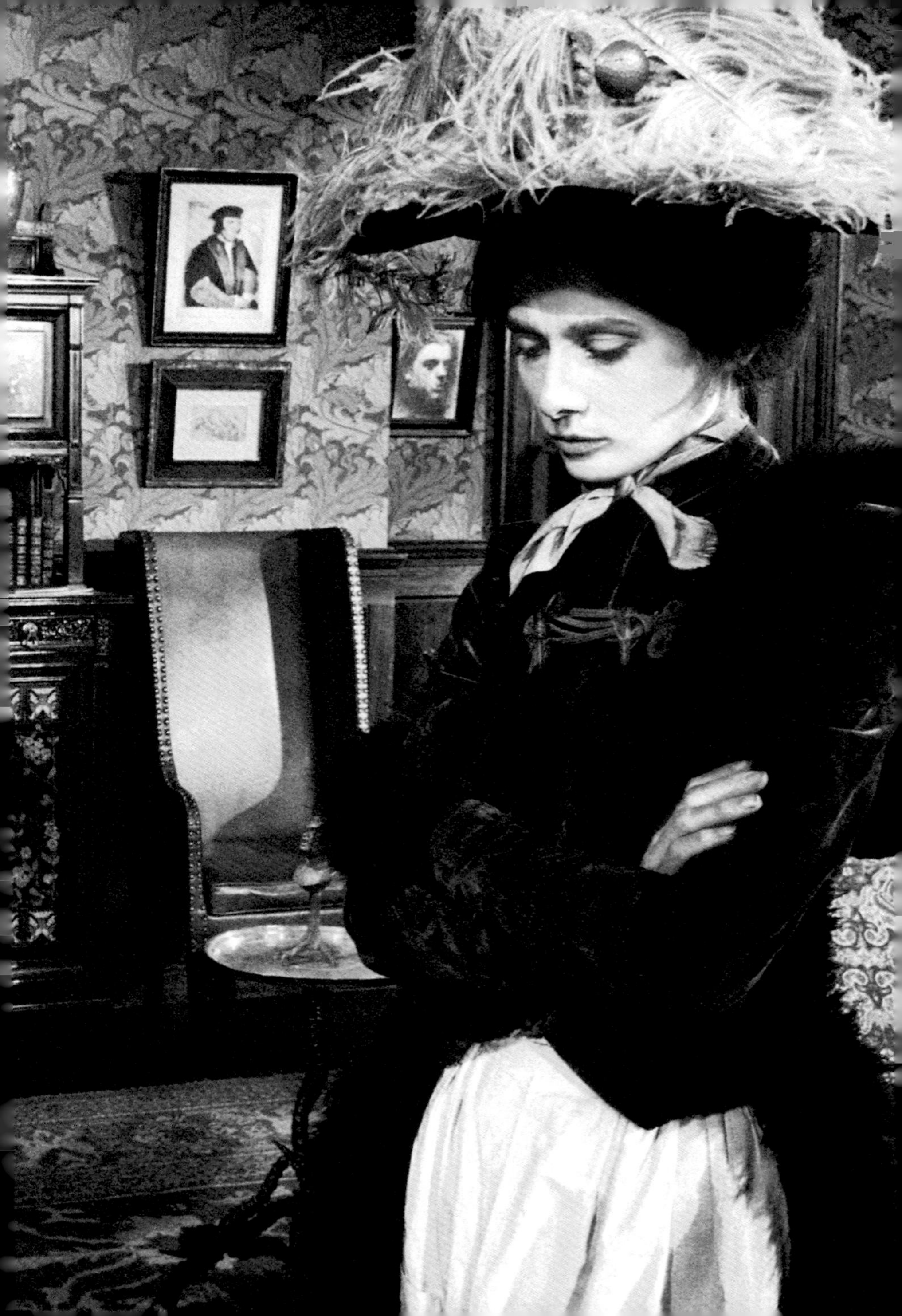

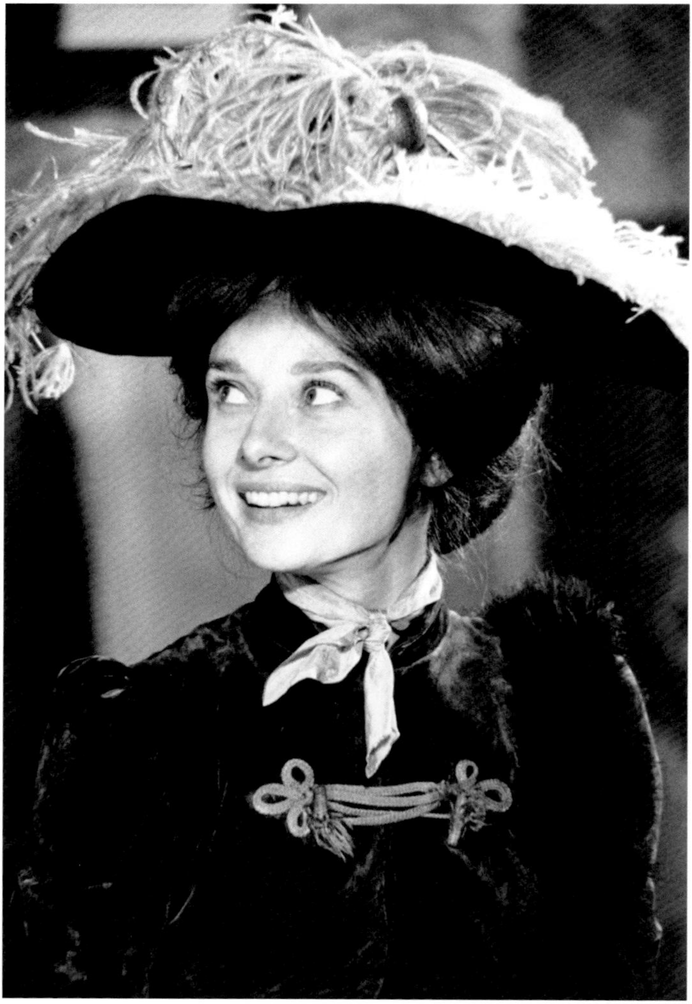

Eliza visits Professor Higgins for the first time.

Hepburn and Harrison wait on the stairs for shooting to resume.

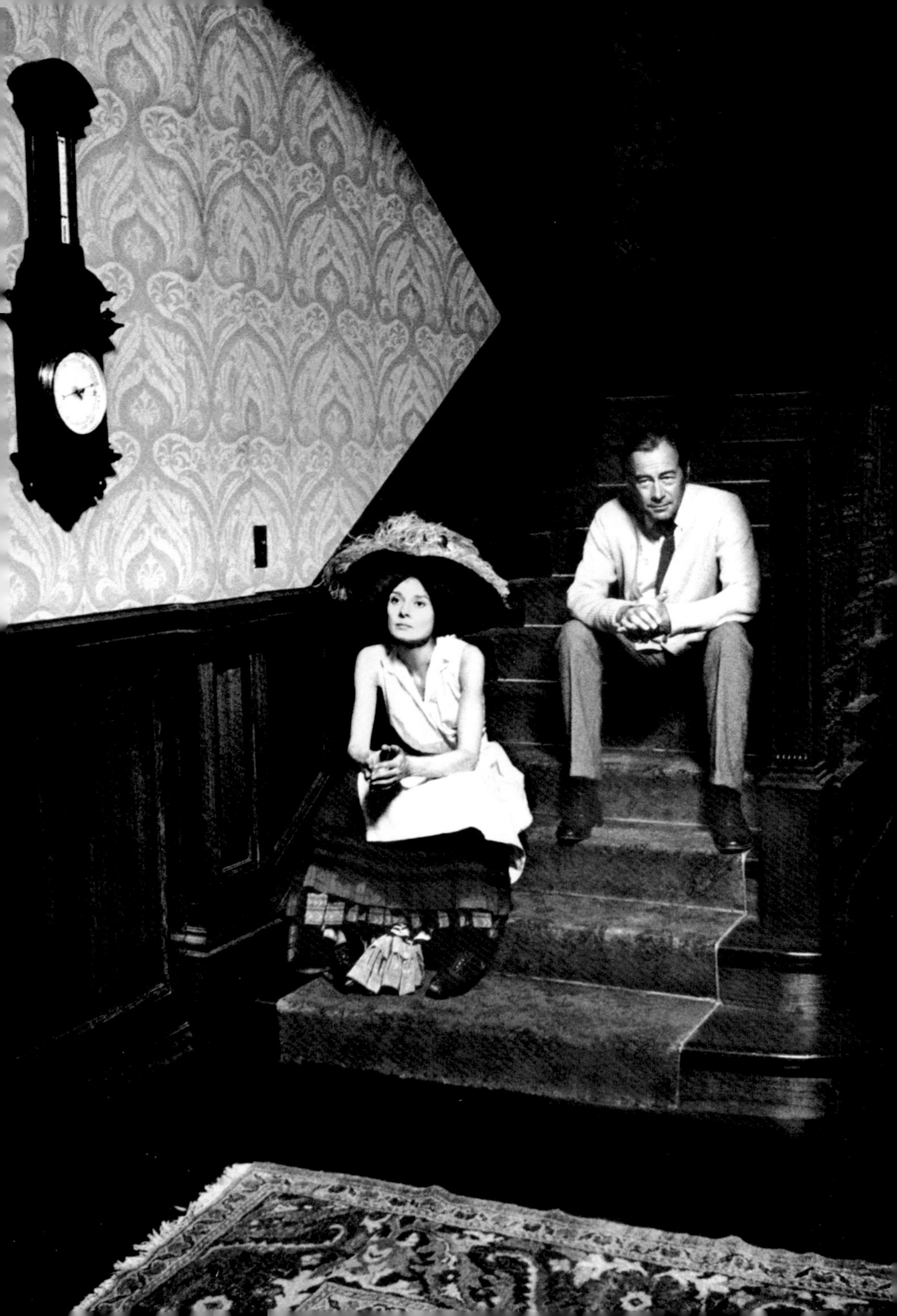

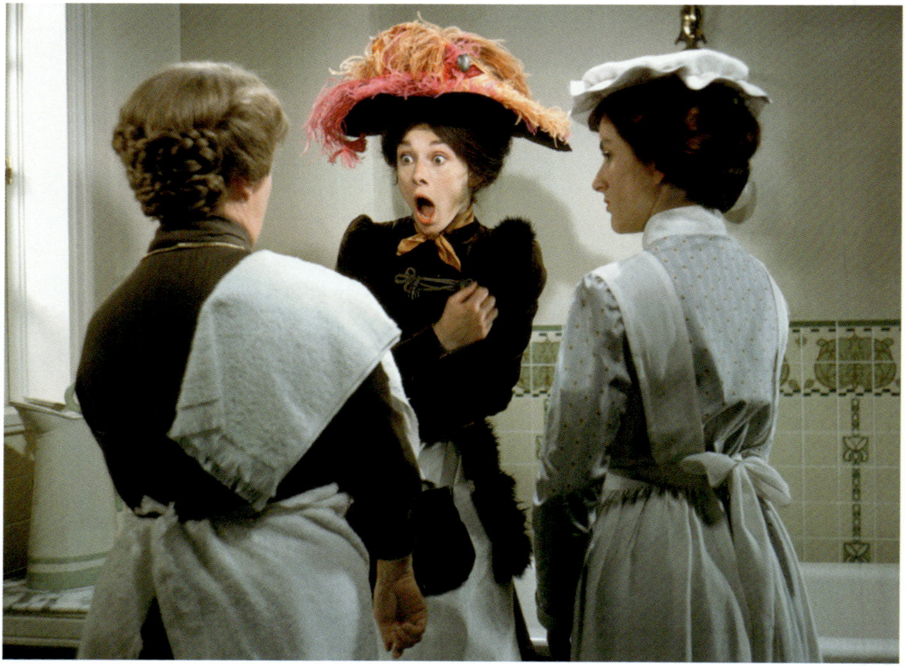

Eliza is appalled at the suggestion that she should get undressed for a bath.

Eliza is manhandled into the bath.

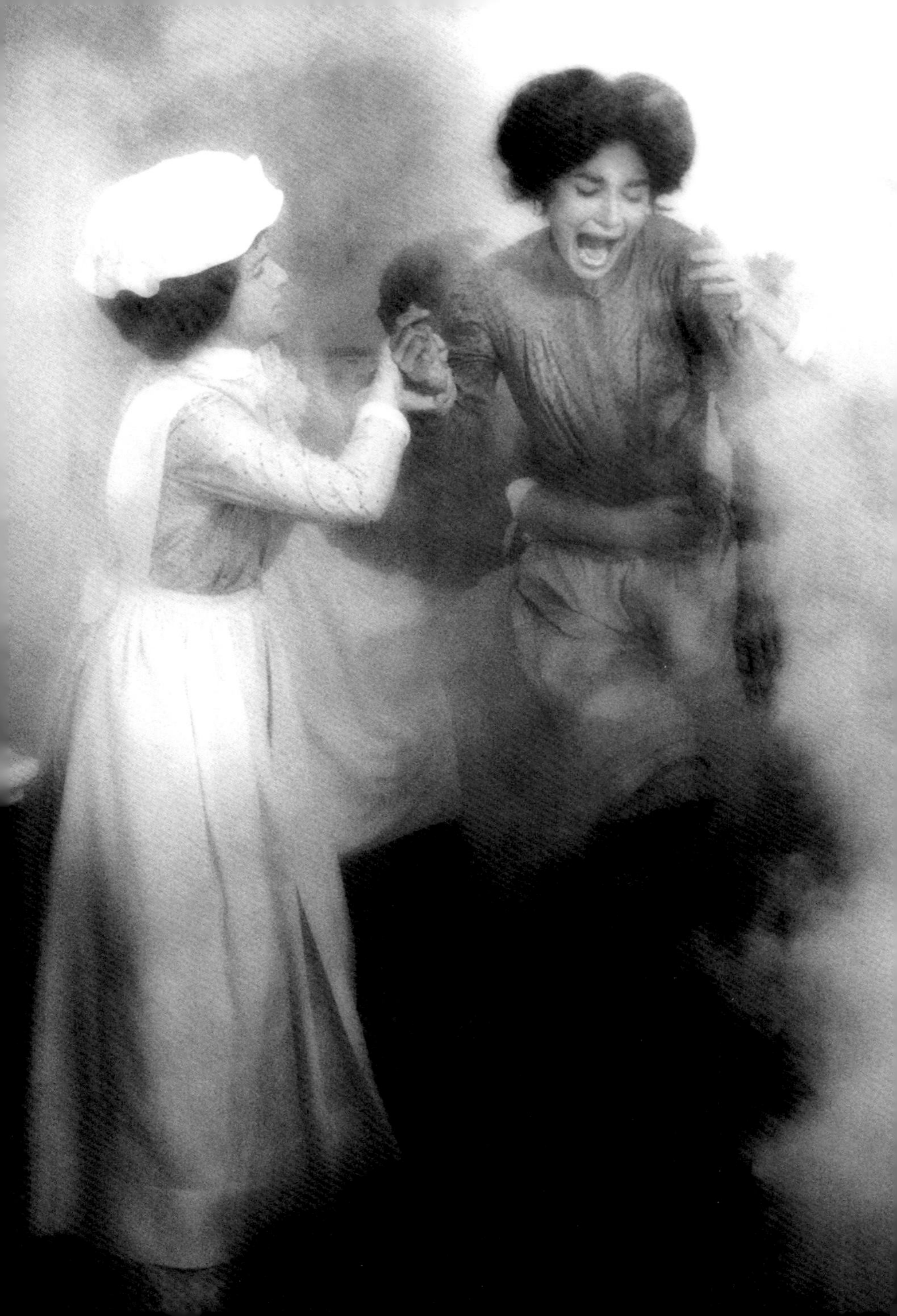

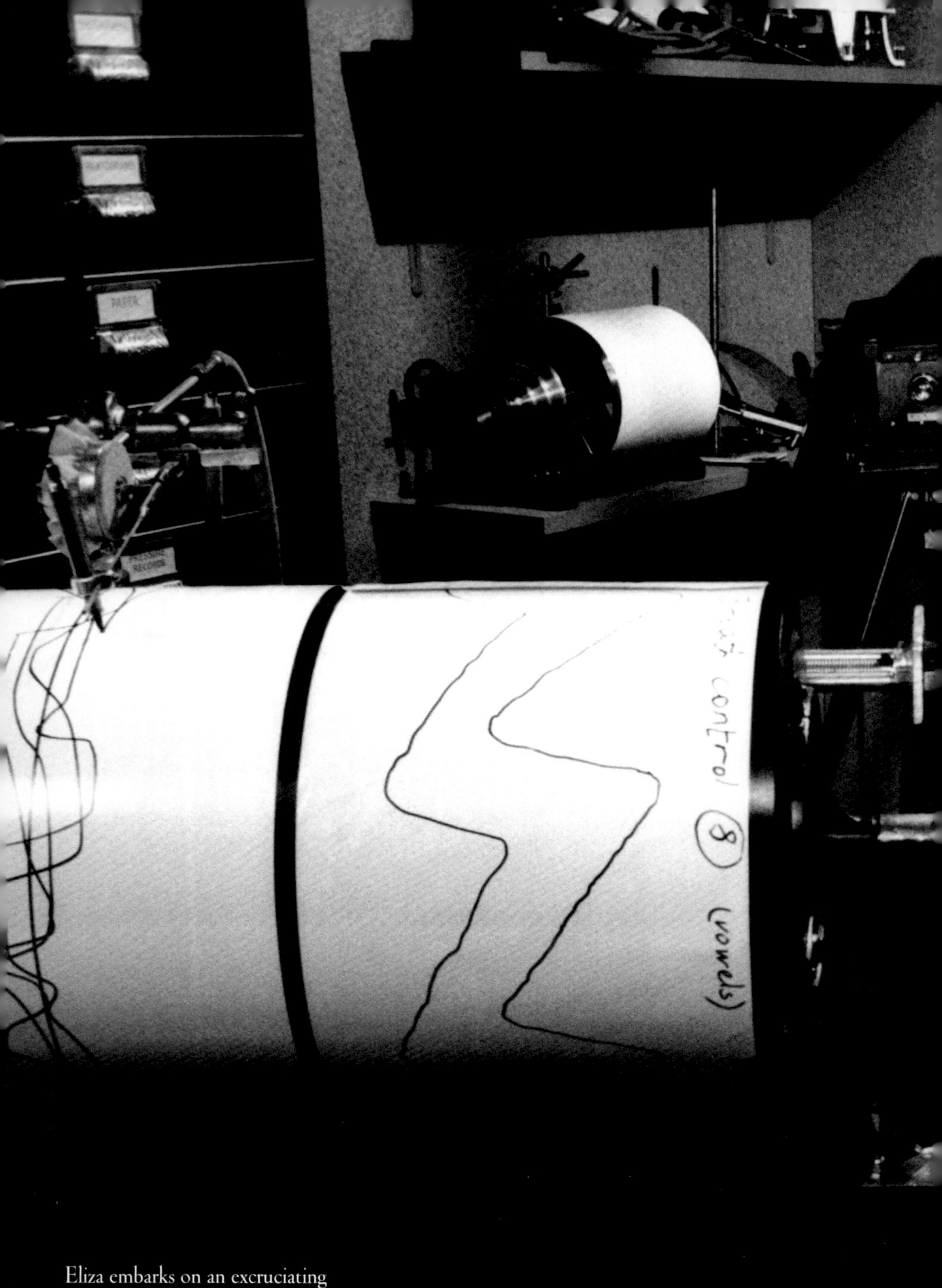

Eliza embarks on an excruciating
regimen of phonetics exercises.

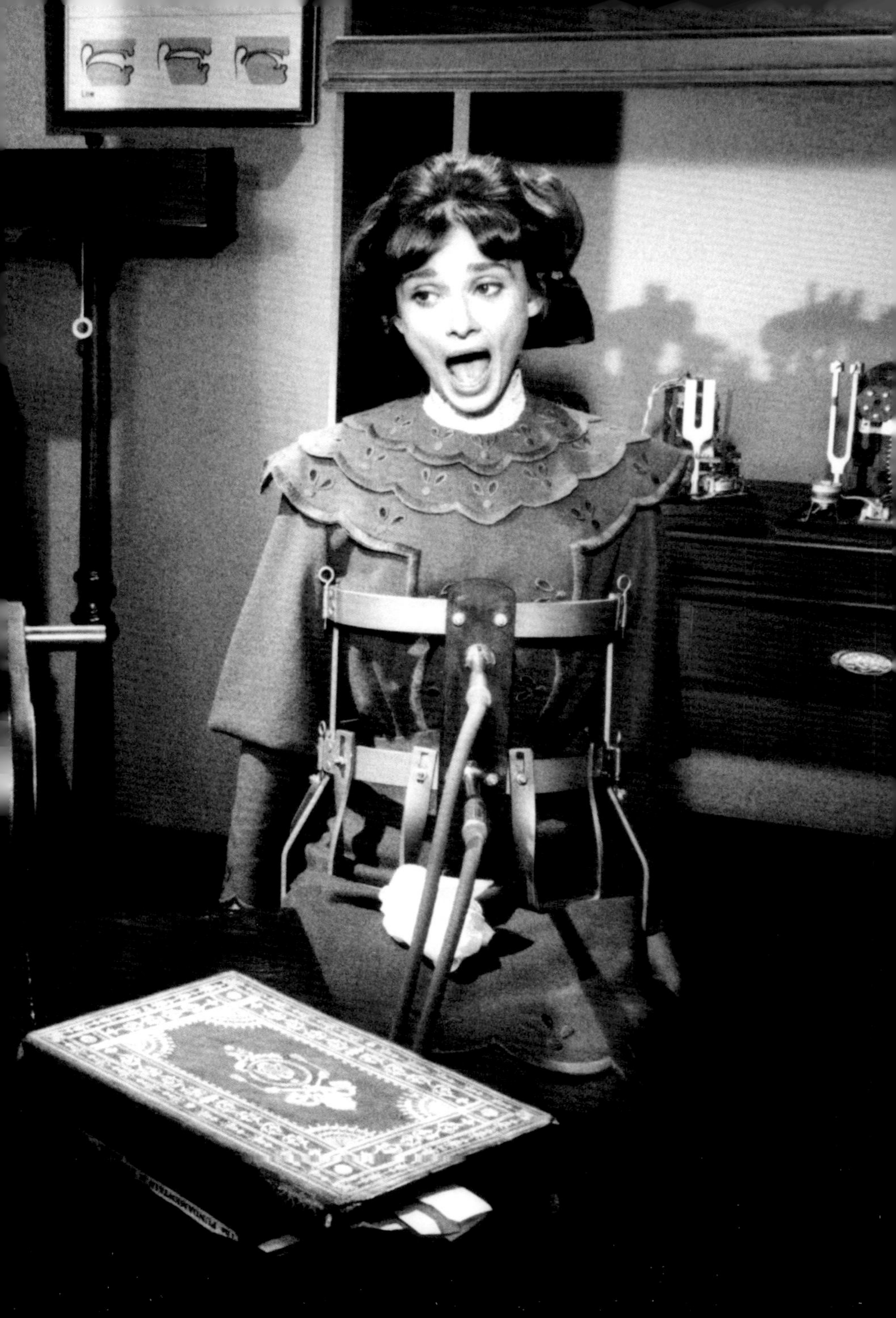

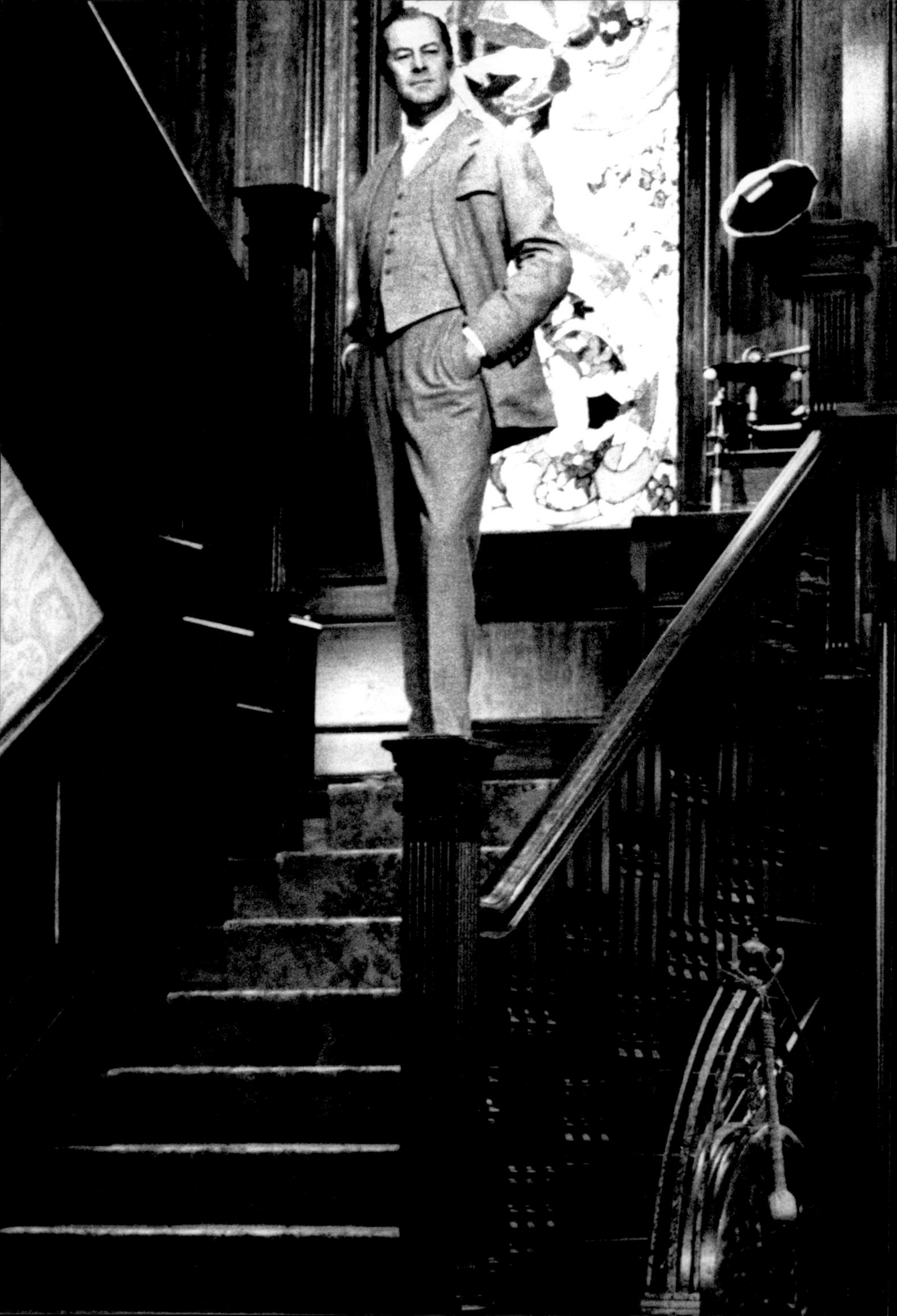

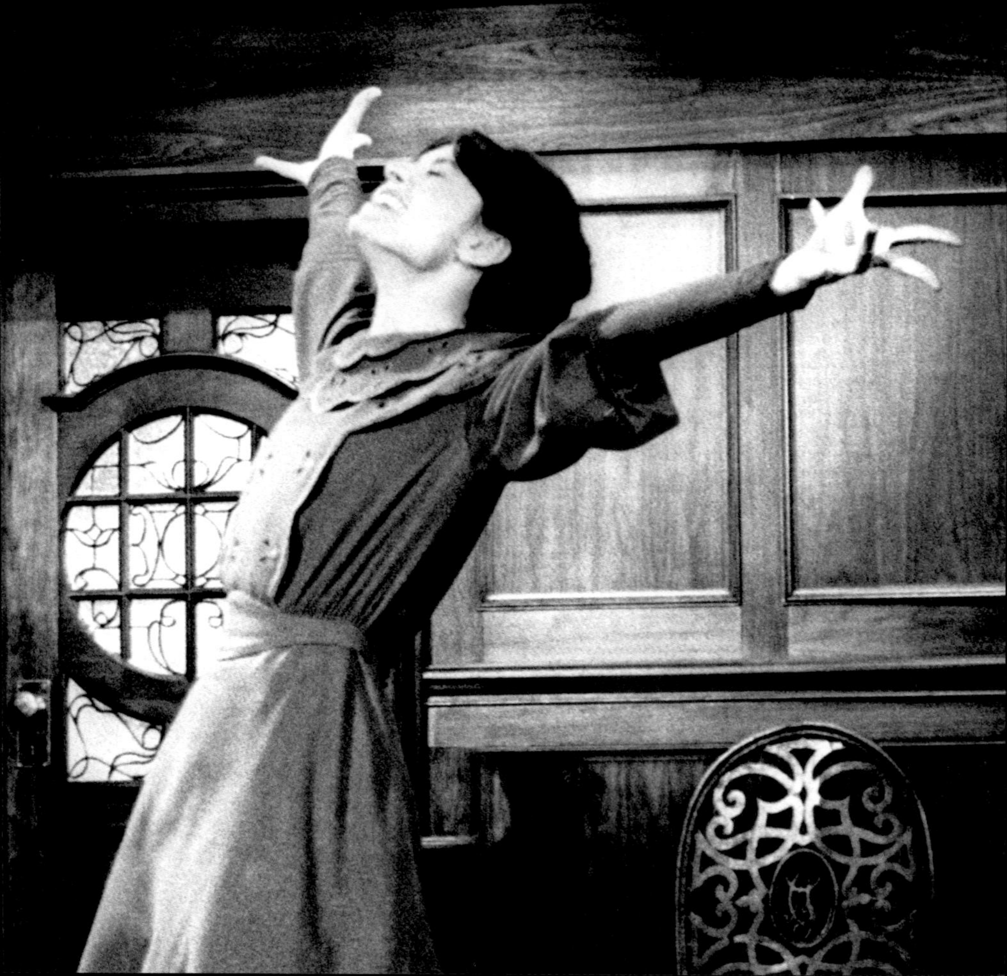

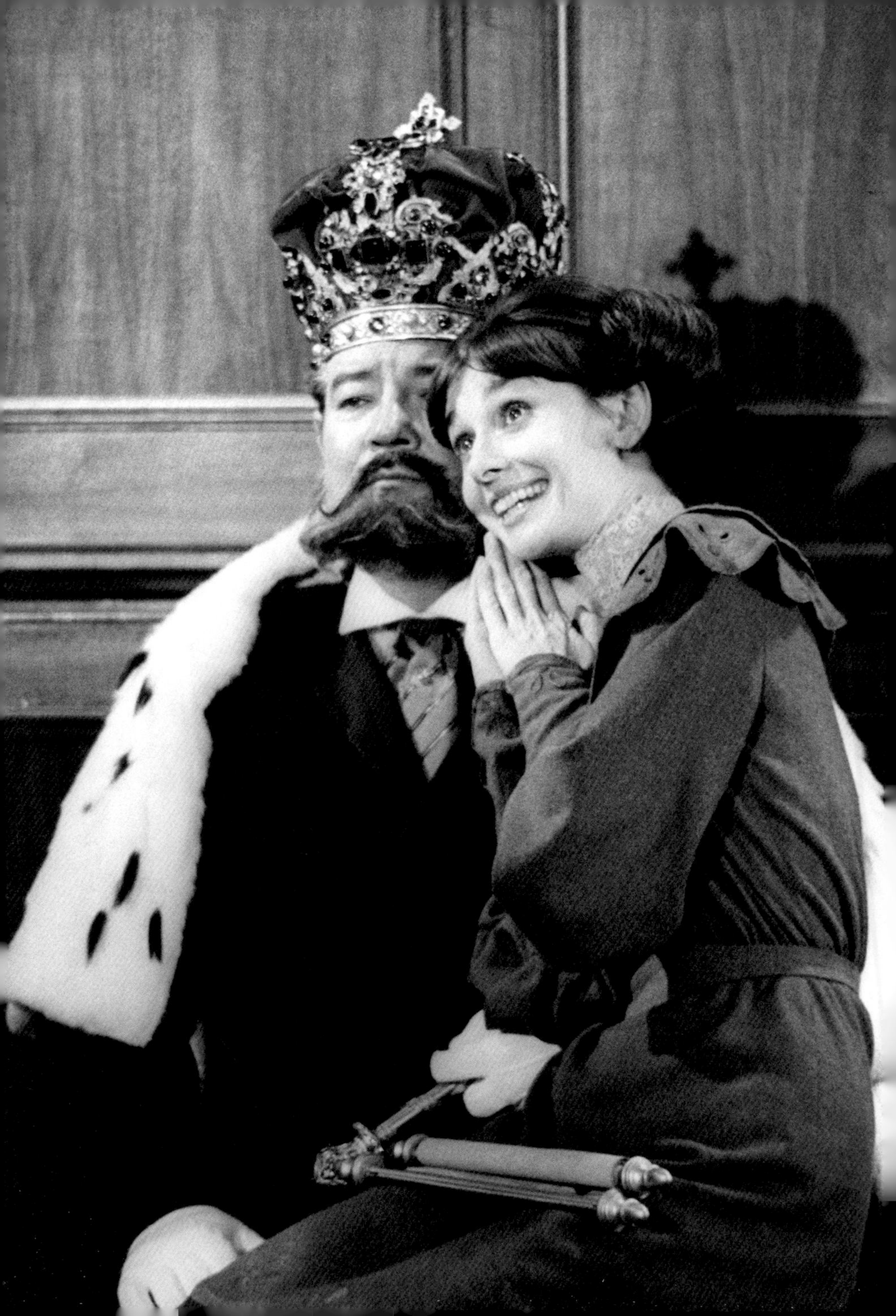

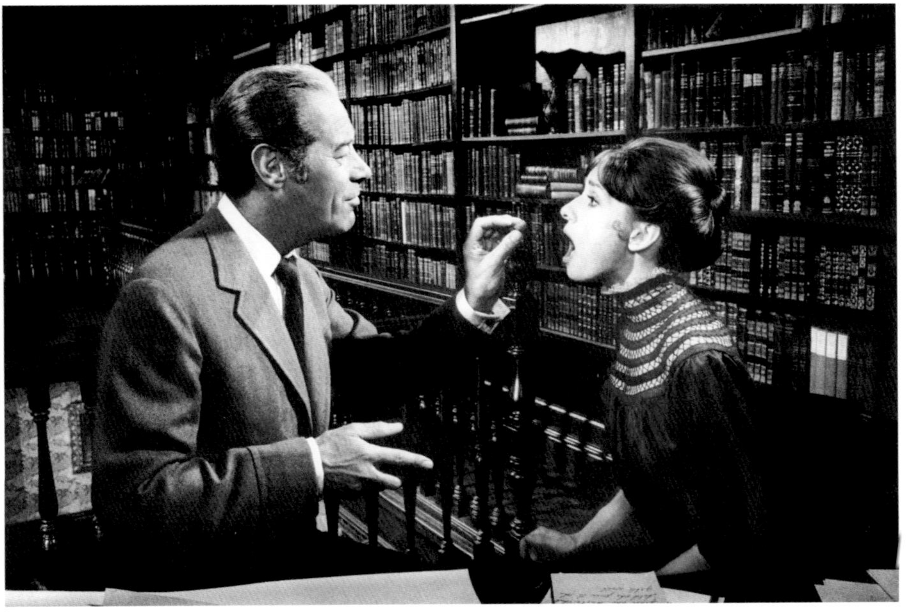

Previous spread:
"Just you wait, 'enry 'iggins, just you wait!": Eliza fantasizes about Higgins's execution.

Opposite:
In the song "Just You Wait," Eliza asks the king for Higgins's head.

Above:
Higgins tentatively feeds sweets to a hungry Eliza.

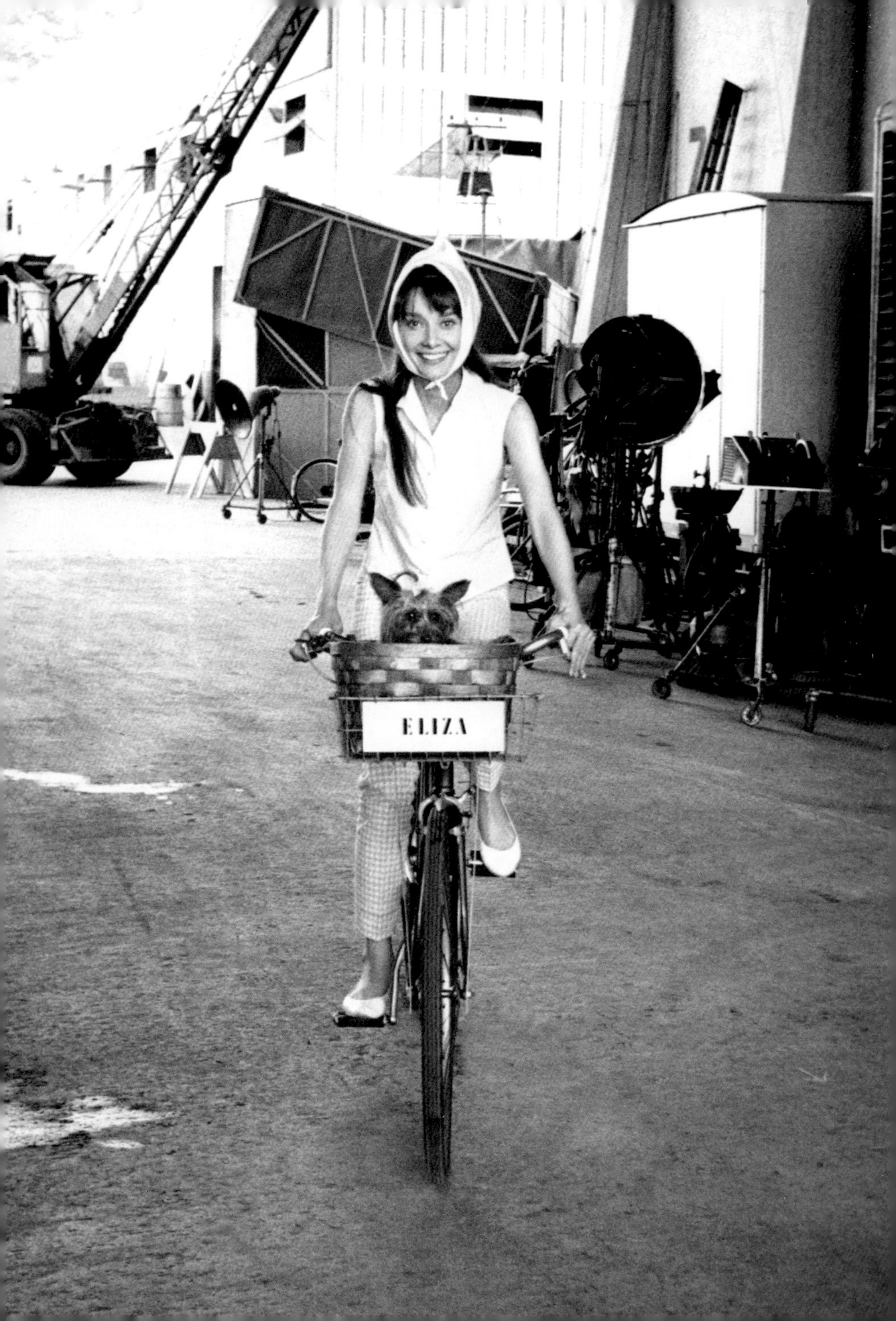
ELIZA

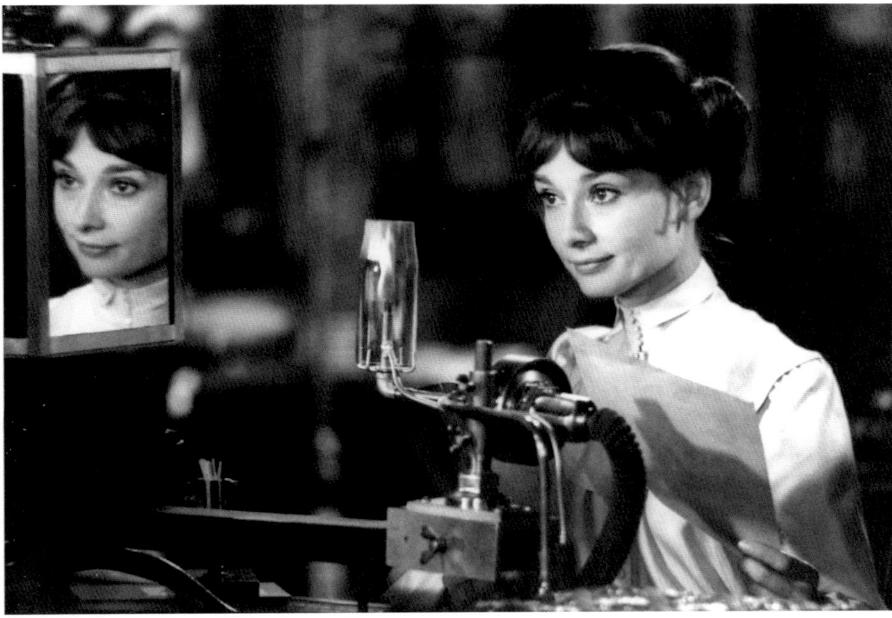

Audrey cycling between the wardrobe and the set.

Another machine designed by Higgins to test both Eliza's pronunciation and her determination.

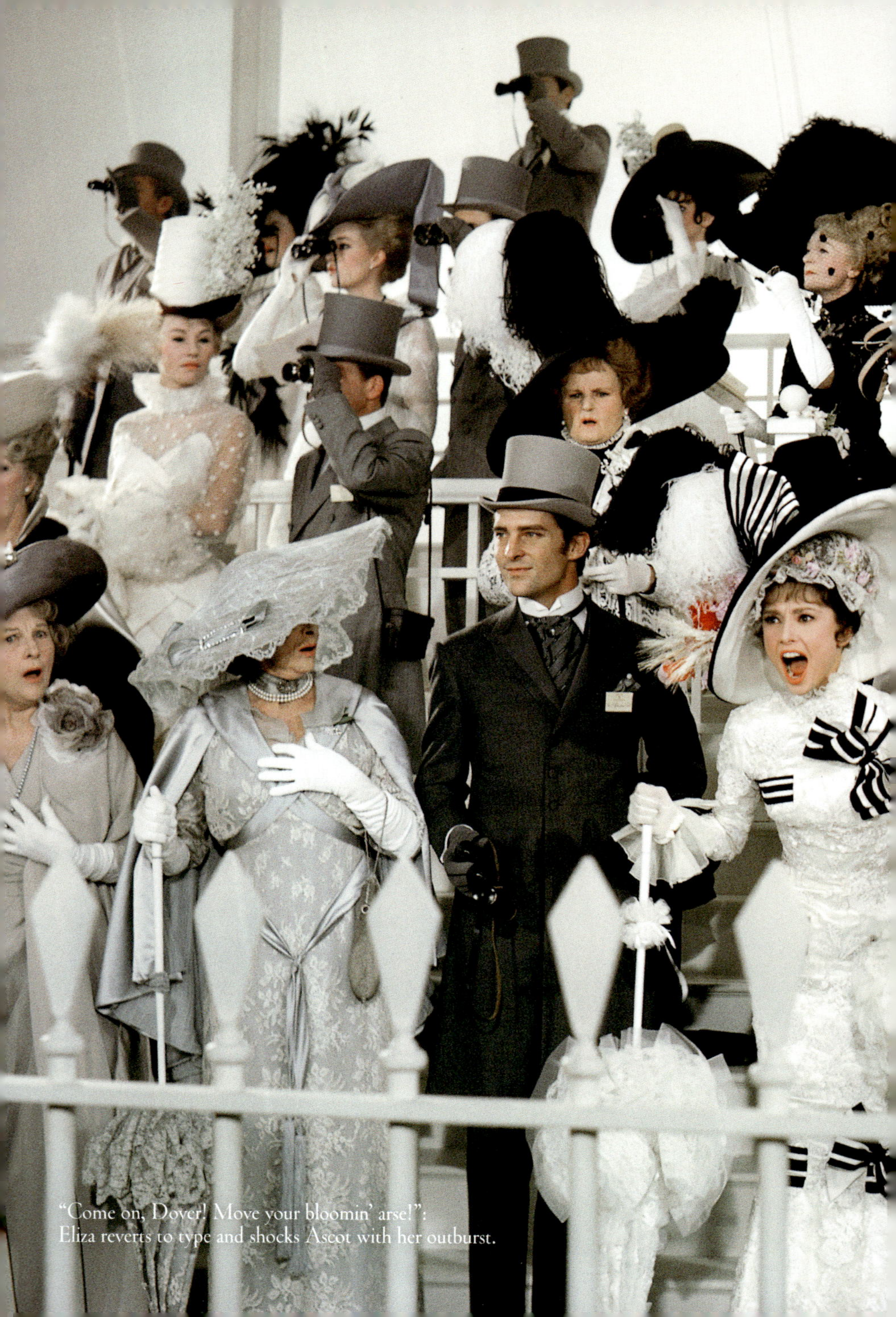

"Come on, Dover! Move your bloomin' arse!":
Eliza reverts to type and shocks Ascot with her outburst.

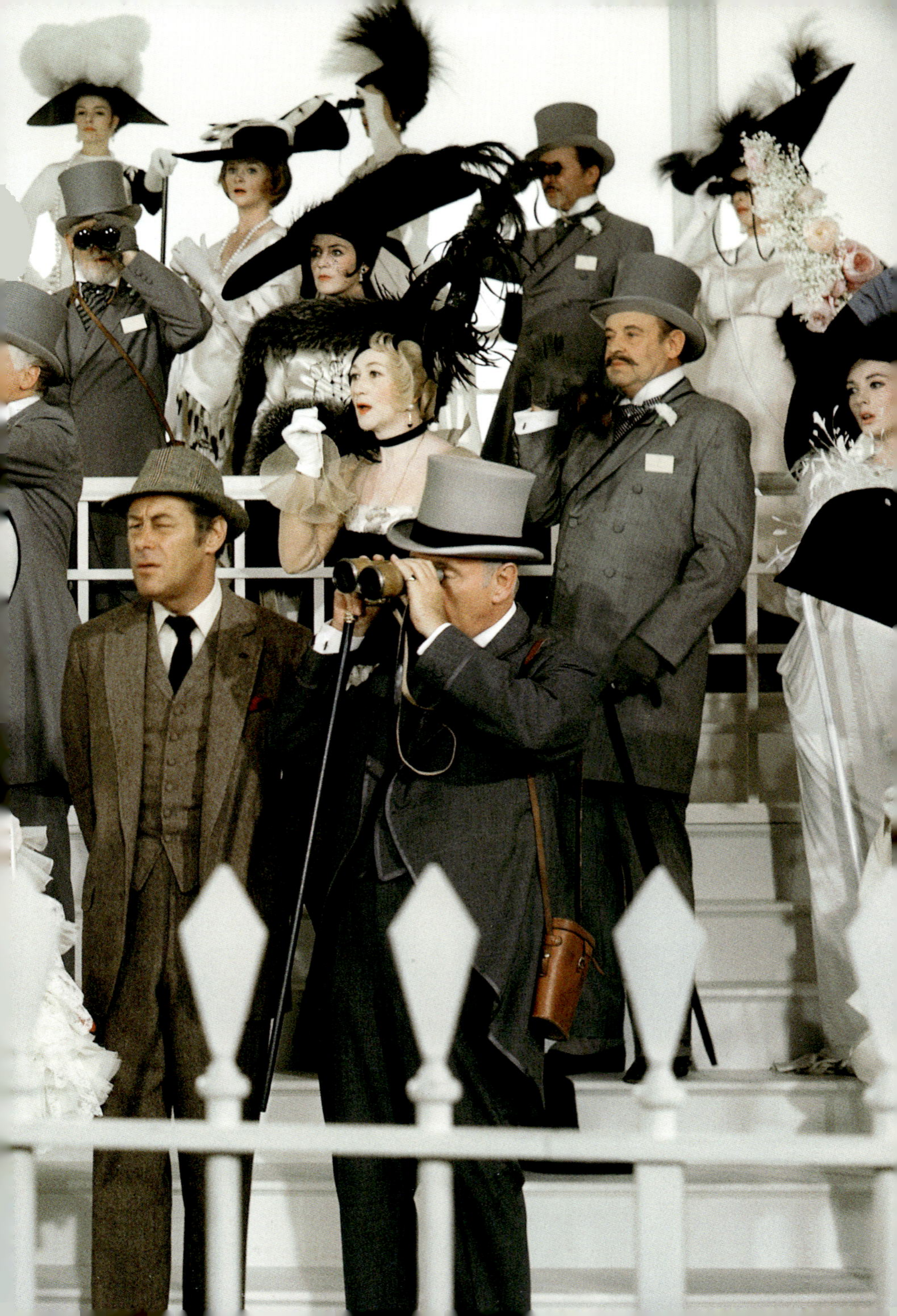

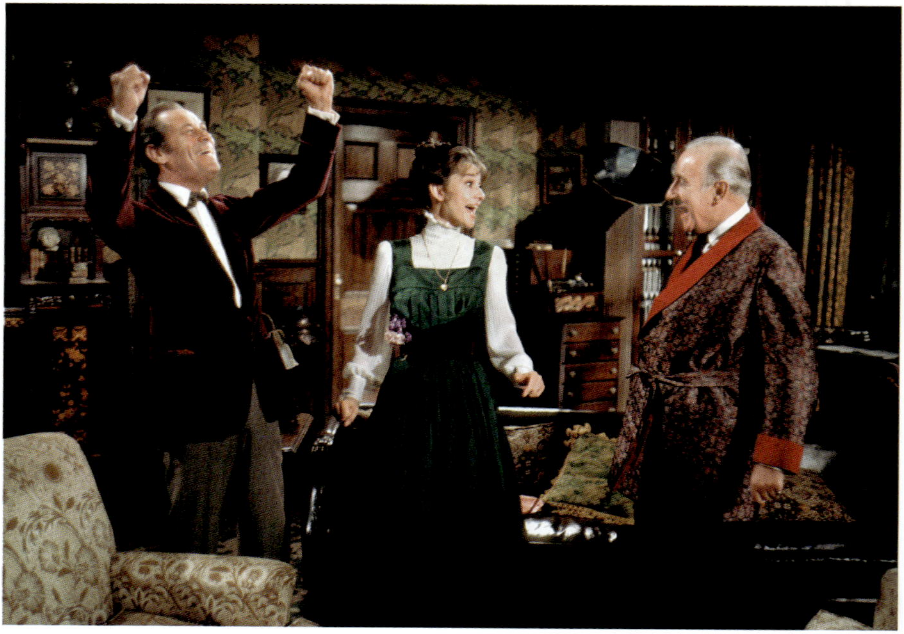

"By George, she's got it!": Eliza sings "The Rain in Spain" with perfect pronunciation.

Higgins and Eliza dance for joy.

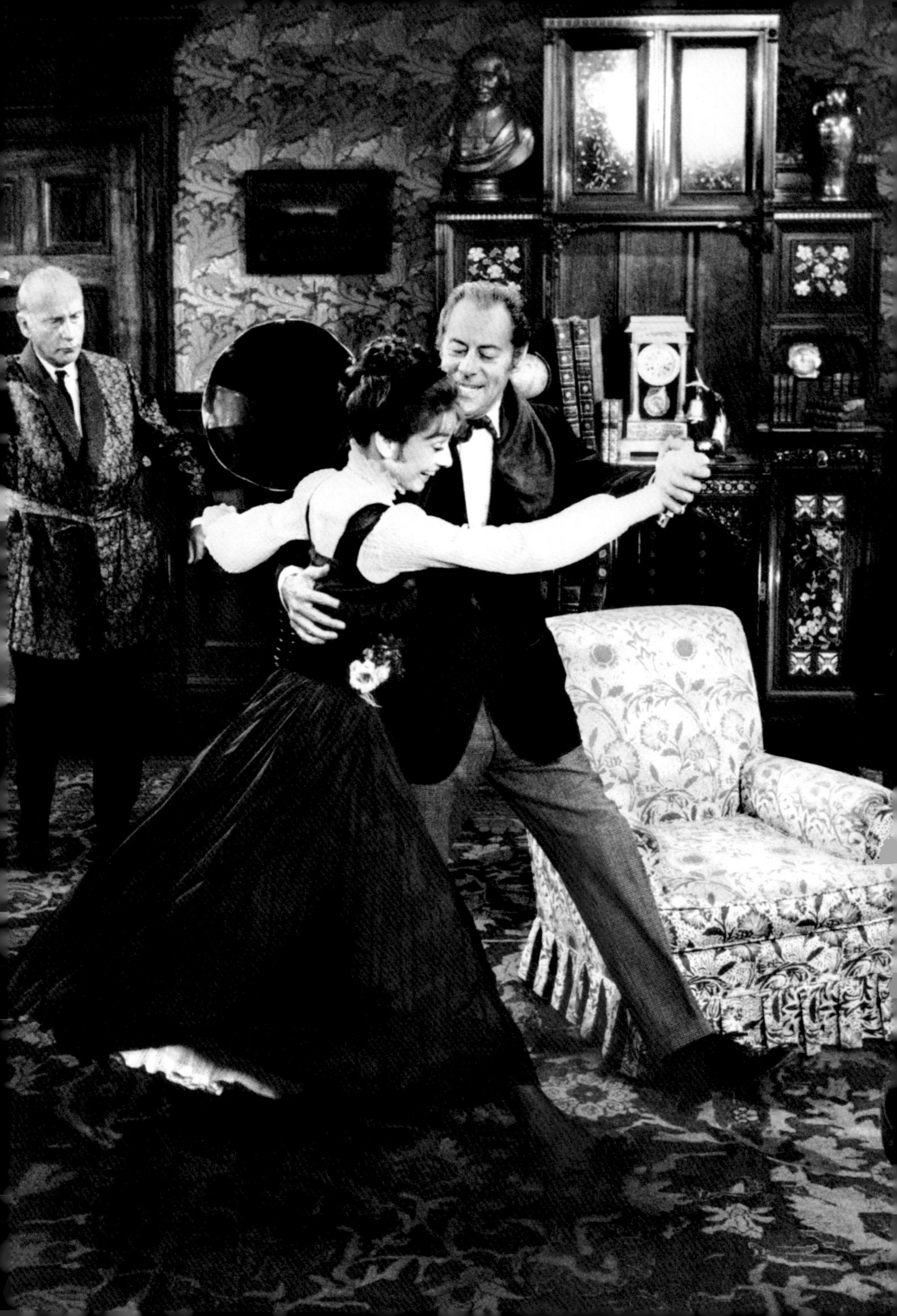

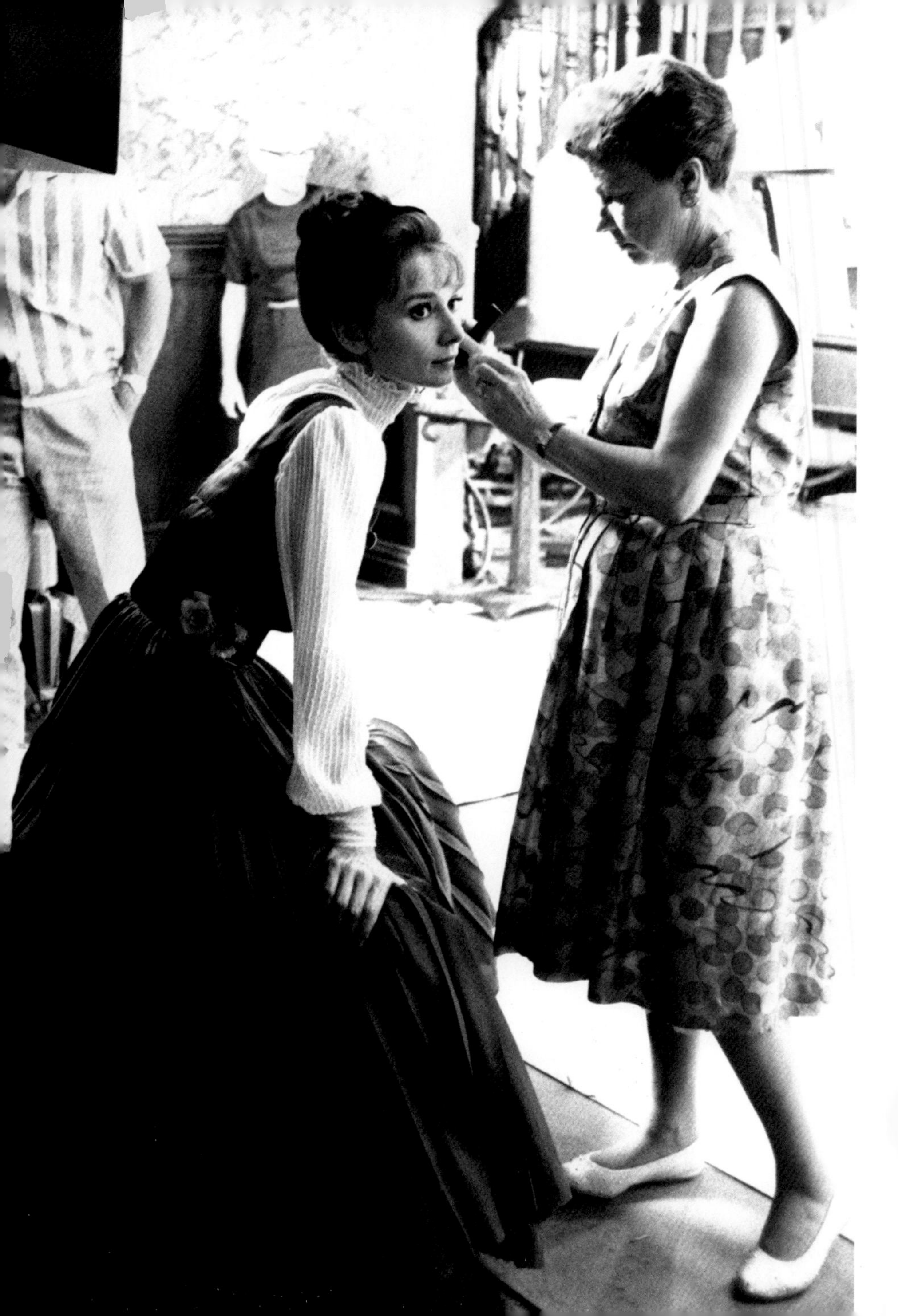

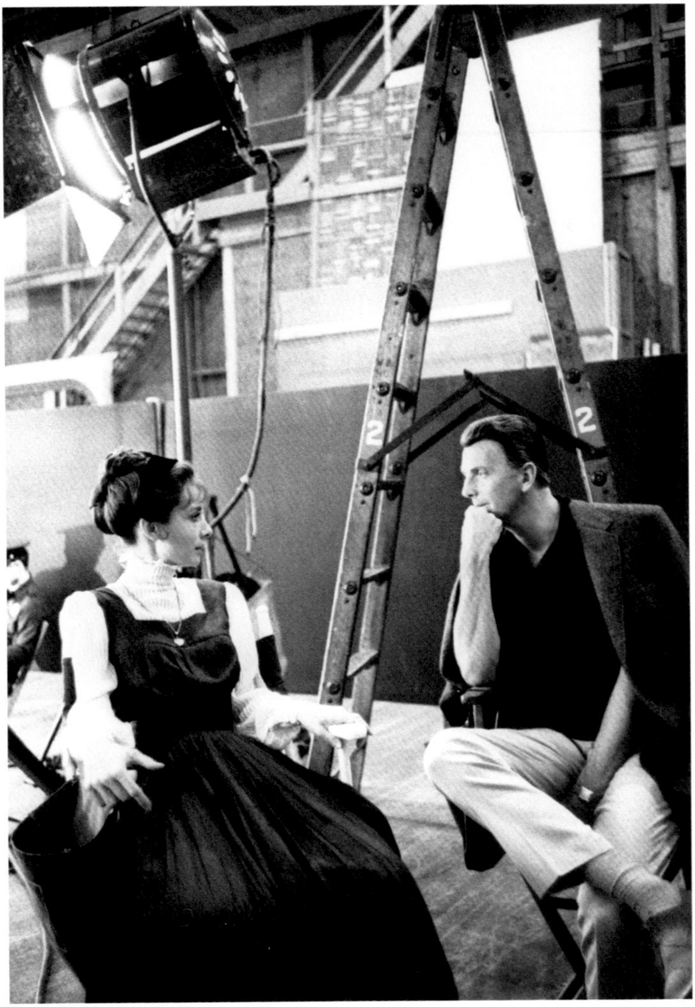

Audrey's makeup is retouched.

Audrey takes five and chats with her dear friend Hubert Givenchy.

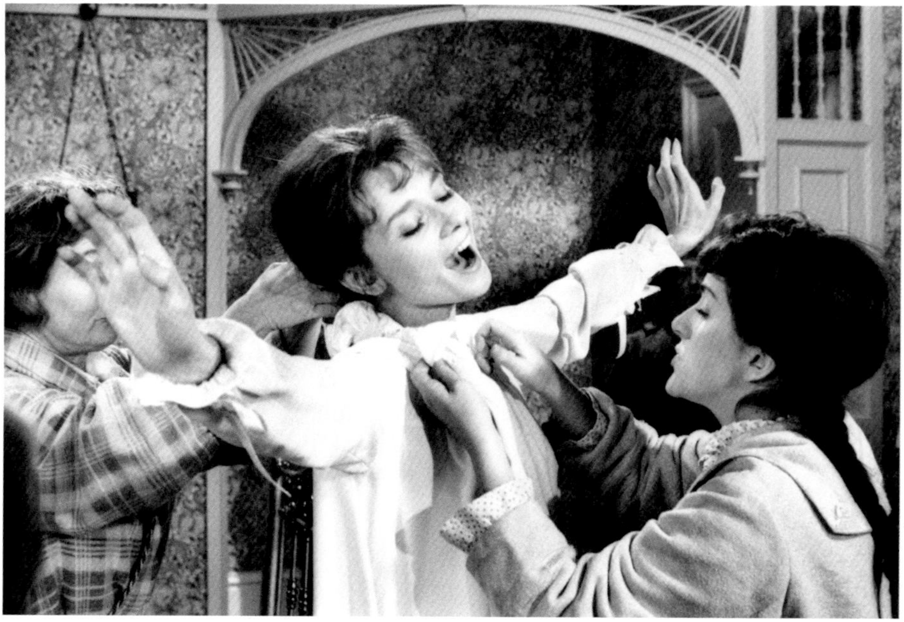

Eliza continues to sing and dance happily as she is dressed for bed.
Higgins has finally treated her like a lady.

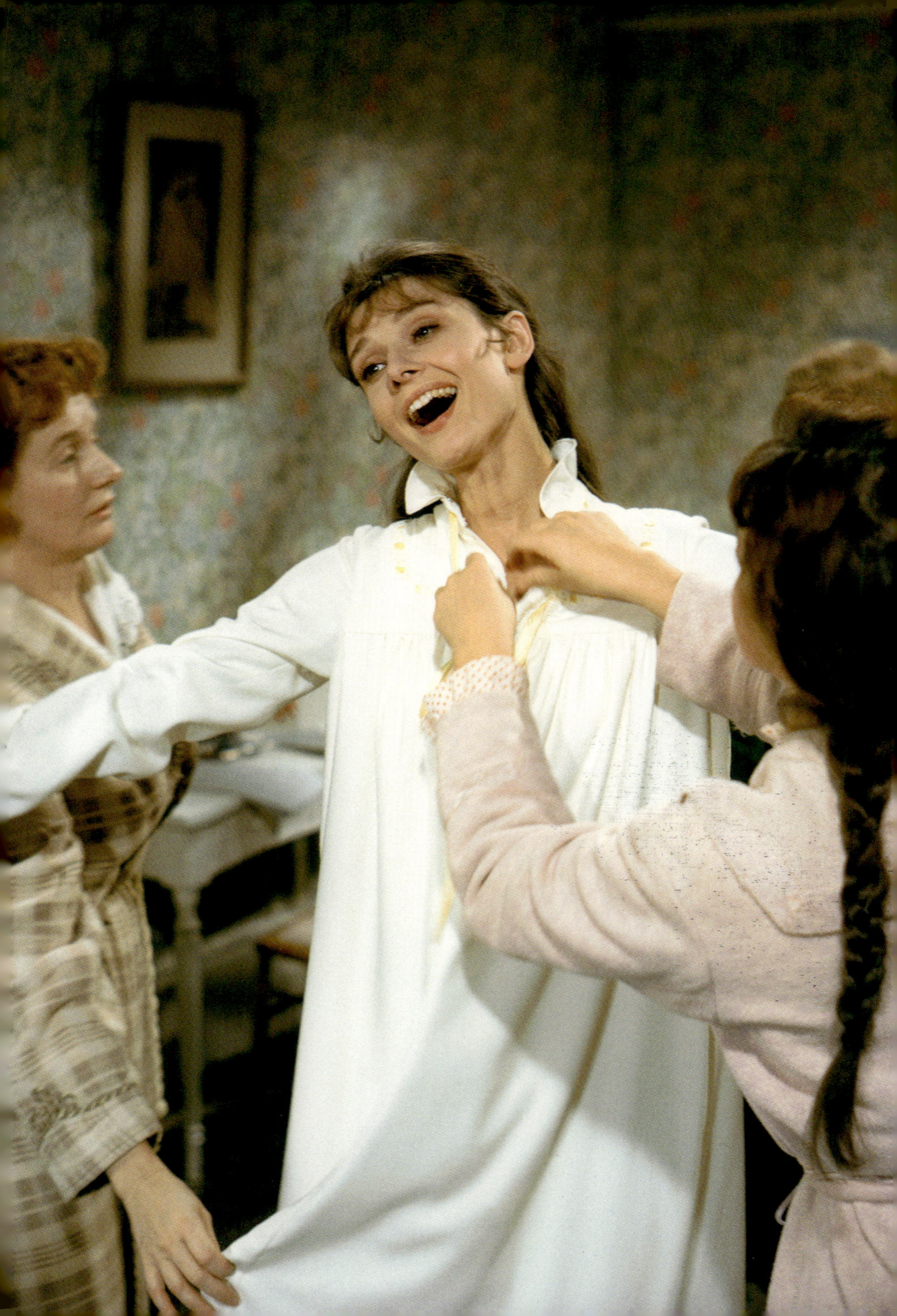

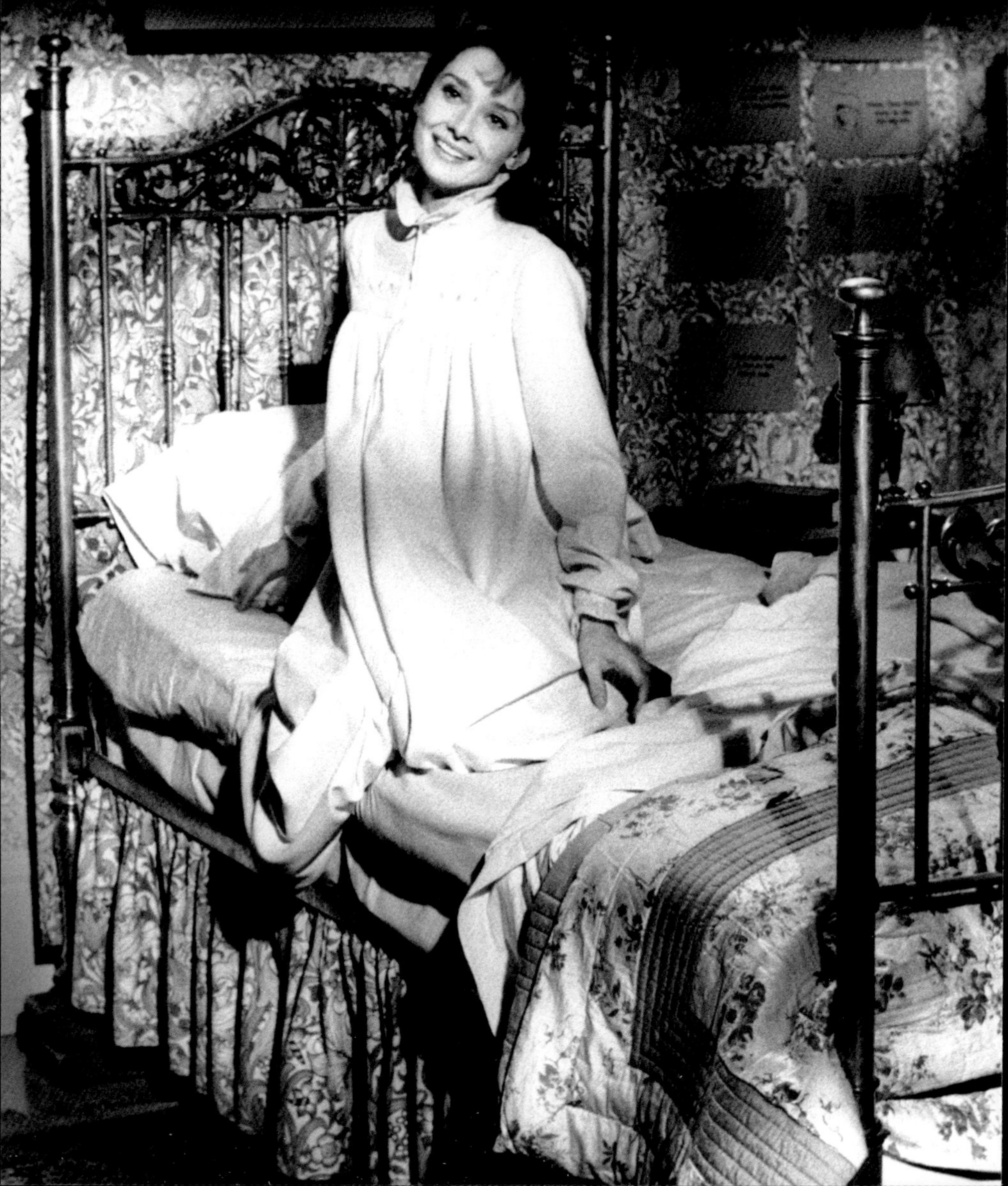

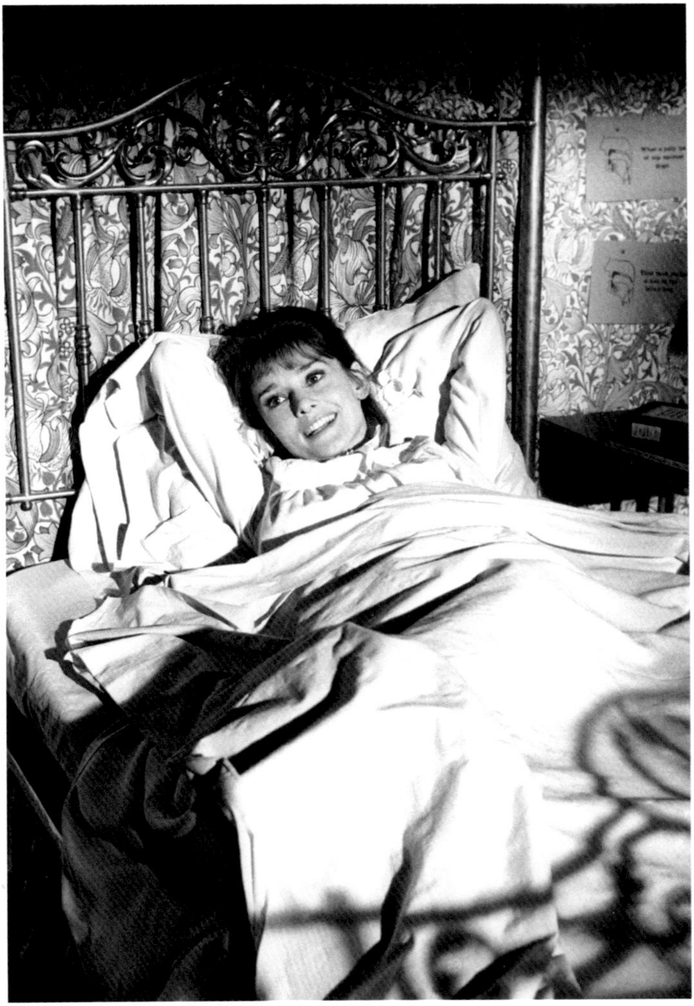

Although it's late, Eliza takes some time to calm down
after the night's exciting events.

Audrey alone on the steps in a
contemplative mood.

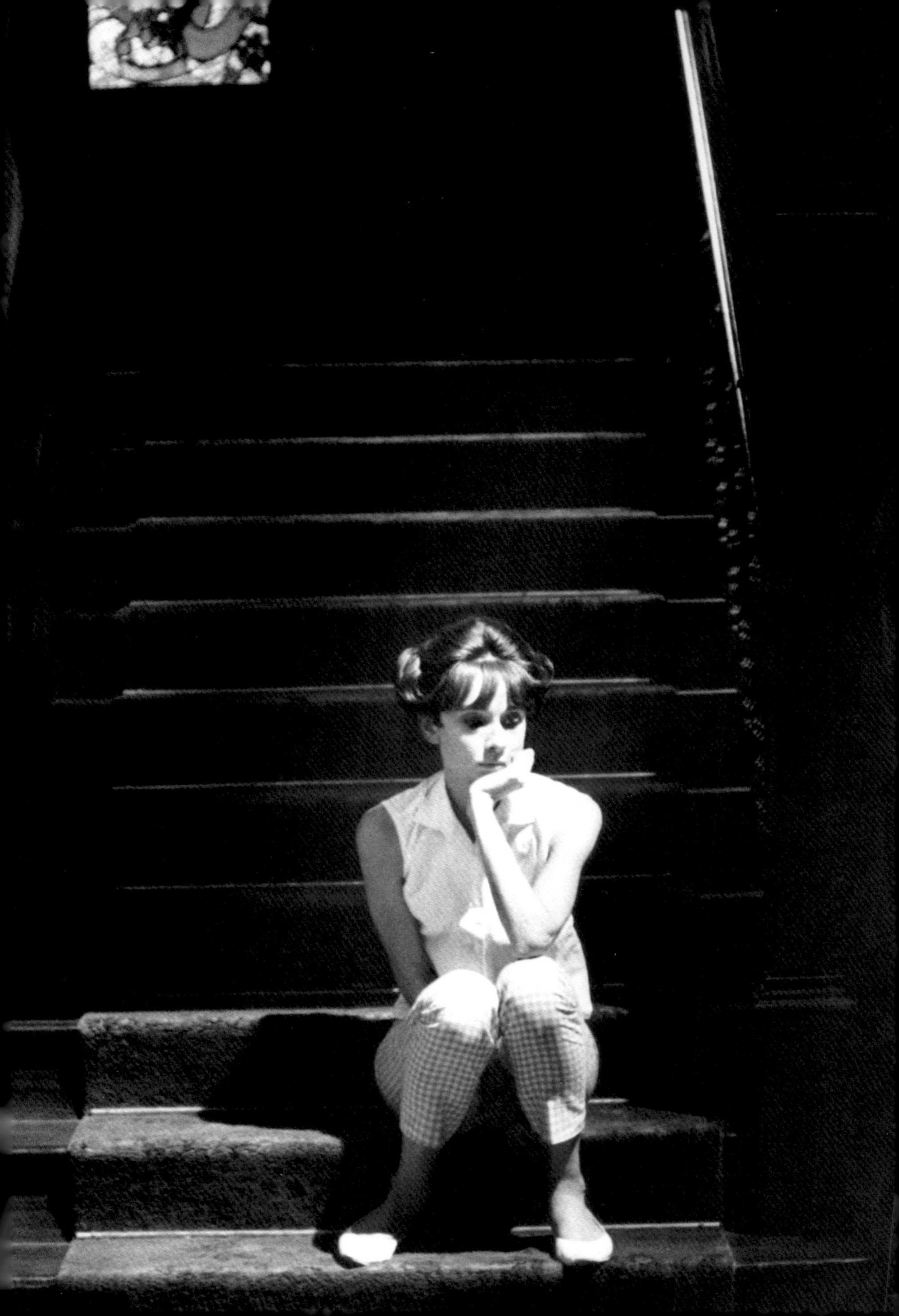

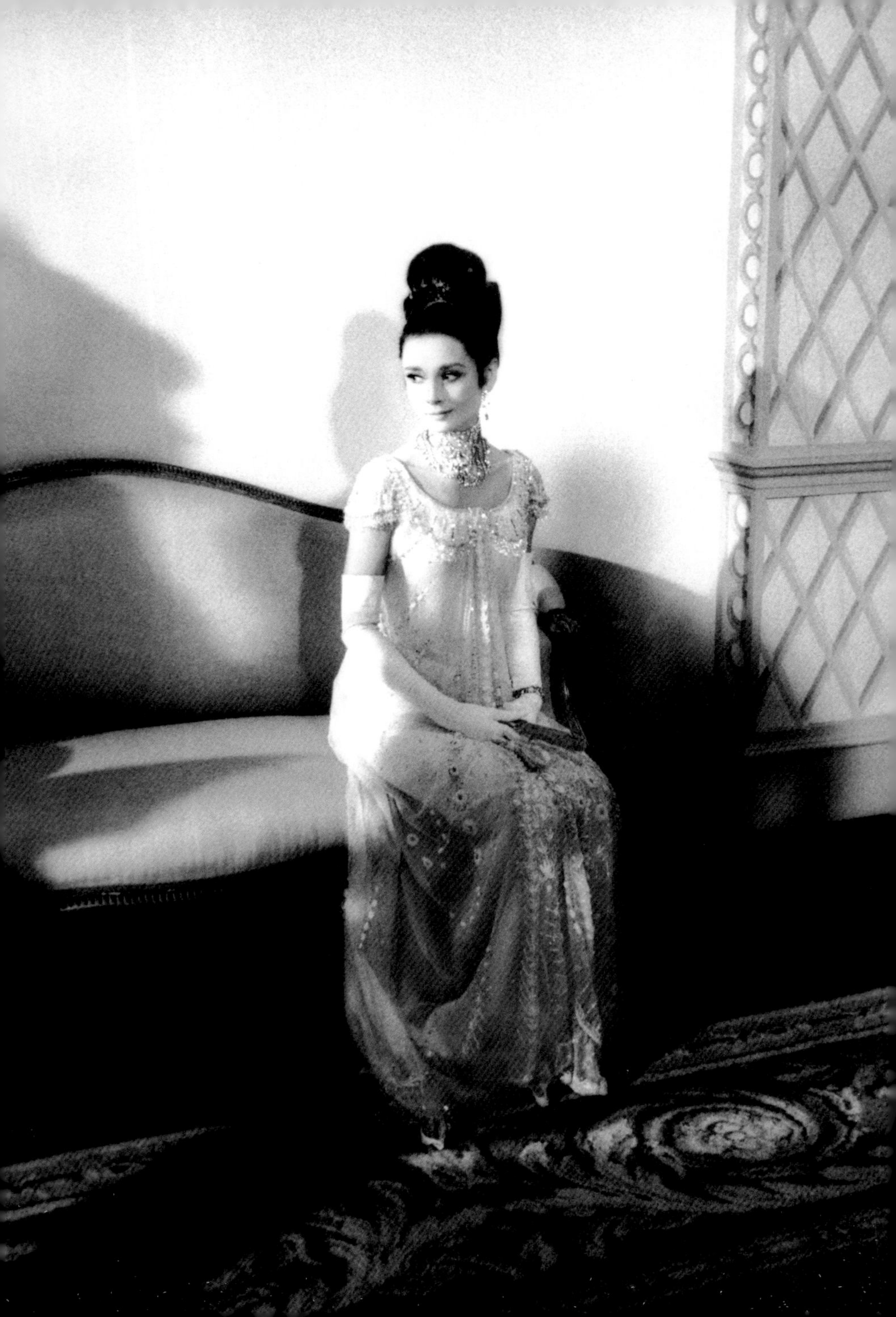

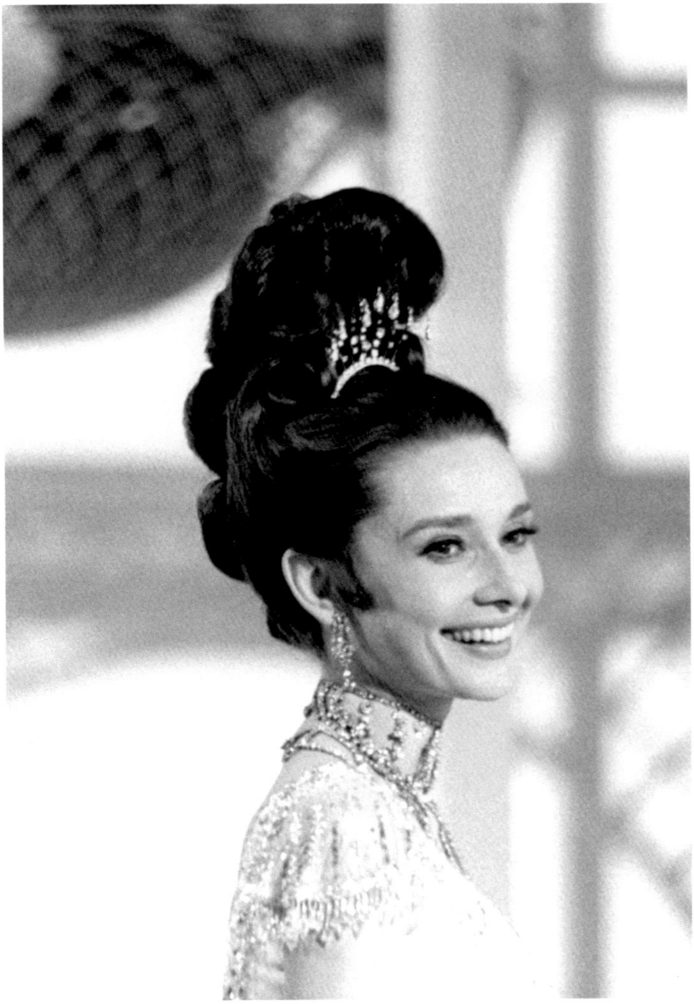

Eliza is radiant as a princess in jewelry,
tiara, and ball gown.

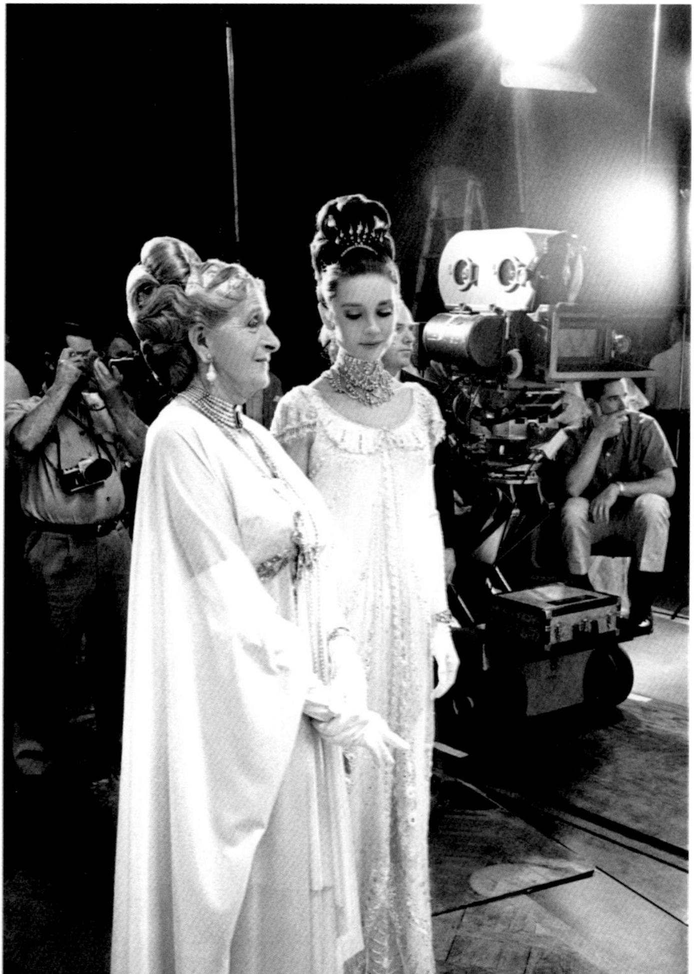

Audrey with Gladys Cooper.

Reporter Art Seidenbaum interviews Audrey for *Life* magazine, 1963.

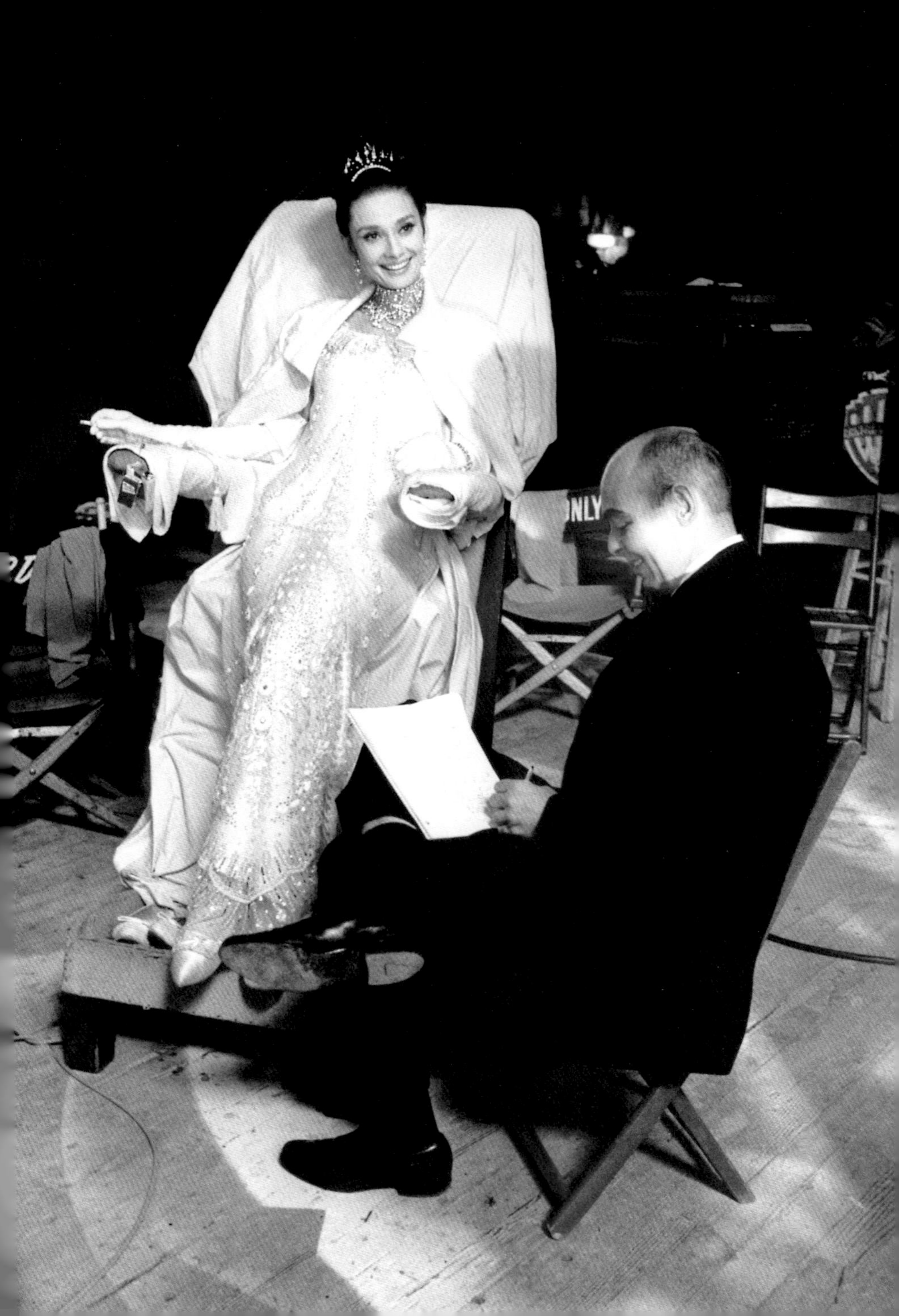
ONLY

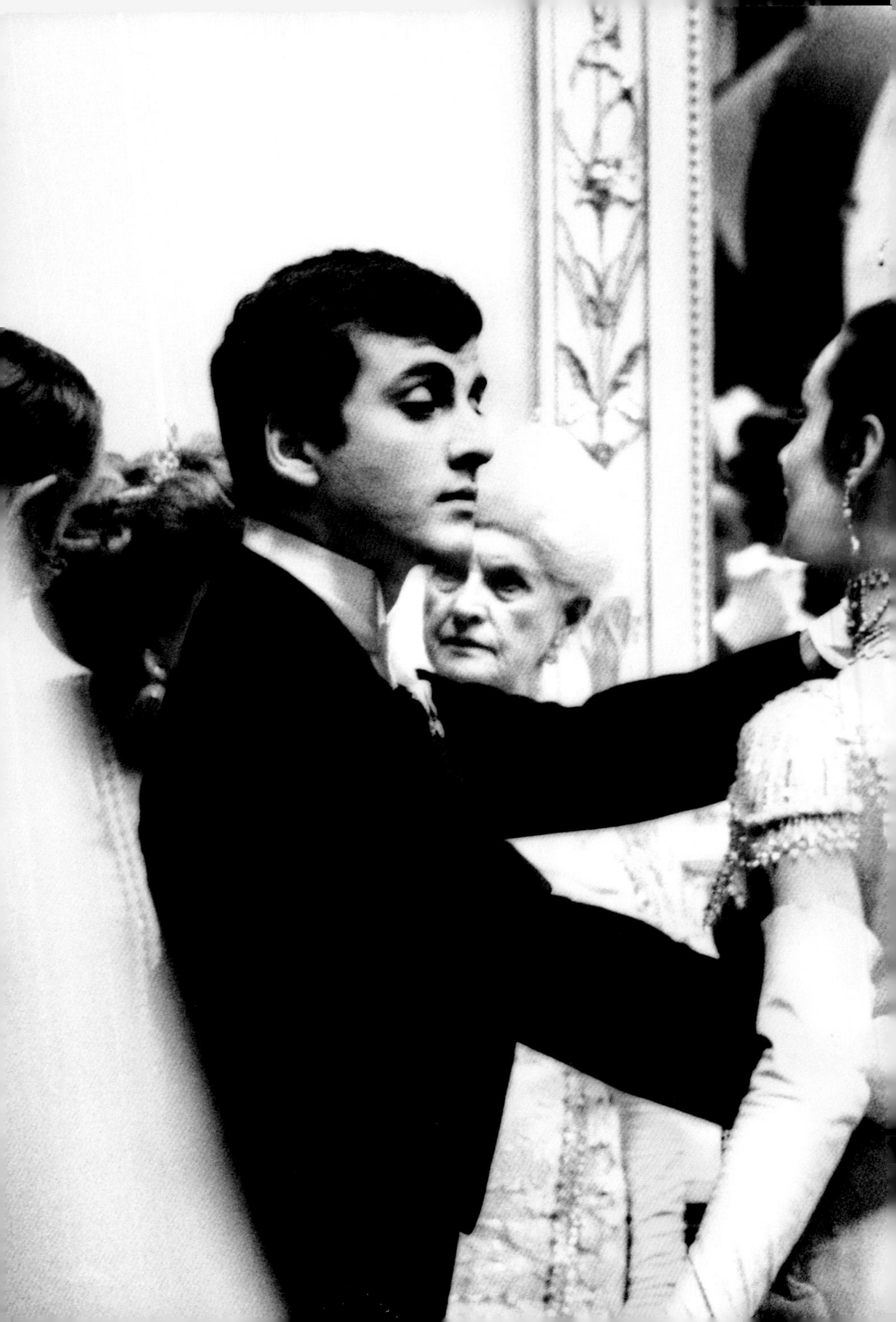

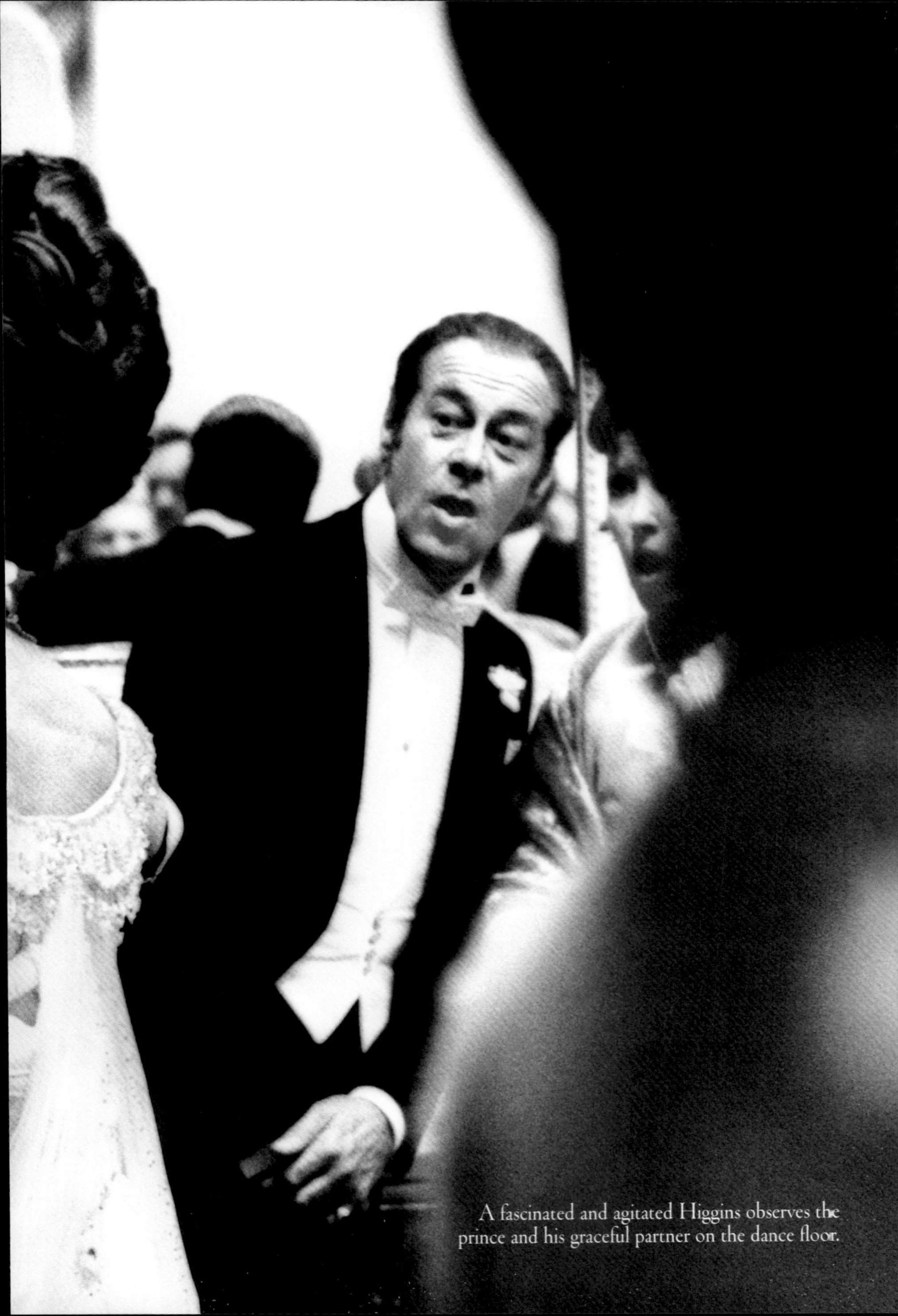

A fascinated and agitated Higgins observes the prince and his graceful partner on the dance floor.

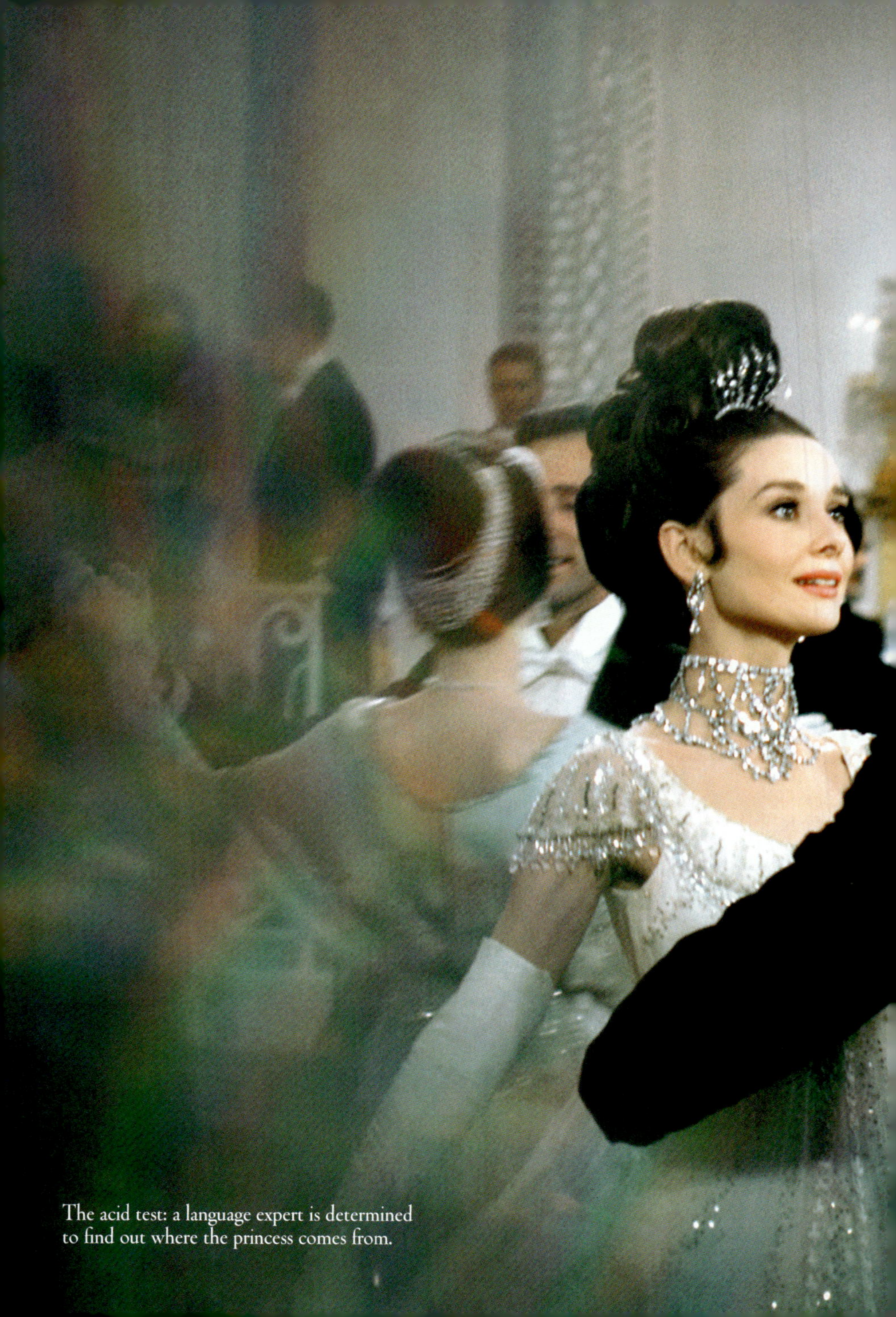

The acid test: a language expert is determined to find out where the princess comes from.

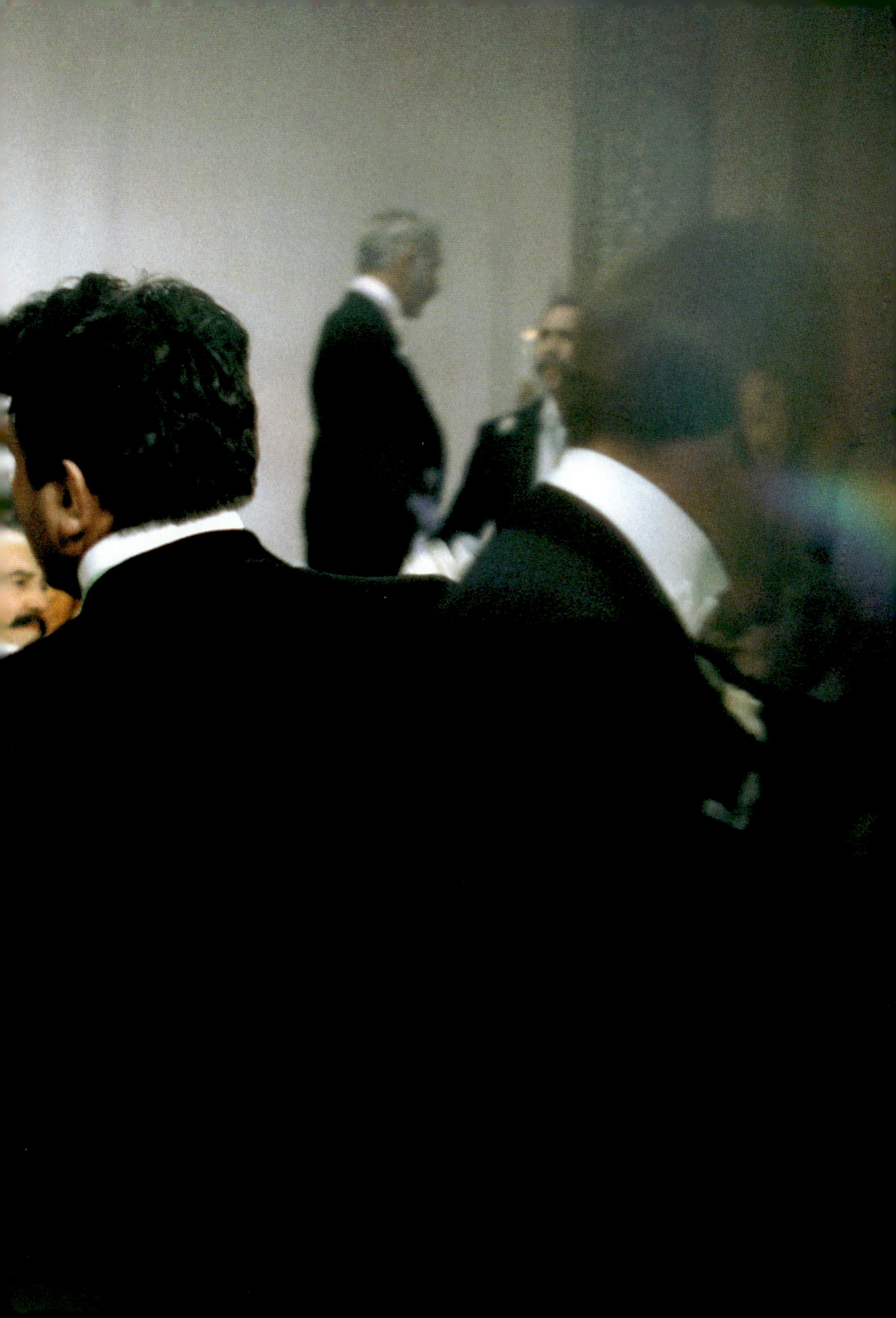

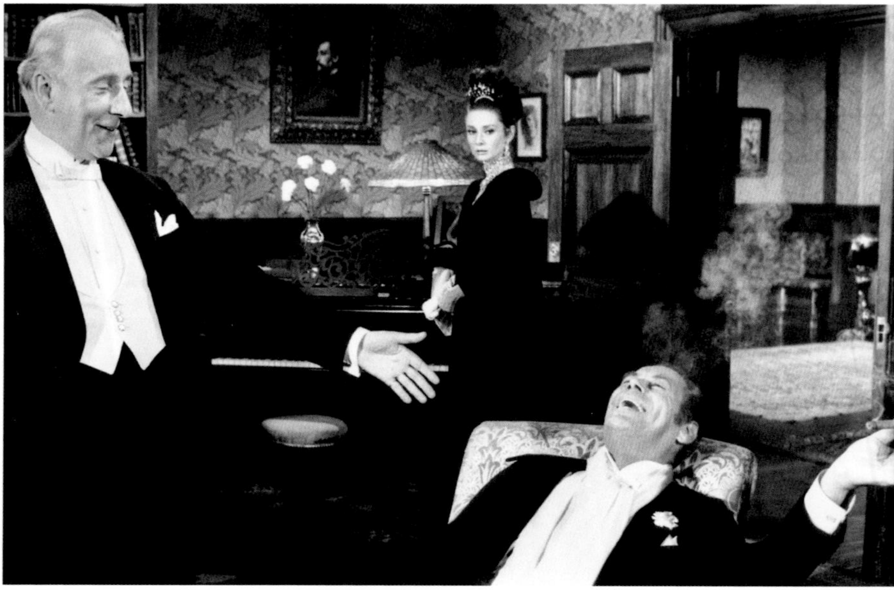

Pickering congratulates Higgins on his success.

Eliza leaves Higgins and returns to her roots, only to find she is no longer recognized.

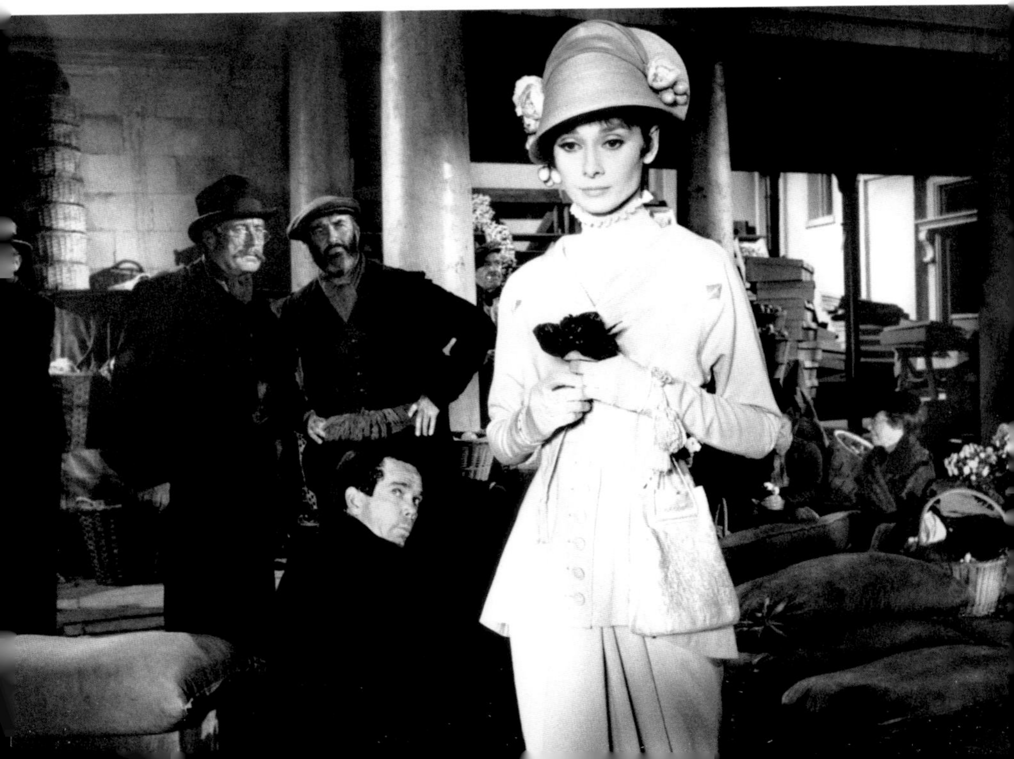

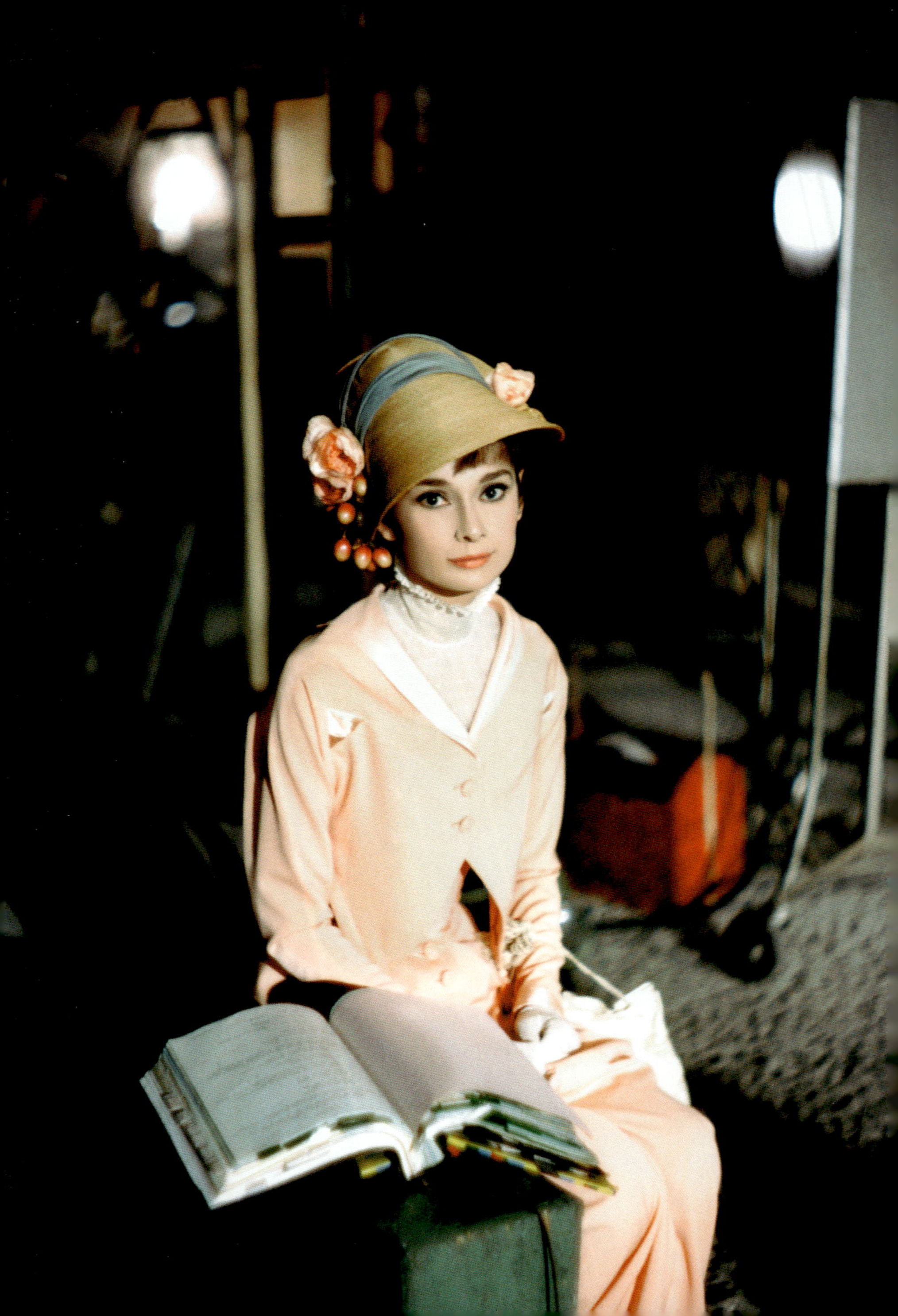

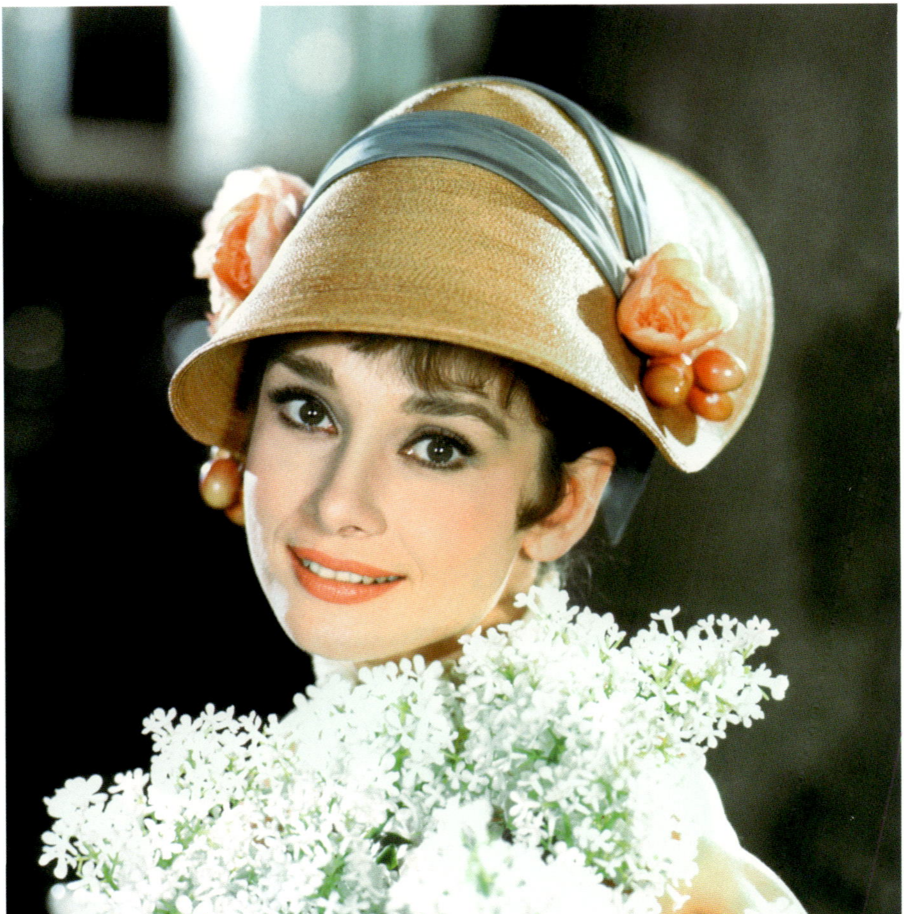

Audrey wears a pink dress with a flower-bedecked hat.

"Are there lilac trees in the heart of town?":
Audrey poses with white lilacs.

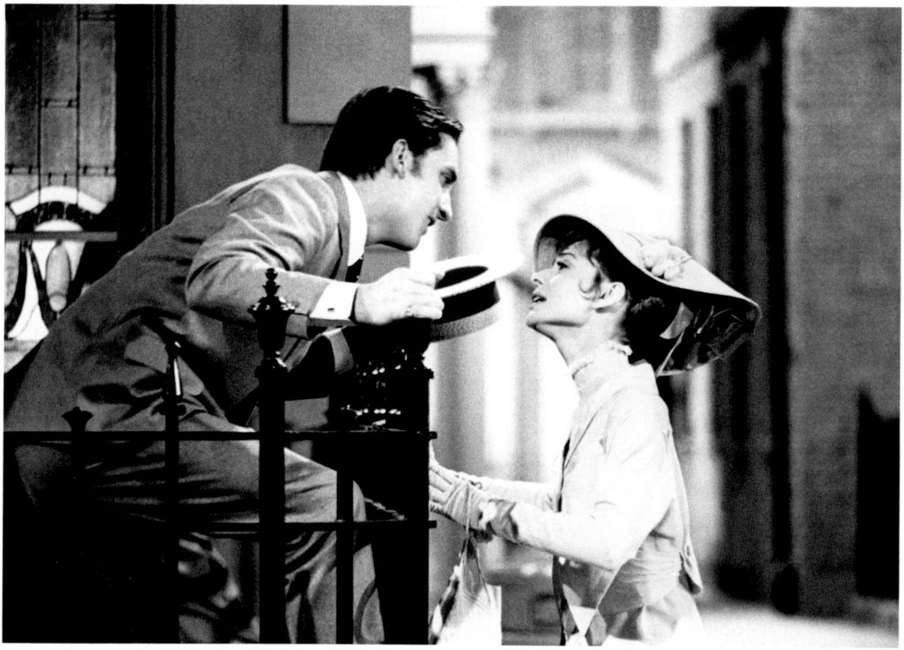

"No it's just on the street where you live":
Freddy, played by Jeremy Brett, has been waiting for Eliza to return.

George Cukor explains what he wants from a scene.

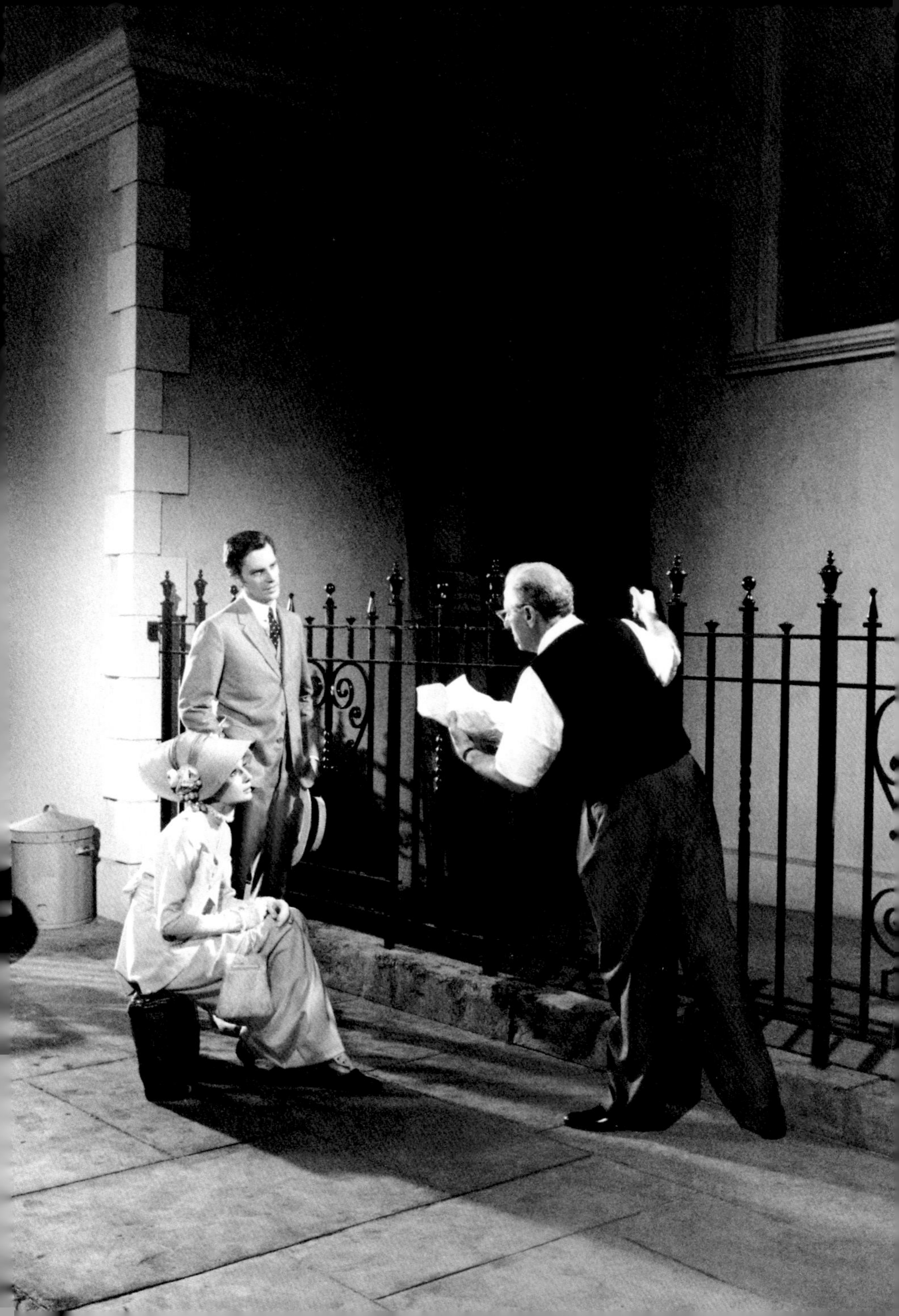

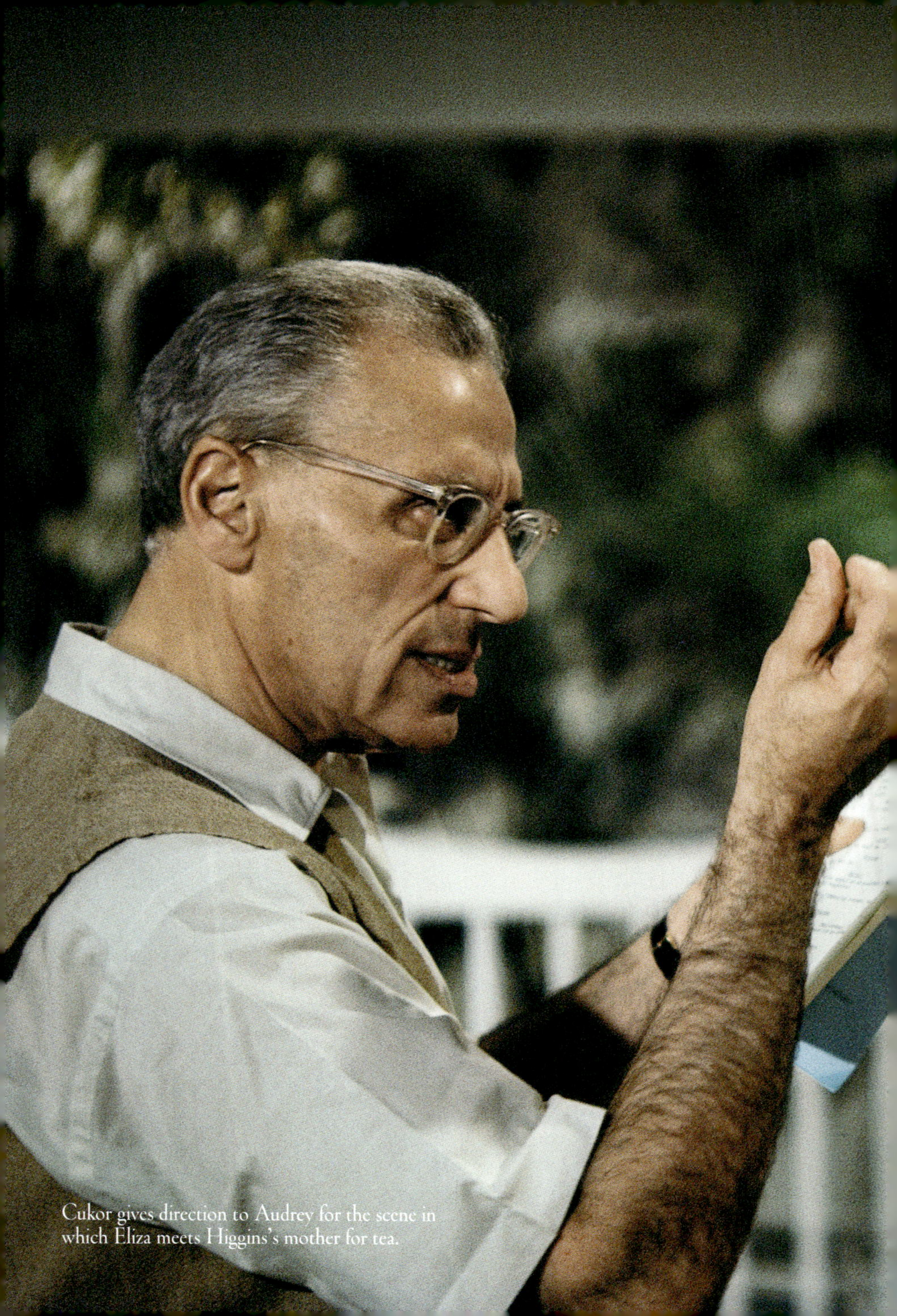

Cukor gives direction to Audrey for the scene in which Eliza meets Higgins's mother for tea.

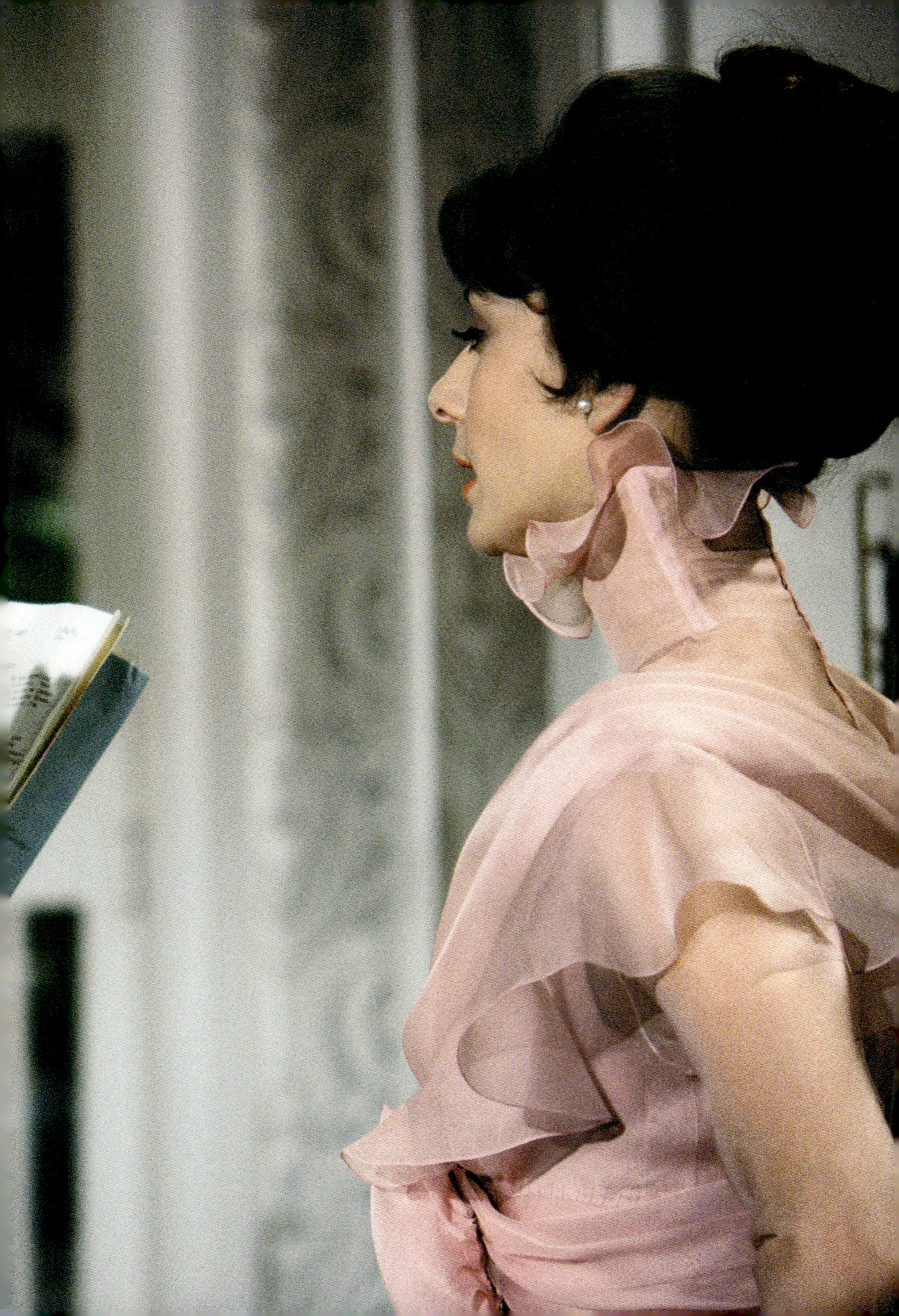

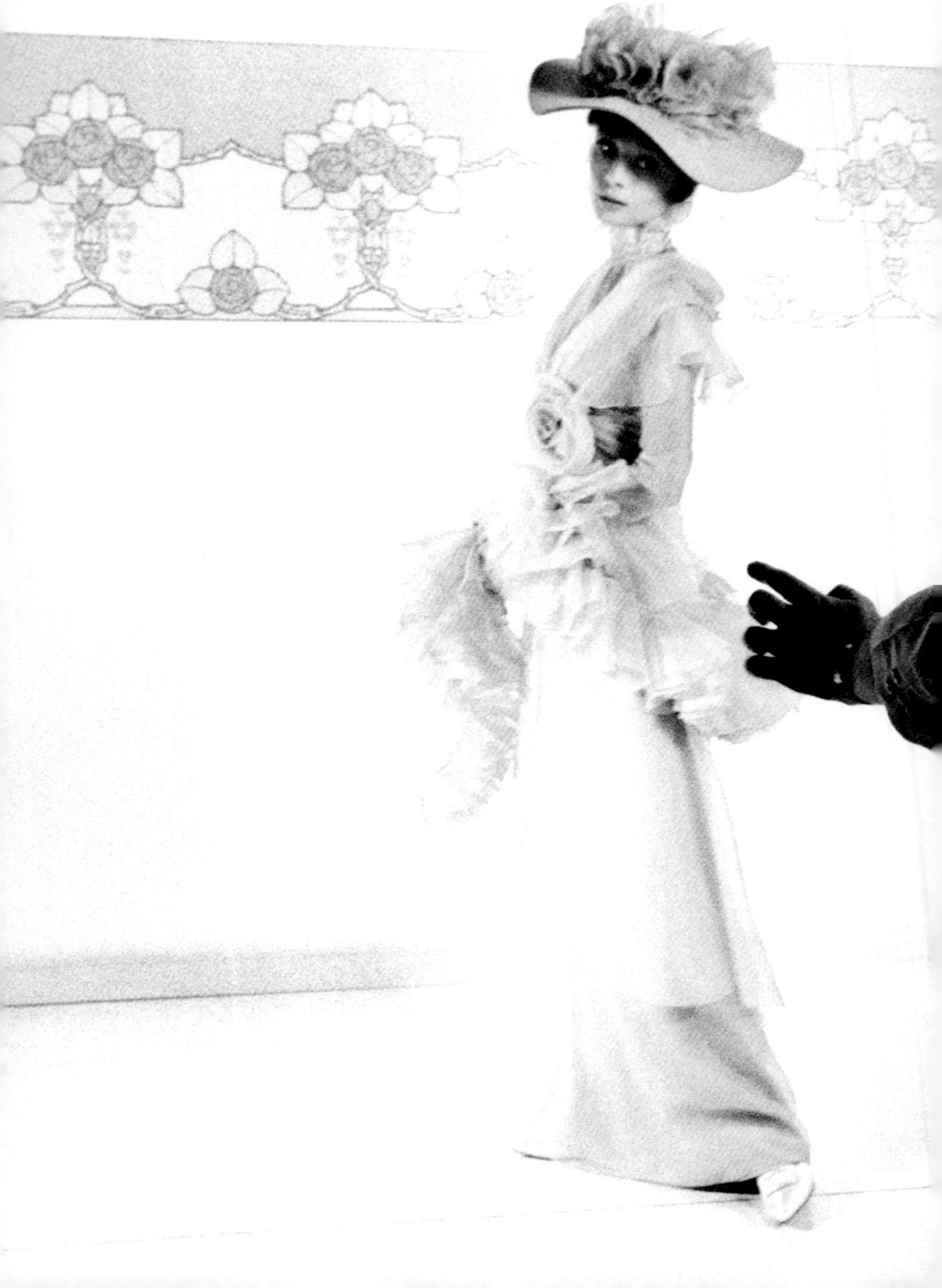

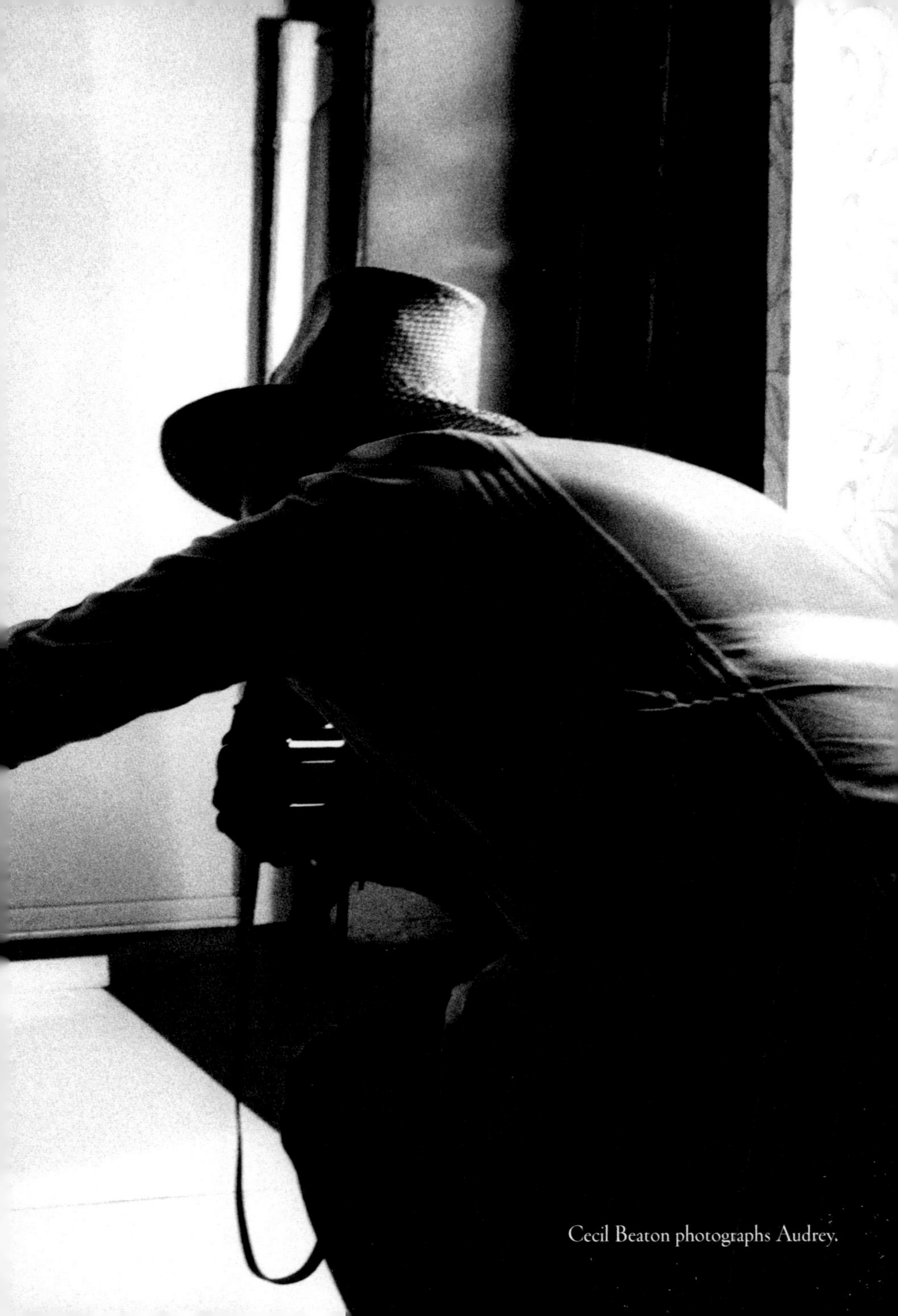

Cecil Beaton photographs Audrey.

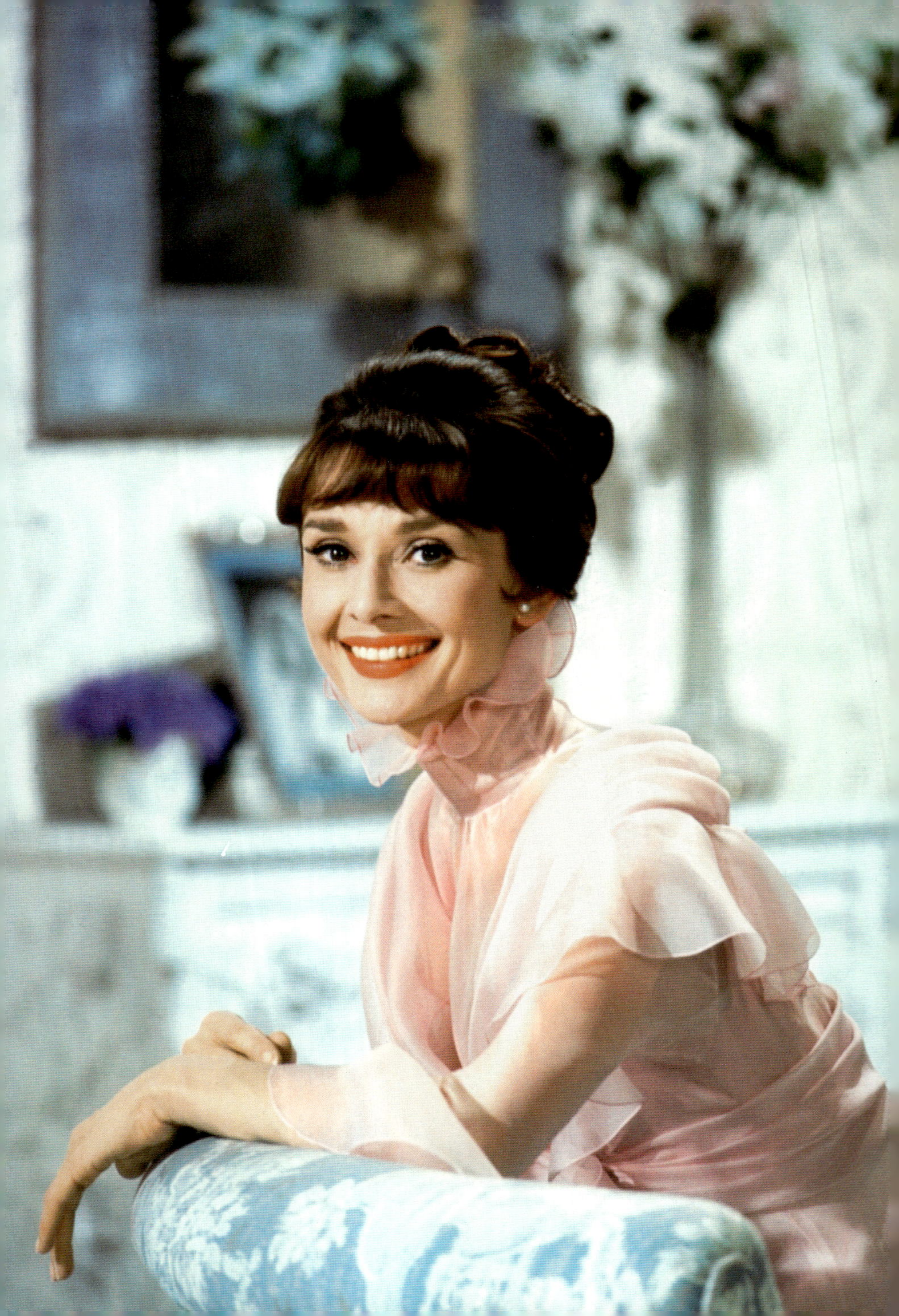

"She wouldn't even let me visit her
on the set while she was in
that bedraggled flower-girl characterization.
But even at her dirtiest, she sprayed
herself with Joy, a $100-an-ounce perfume.
'I may look dirty,' she'd say, 'but
I am to smell pretty.'"

Mel Ferrer

Eliza meets Higgins's mother, who is completely on her side.

Following spread:
Audrey laughs during a rehearsal
for *Two for the Road* with Albert Finney.

TWO FOR THE ROAD

1966

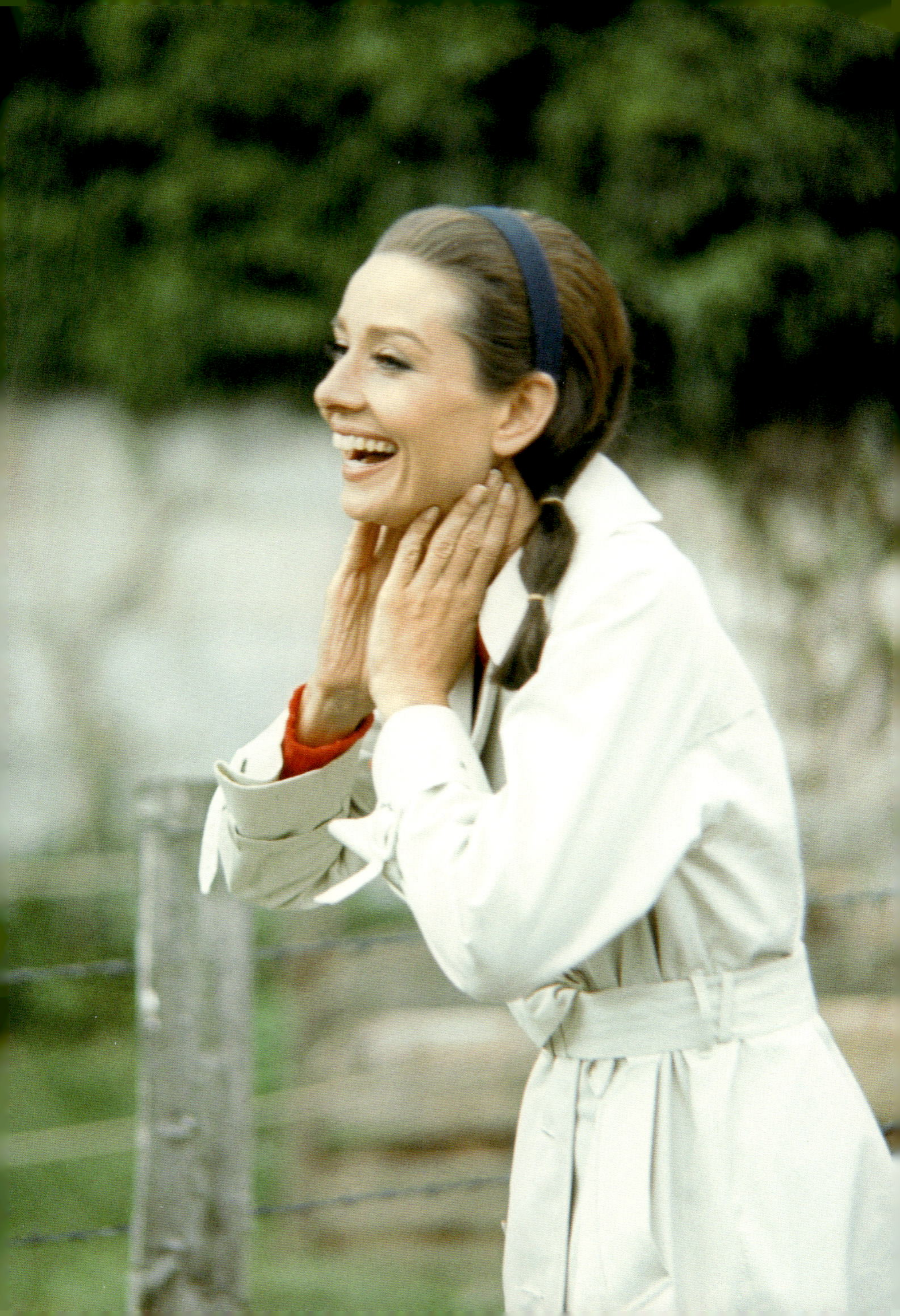

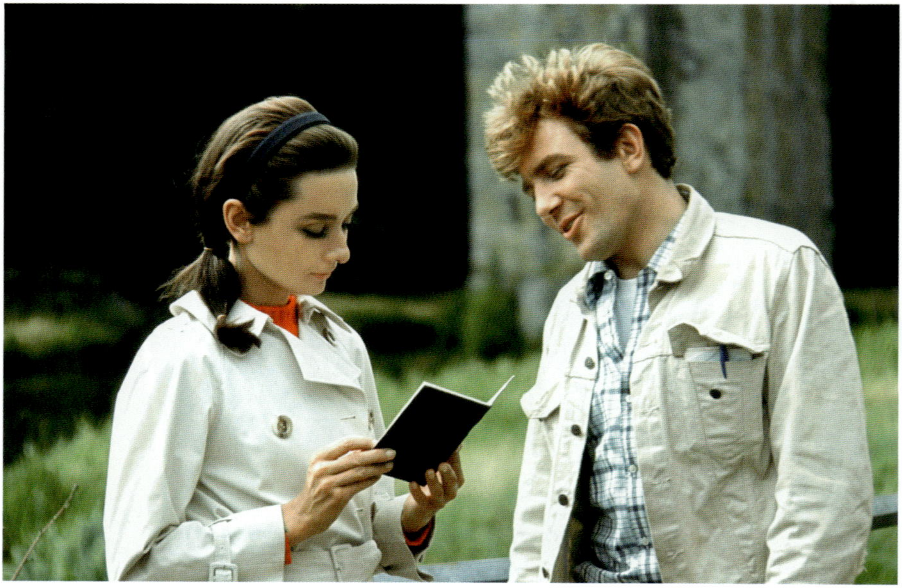

Finney shows Audrey his passport.

The chemistry between Audrey and Albert Finney is palpable.

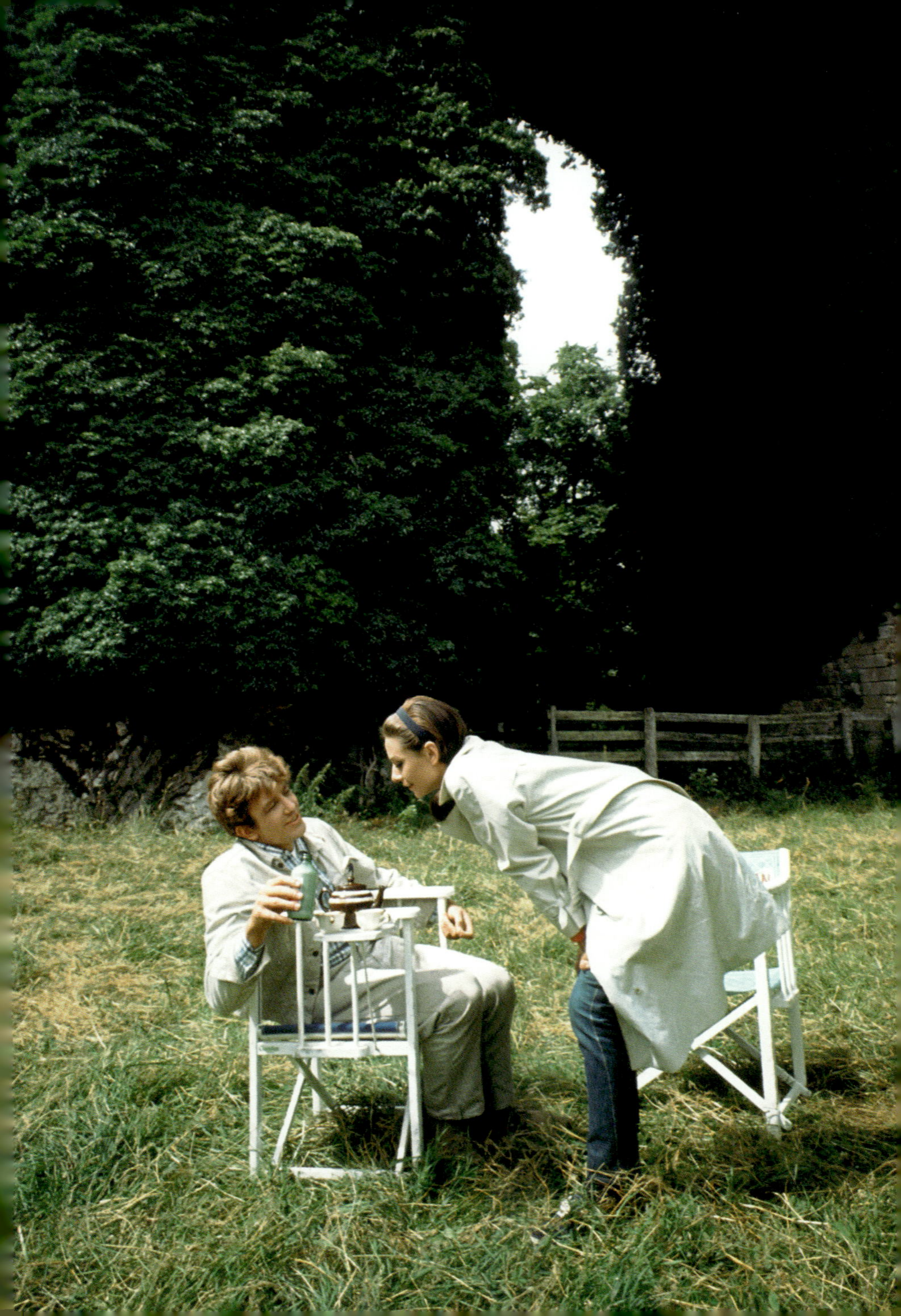

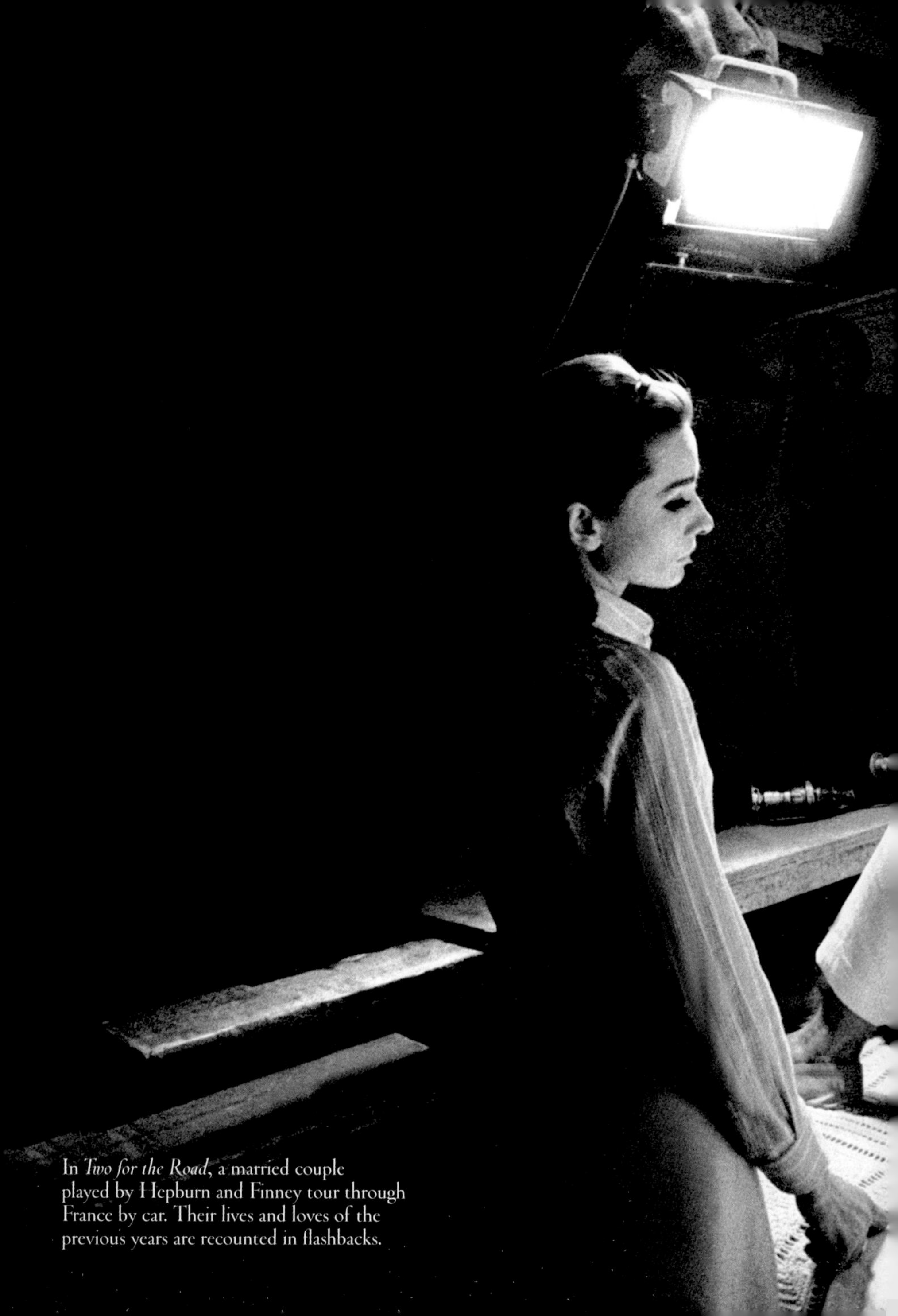

In *Two for the Road*, a married couple played by Hepburn and Finney tour through France by car. Their lives and loves of the previous years are recounted in flashbacks.

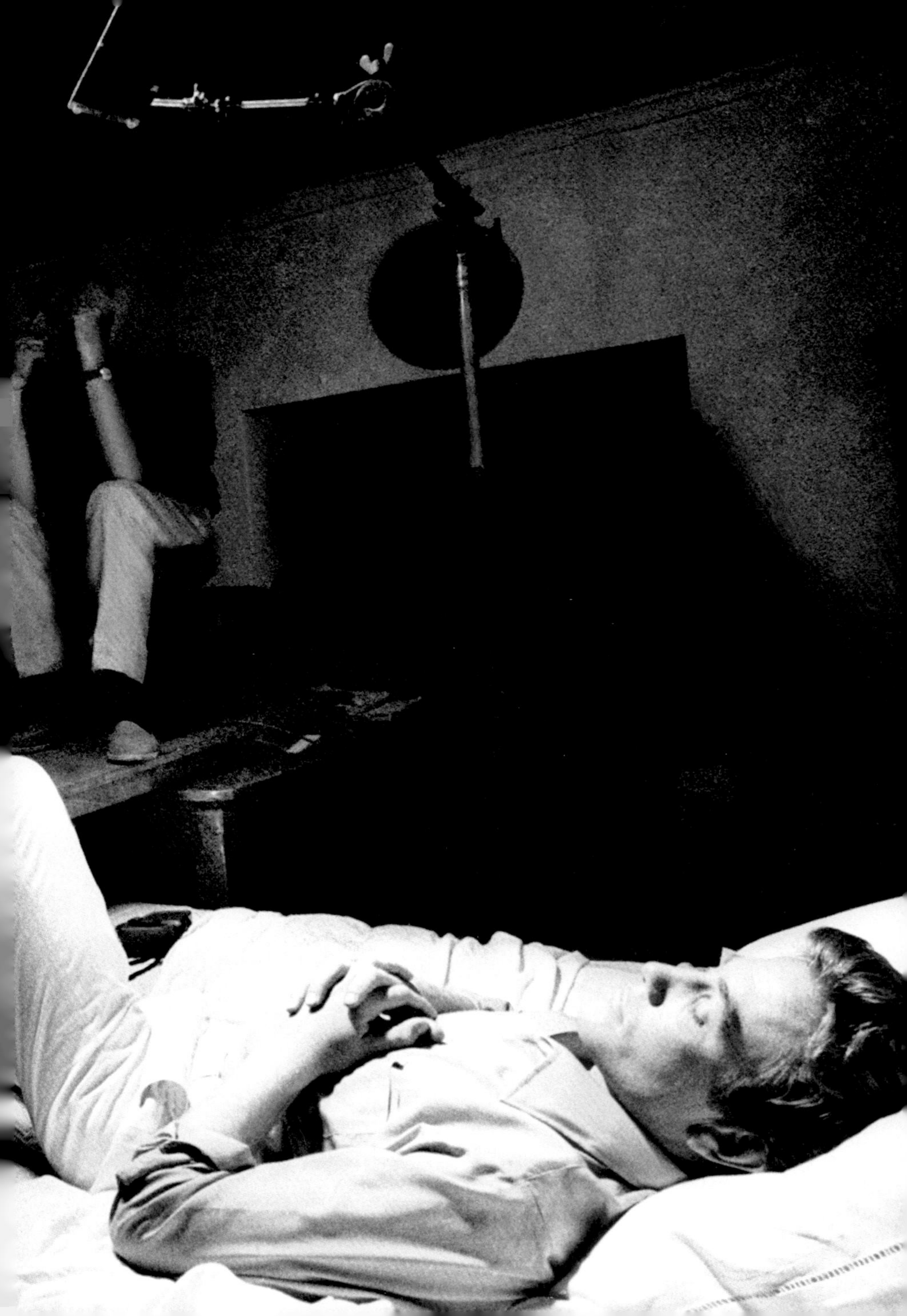

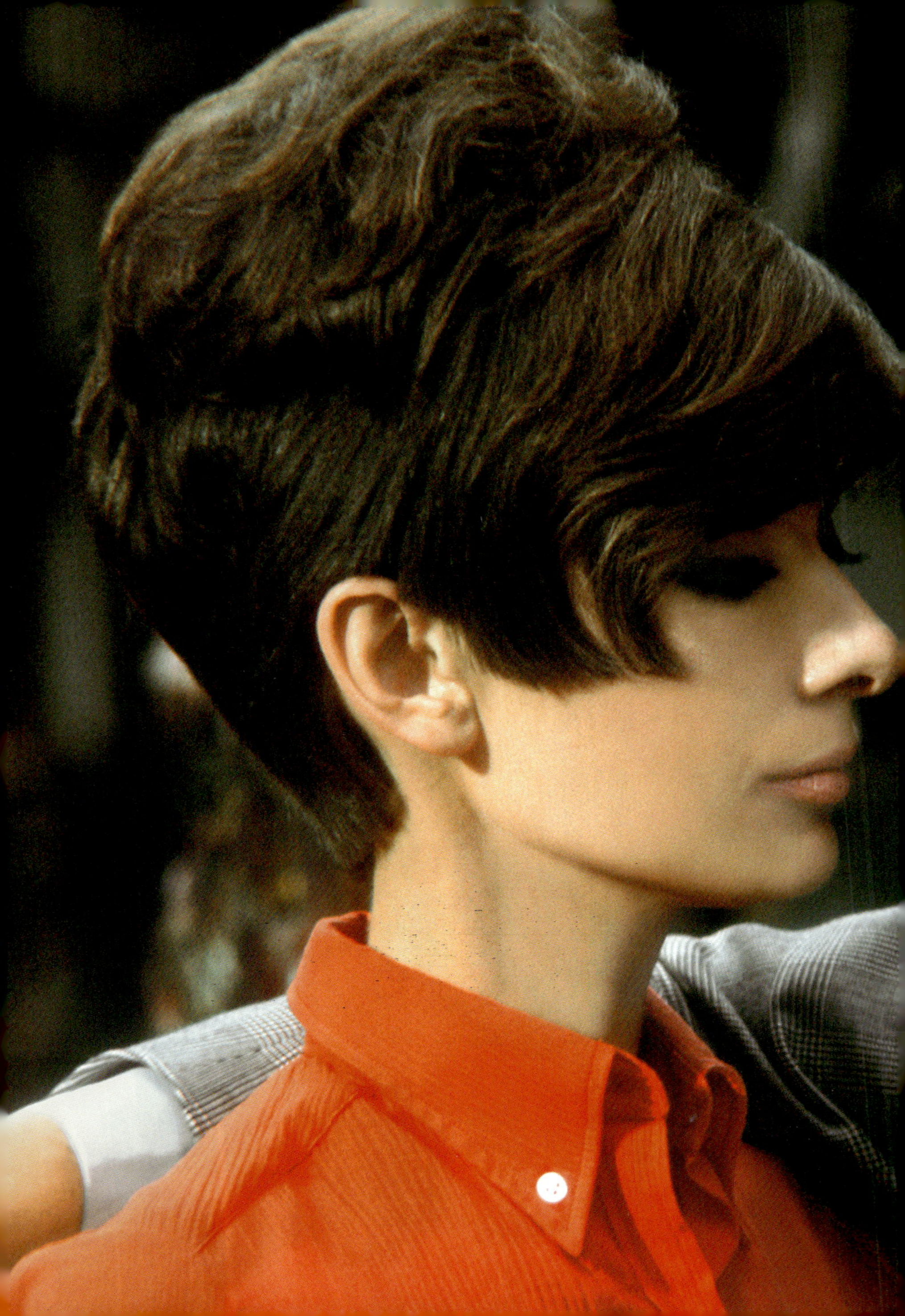

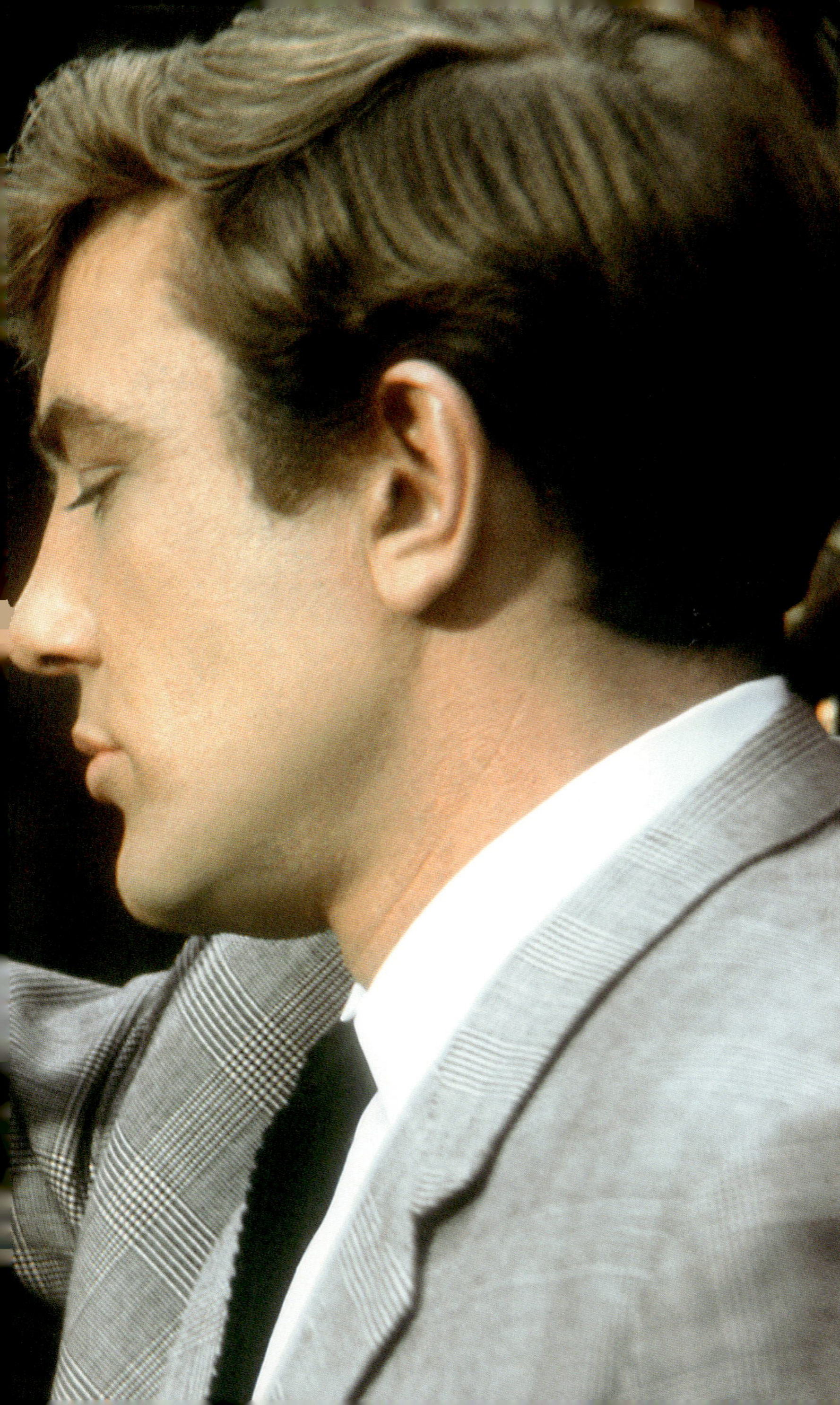

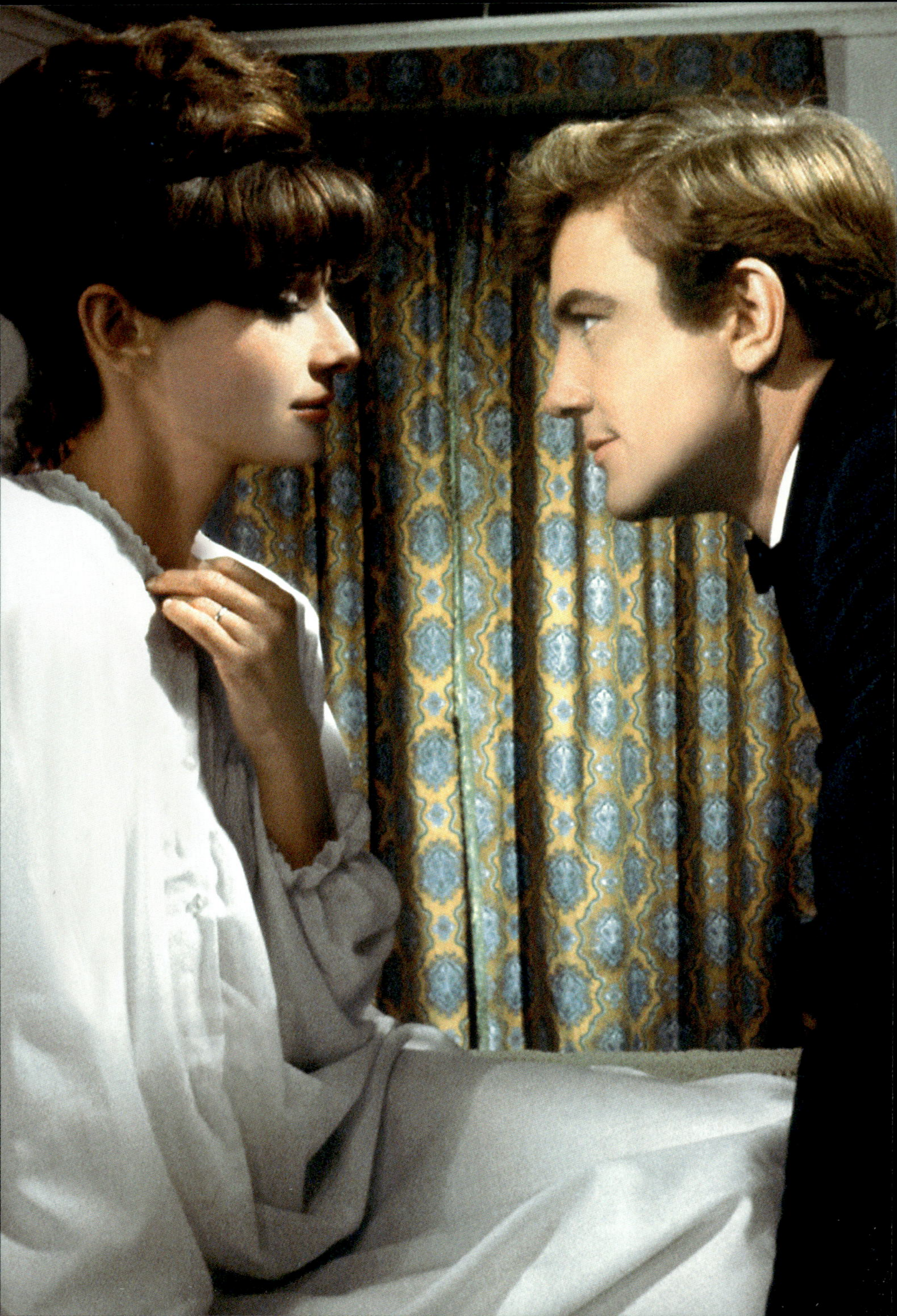

"I was crazy about *Two for the Road* and thought she really let her defenses down in it. ... Actresses usually all try to protect themselves, that's the nature of the beast, but she's really real in that movie."

Audrey Wilder

Previous spread:
Audrey and Albert Finney in a love scene in *Two for the Road.*

Opposite:
Albert stares intently at Audrey in a bedroom scene in *Two for the Road*.

APPENDIX

FEATURED FILMS

Green Mansions (1958)
In this film directed by her husband Mel Ferrer, Audrey Hepburn plays South American jungle girl Rima, who loves and cares for the animals that surround her. She falls in love with Abel (Anthony Perkins) after saving his life, but they are subsequently caught up in a devastating conflict. It was a rare critical and commercial failure for Hepburn and prevented further collaborations with her husband.

The Children's Hour (1961)
Plagued by a spiteful student who accuses them of a lesbian affair, teachers Martha Dobie (Shirley Maclaine) and Karen Wright (Audrey Hepburn) find their school and their lives thrown into hopeless despair. Karen's fiancé Dr. Joe Cardin (James Garner) doubts her fidelity and their engagement is broken, while Martha reveals that she is in love with Karen. First-class acting in William Wyler's film adaptation of Lillian Hellman's play.

Paris When It Sizzles (1962)
Jaded playboy screenwriter Richard Benson (William Holden) has two days to write his next screenplay so he hires secretary Gabrielle Simpson (Audrey Hepburn) to take down his words of wisdom. Trapped in his Parisian hotel room, the pair construct numerous generic plots which they enact as they slowly, and inevitably, fall in love.

My Fair Lady (1963)
Based on George Bernard Shaw's play *Pygmalion*, and Lerner and Loewe's hit Broadway musical, George Cukor's film follows Eliza Doolittle (Audrey Hepburn) as she attempts to lose her Cockney accent so that she can work in a flower shop. Arrogant professor of phonetics Henry Higgins (Rex Harrison) is happy to teach her since it will help him puncture the pretentiousness of the upper classes. However, in the end, they find themselves drawn to each other despite their class differences.

Two For The Road (1966)
Architect Mark (Albert Finney) and his wife Jo (Audrey Hepburn) are traveling through France to meet one of his clients, on a journey they have completed several times before. Jumping back and forth in time from one journey to another, the film follows the couple's relationship from first love, to married bliss, and eventually to infidelity, before they resolve their mutual fears and insecurities at the film's denouement.

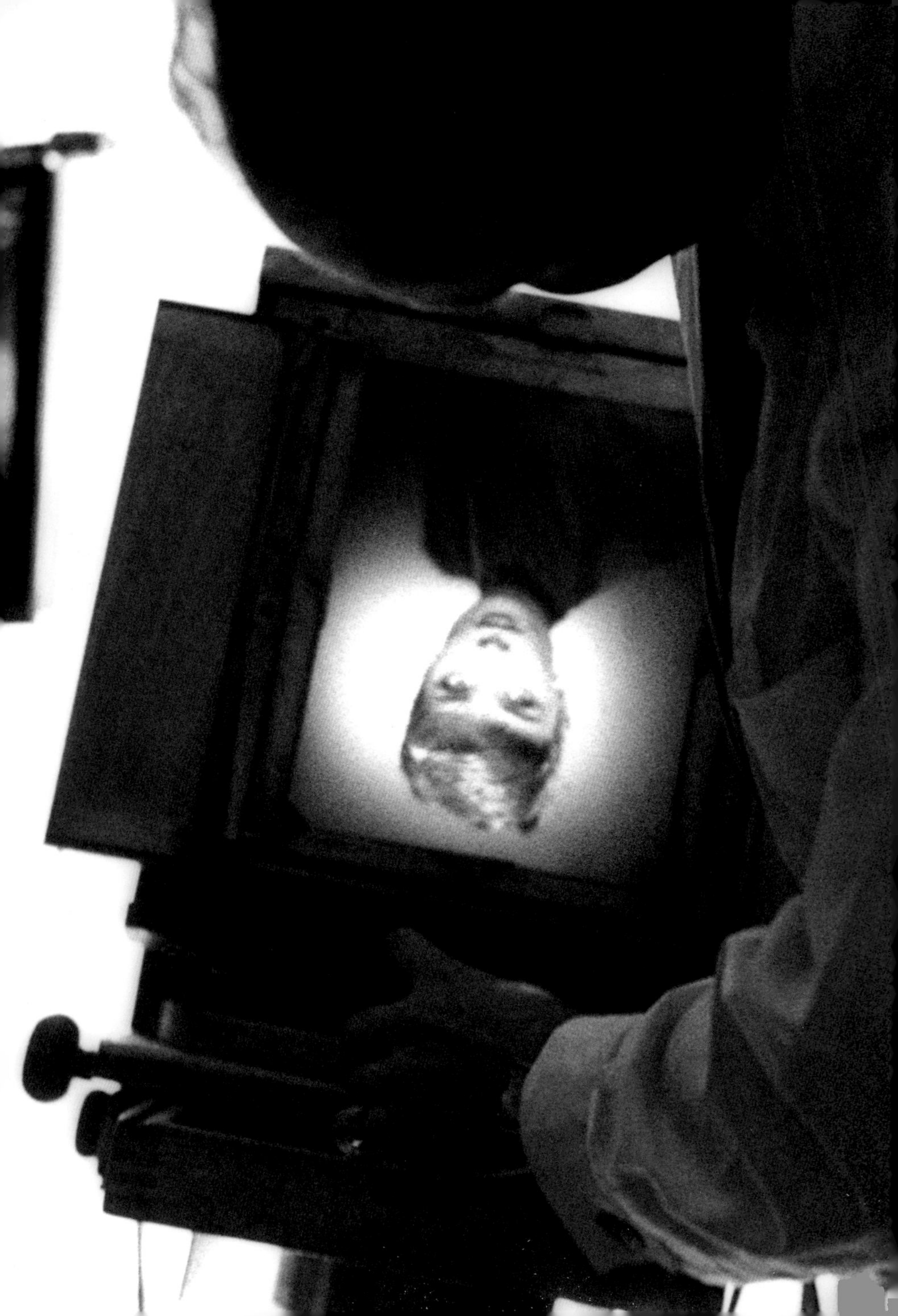

BOB WILLOUGHBY

Bob Willoughby, born in Los Angeles in 1927, studied film at the USC Cinema Department and design with Saul Bass at the Kann Institute of Art. At the same time, during the late 1940s, he apprenticed with many Hollywood photographers, including Wallace Seawell, Paul Hesse, and Glenn Embree. His first magazine assignments were with *Harper's Bazaar* in the early 1950s.

He was soon discovered by the film studios, and was the first "outside" photographer hired to get space for them in magazines, beginning in 1954, when Warner Bros. asked him to photograph Judy Garland in the final number of *A Star Is Born*. This proved successful for them both, (with Willoughby getting his first *Life* magazine cover) and it began a 20-year collaboration with the publicity departments of all the major studios, and provided a new link to the great magazines of the day.

Popular Photography called him "the man who virtually invented the photojournalistic motion picture still." During his 20-year career in films, his work literally never went out of print for a single week. In 1972 he moved to the south of Ireland with his wife, four children, and mother-in-law Quig. They lived for 17 years in a castle on Courtmacsherry Bay, where he translated a book of early Irish poetry, *Voices From Ancient Ireland*. With children and grandchildren scattered across many parts of the world, Willoughby lived with his wife Dorothy in the south of France until his death on December 18, 2009.

His photographs can be found in the collections of the National Portrait Gallery, Washington, D.C.; the National Portrait Gallery, London; the National Museum of Photography, Bradford, UK; Bibliothèque Nationale de France, Paris; Musee de la Photographie, Charleroi, Belgium; the Academy of Motion Picture Arts & Sciences, Beverly Hills, California; The Museum of Modern Art, Film Department, New York; Tate Gallery, London; and Museé de la Photographie et de l'Image, Nice.

Photographer Bud Fraker looks at Audrey
through his camera at the Paramount Studio Portrait Gallery.

Front cover: Audrey wears a pink dress with matching ribbon and elegant white gloves.
Page 2: Audrey poses with a phone during a 1953 photo session at Paramount Studios.
Page 4: Audrey with a bouquet of azaleas and wearing a blouse from the touring stage play *Gigi*, which was playing in Los Angeles at the time.
Page 6: Still from the opening titles of MGM's *Green Mansions*, 1958.
Back cover: Bud Fraker positions Audrey for a shot.

EACH AND EVERY TASCHEN BOOK
PLANTS A SEED!

Each year, we offset our annual carbon emissions with carbon credits at the Instituto Terra, a reforestation program in Minas Gerais, Brazil, founded by Lélia and Sebastião Salgado. To find out more about this ecological partnership, please check: *www.taschen.com/institutoterra.*
Inspiration: unlimited. Carbon footprint: (almost) zero.

Want to see more?
Visit *taschen.com* to view our current publications, browse our latest magazine, and subscribe to our newsletter.

Hohenzollernring 53, 50672 Köln, Germany
www.taschen.com

Printed in Italy
ISBN 978-3-8365-9709-8